THE SHIITES

Also by David Pinault

Story-Telling Techniques in the Arabian Nights

THE SHIITES

Ritual and Popular Piety in a Muslim Community

David Pinault

St. Martin's Press
New York

First published in the United States of America in 1992
First paperback edition 1993

Printed in the United States of America

ISBN 0-312-07953-2 (cloth)
ISBN 0-312-10024-8 (paper)

All photos are by the author

Library of Congress Cataloging-in-Publication Data

Pinault, David.
  The Shiites : ritual and popular piety in a Muslim community /
David Pinault.
        p. cm.
      Includes bibliographical references and index.
      ISBN 0-312-07953-2
      1. Shi' ah—India—Hyderabad. 2. Shi' ah. 3. Hyderabad (India)—Religious
      life. I. Title.
      BP192.7.I4P56   1992
      297'.82'095484—dc20   92-5210
                                                                   CIP

To my mother and father

Madeleine Lajoie Pinault
George Joseph Pinault

CONTENTS

Part I
An Introduction to the Shiite Tradition in Islam

Part II
Ritual and Popular Devotion in a Shiite Community:
Muharram Liturgies of Hyderabad

Part III
Conclusion

PREFACE

This book grew out of two summers' residence in the Indian city of Hyderabad, where I learned something of the religious practices surrounding Muharram. It is during this liturgical season that Shiite Muslims perform their annual lamentation rituals to commemorate the seventh-century battlefield death of the Imam Husain, beloved grandson of the Prophet Muhammad. While living in India in 1989 and 1991 I came to know members of six of Hyderabad's numerous *matami guruhan,* the Shiite men's guilds which organize many of the city's Muharram liturgies and supervise communal expressions of grief in acts of self-mortification.

Numerically Shiites comprise only a small percentage of Hyderabad's population, some eighty thousand in a city of three to four million; but they are a highly visible minority, in part because of their continued custom of gathering for mass liturgical displays of public mourning at Muharram. This is particularly so on Ashura, the tenth day of the month of Muharram, when a procession of thousands of mourners marches through the streets of Hyderabad's Old City neighborhoods, in a parade of camels and horses, elephant-borne battle-standards, and razor-wielding flagellants from the men's guilds. Crowds line the streets; beggars, fruit-sellers, and tradesmen with votive-banners for sale work the throng; and members of other faith-communities—Hindus, Sunni Muslims, Parsees, and Christians—come to the Old City to watch.

Some onlookers come for more than amusement; as I discuss later in this book, many Hindus visit Shiite shrines during Muharram to offer veneration to Husain. This tradition of intermingling made matters easier for me when I first located the Old City headquarters of the guruhan and asked their officers if I might follow them about and attend their meetings. Many members asked whether I was Muslim; but when I identified myself as Roman Catholic this created no particular problem (and for my part, my own upbringing in an intensely liturgical tradition helped predispose me, I feel, to an interest in a community structured by religious ritual). True, I did occasionally meet men who were suspicious of my presence at the shrines. This was especially so in the summer of 1991, in the aftermath of the Persian Gulf War, when numerous Shiites in conversations with me voiced their bitterness against the American government for standing by while Saddam Hussein crushed the Shiite rebellion in southern Iraq. Nevertheless, throughout my time in India most guild members remained unstinting in their welcome. Thanks to them I was able to interview individual men, attend liturgies of all kinds (private devotions held in members' homes as well as outdoor services held at the great shrines), and even watch the closed rehearsal sessions (perhaps most fascinating of all) where boys and young men are trained in the roles they are to play in the public liturgies supervised by the *guruhan*. All of this I describe in the chapters that follow.

I have organized this book into two sections. Part I is an introduction to Shiism. It is not an exhaustive treatment; nor is it meant to be so. Instead I limit myself to a discussion of selected essential doctrines, including beliefs held commonly in both the Shiite and Sunni forms of Islam as well as dogmas which differentiate one from the other. Of necessity I devote a good deal of attention to the Quran, the life of the Prophet Muhammad, and commonly shared Islamic views of the nature of prophethood. I have included this material in part to make my subject more accessible for readers with no prior experience of Islam. I go on to an examination of historical events identified as crucially important in the Shiite tradition, especially the question of the Imam Ali's succession to the caliphate and Husain's death at Karbala in the year A.D. 680. From here I discuss the worldviews and interpretations of sacred history elaborated by Shiites of later generations who meditated on the persecutions suffered by the Prophet's family. In the process I describe briefly the various denominations of Shiism—Twelver, Ismaili, and Zaydi— as well as the heterodox sects known collectively as the *ghulat* or "doctrinal extremists."

I discuss Shiism's historical legacy at length because a knowledge of the events of the seventh century is essential to any understanding of Shiite liturgy as it is practiced today. Shiite communal rituals are meant to preserve the memory of Karbala and other key historical events and pass this memory on from one generation to the next; furthermore, the form of these liturgies encodes the significance assigned these events by the Shiite community. Part II focuses attention on Muharram liturgies and attempts to show how historical understanding and worldviews are reflected in communal ritual. I do this by describing what I witnessed in Hyderabad among the *matami guruhan*; wherever possible, I describe not only religious practices but also the meaning given to these rituals by the Shiite men themselves whom I interviewed.

In writing this book I kept in mind the example of Lis Harris, author of *Holy Days: The World of a Hasidic Family* (Collier: 1985), who used her personal experiences visiting Jewish families in Brooklyn to introduce readers to the tradition of Hasidism. I envision two audiences for this study.

I wrote *The Shiites* first for the general reader who wishes an introduction to the Shiite form of Islam and who wants to understand something of Shiite religious practices. For this reason I have translated into English all passages cited from Arabic, Persian, and Urdu sources; for simplicity's sake I have also omitted diacritical marks in the terms I have transliterated from these languages. Part II of my work should be of interest as well to scholars concerned with the phenomenology of Shiite devotion. Relatively little has been published to date on this subject in general, and Hyderabad's Shiite community has received almost no scholarly attention at all.

A book of this kind could never be written without the help of many patient and good-natured individuals willing to tolerate at their elbow a notebook-wielding interrogator. I thank first of all the officers and members of the following *guruhan*: Anjuman-e Masoomeen; Guruh-e Ja'fari; Anjuman-e Parwaneh Shabbir; Guruh-e Husayniyah; Guruh-e Haydariyah; and Anjuman-e Ittihad-e Iraniyan-e Dekkan. Luckily for me, many members of these groups are fluent in English; as an Arabist only recently introduced to India, my facility in speaking Urdu was very limited indeed. Thus almost all my interviews were conducted in English (in a few instances, when chatting with religious scholars, I conversed in Arabic). Officers of the *guruhan* frequently offered their help as interpreters when I interviewed non-English speaking members of the guilds.

Dr. Omar Khalidi of the Hyderabad Historical Society provided bibliographic assistance, and of the many people who granted extensive interviews, these in particular should be singled out: Professor Sadiq Naqvi of Osmania University; S. Abbas Ali, founder of the Imam-e Zamana Mission; Ali Muhsin Khan of the Elia Theological Association; Allamah Akhtar Zaydi and his son Hyder Zaydi, both well known in the Old City as outstanding Muharram orators; and S. Naimatullah Moosavi, administrator of Hyderabad's Hauzat al-Mahdi religious school.

Throughout my two summers' stay, numerous individuals of Hyderabad's Shiite community supported me with their friendship and lively interest in my work. Ansar Hyder Abedi acted as liaison in arranging interviews and invited me to serve as a paramedic at his first-aid station outside the Hazrat Abbas shrine on Ashura 1991. I was able to interview the Iranian vice-consul in Hyderabad only through the very active intercession of Agha Mohammed Hussein. Shaukath Husain of A. A. Husain Booksellers gave me some memorable motorcycle rides through Hyderabad and very kindly invited me to liturgies held by the Nimatullahi Sufi order. Hasan Abbas Rizvi, poet and chanter in the Anjuman-e Parwaneh Shabbir, welcomed me to his home with great hospitality, and S. Ahmed Ali, president of Parwaneh Shabbir, answered endless questions with great patience and unfailing good humor. Mir Sabir Ali Zawar, founder and secretary of Anjuman-e Masoomeen, talked with me at length and allowed me to observe rehearsal sessions at his guild's headquarters.

Hyderabad's Henry Martyn Institute of Islamic Studies played a special role in my research. It was an article by the Institute's former director, the Reverend David Lindell, that first drew my attention to the *matami guruhan*. The Institute's present associate director, Dr. Andreas D'Souza, and his wife Diane D'Souza offered encouragement, affection, and active support in both 1989 and 1991. Andreas accompanied me on many visits to the Old City and acted as interpreter in several interviews. I am not alone in attesting the D'Souzas' generosity of spirit: during the Old City riots of December 1990 Andreas and Diane worked at considerable personal risk to build interfaith reconciliation in the Muslim and Hindu neighborhoods of Hyderabad.

Closer to home, David Hughes and Ann Ackerson of Colgate University's Interlibrary Loan Division expedited hair-raising last-minute bibliographic requests with aplomb. Technical support was cheerfully provided by Darryl Simcoe, director of Colgate's Audio-Visual Services, who helped in the preparation of photographic material, and by Peter Jörgensen, microcomputer specialist at Colgate, who answered a number of questions concerning the text's format.

Colgate's Research Council awarded me a Picker Grant in 1991, thereby facilitating a return to Hyderabad for a second season of work. I acknowledge with gratitude the Council's generosity. A Fulbright grant for Arabic and Persian manuscript research, awarded by the Indo-U.S. Subcommission, made possible my initial visit to India.

The work of composing this book in the fall of 1991 was made easier because of the encouragement I received from many friends, especially John Shuler, Karen Gegner, and Constance Harsh, all of the Colgate community. Michael Coyle of Colgate's English Department acquainted me with the writings of A.E.W. Mason and the 1938 film version of *The Drum*. I thank him for several enjoyable conversations on British imperial fiction. In particular I thank my colleague Steven Kepnes from Colgate's Philosophy and Religion Department for a suggestion made one day over lunch at the Merrill House faculty club, a suggestion which led to the writing of this book.

Theodore P. Wright, Jr., professor of political science, State University of New York at Albany, gave very valuable bibliographical suggestions with regard to the political history of Hyderabad State.

Enduring the copy editing and production stages of publication was made easier by the courteous, ongoing help of senior editor Simon Winder and editorial assistant Laura Heymann, both of the Scholarly and Reference Division at St. Martin's Press. In 1990 Simon took the initiative to approach me with the idea of a volume on Shiite piety; his enthusiasm and imaginative vision helped bring this project to completion.

Bibliographic advice and helpful suggestions came from old friends in Philadelphia, most notably Frank Korom and Basilides Elatinos. I salute my Urdu tutors in Philadelphia, Iffat Farah and Aliya Azam Khan, for their patience and skilled teaching. Wayne Husted of Pennsylvania State University offered very valuable suggestions for improving my translations of Urdu lamentation chants; I thank him for his generosity and enthusiastic help. And reading Persian poetry some years ago with Birch Miles of the University of Pennsylvania helped stimulate many of the ideas to be developed in the writing of this book; I recall with gratitude our evenings working on Hafez and Firdawsi.

Under fatiguing field conditions moral support is everything. That I persevered is a blessing I attribute to my wife, Dr. Jody Rubin Pinault, who accompanied me to Hyderabad on my first visit in 1989. Some of my comments on women's rituals stem from her observations when she sat in purdah attending liturgies with Shiite women acquaintances. The text of each chapter benefited from her perceptive and sensitive comments. To her more than anyone else I owe thanks.

Hamilton, New York
December 1991

1. Members of the Hazrat Abbas procession at the Husseini Kothi palace, Hyderabad, eighth of Muharram, 1991.

2. Members of the Hazrat Abbas procession at the Husseini Kothi palace, Hyderabad, eighth of Muharram, 1991. The votive cloth and garlands are draped over the rider's standard.

3. *Alams* carried in procession at the Husseini Kothi palace, Hyderabad, eighth of Muharram, 1991. Individuals press forward to touch the *alams* in an act of veneration.

4. Boys performing *matam* with razor blades, Husseini Kothi palace, Hyderabad, eighth of Muharram, 1991. The boy's headband reads "Hail, Husain!"

5. Sabil erected annually in Hyderabad's Old City for dispensing of water and other refreshments to passersby during Muharram season. The lettering immediately beneath the blood-dripping sword reads *piyas*, "thirst." The three dots forming part of the Urdu letter *p* are shaped to resemble an arrow-pierced *mashk*, the waterskin carried by Abbas at Karbala. The letter *y* of this same word is dotted with two diacritical points in the shape of terra-cotta waterjars which catch the martyrs' blood as it flows from the blade.

6. *Ashurkhana* in Hyderabad's Old City. Lettering above entrance reads "The shrine of Abu al-Fadl al-Abbas." Garlands and votive cloths are for sale beneath awning.

7. Entrance to *ashurkhana* in Hyderabad's Old City. The painted figures symbolize the first Shiite Imam, Ali ibn Abi Talib, and his honorific title of *sher-e
Khoda*, "the tiger of God." The *panje* or mystic protective hand and the parasol
represent spiritual and worldly sovereignty.

8. Shrouded *alams* at the shrine housed within the Inayat Jung palace, Hyderabad. The crests are ornamented with the word *Allah* and the names of members of the Prophet's household.

9. Dragon-headed *alams* draped with garlands at *ashurkhana* in Hyderabad's Old City.

10. Men performing *matam* in evening *ziyarah* at Shiite shrine in Hyderabad's Old City, seventh of Muharram, 1989. Iconography of Dhul fiqar and *panje* in *alams* lining sanctuary wall.

11. Members of Anjuman-e Masoomeen performing *matam* at private *majlis* in Hyderabad's Old City, ninth of Muharram, 1991. Banner reads "Hail, Husain!"

12. Woman with infant outside entrance to Hazrat Abbas shrine, morning of Ashura, 1989. The mother has had her child's forehead cut and bandaged as an act of participation in the sufferings of the Karbala martyrs.

13. *Alams* being brought out for procession during *matam* liturgy at Hazrat Abbas shrine, morning of Ashura 1989. Crests are coated with sandalwood paste.

14. Men performing *matam* at liturgy sponsored by the Anjuman-e Parwaneh Shabbir, shrine of Hazrat Abbas, Ashura 1989.

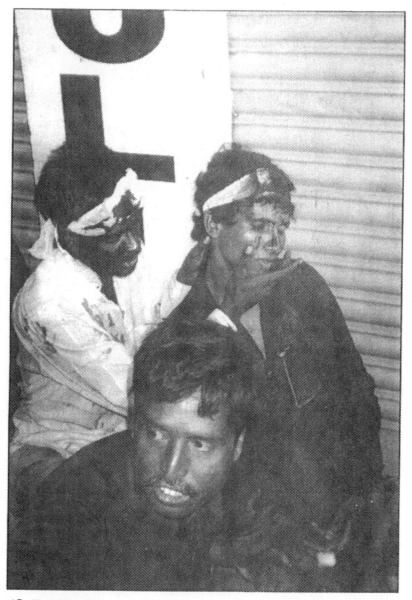

15. Flagellants being treated for self-inflicted wounds at Hyderi Medical Station, situated at the entrance to the Hazrat Abbas shrine in Hyderabad's Old City, Ashura 1991.

16. Shrouded *alams* being brought out for procession at the Inayat Jung palace,
Ashura 1989. This liturgy was sponsored by the Guruh-e Husayniyah.

Part I

———

An Introduction to the Shiite Tradition in Islam

1

Shiism: An Overview

PROLOGUE: EVENING IN HYDERABAD

"**T**ry not to hit the water buffaloes." I didn't wish to play back-seat driver, but Hyder had an unsettling habit of looking back over his shoulder at me while chatting as we rode together on his motorcycle. The herd ahead was distracting me from his argument.

"Oh." We swerved neatly around the animals, who were clearly accustomed to enjoying right of way as they moved slowly along the crowded street. I had a brief impression of blue-black flanks caked with ordure and mud; then we were clear.

"They are a nuisance," he pronounced with a wave of the hand.

Now we passed the Moazzam Jahi Market and were in the surging business center, with its money lenders and tinsmiths, its bookstalls and shops selling striped Eikot fabrics. Hindus, Muslims, Parsees, Jains—all hurried to finish their buying and make their way home.

It was twilight by the time we reached the Salar Jung Bridge, nosing our cycle among the oxcarts and buses and rickshaws. Near the bridge's railing, fruit vendors reclined against their barrows. Below, a glimpse of the sluggish River Musi; downstream, the red stone of the nizam's High Court, with its bulbous cupolas in Victorian Indo-Saracenic style. On the farther shore the minarets and domes of the Old City displayed black banners marked with the name of Husain, the slain Imam. For this was the eve of the first of Muharram, season of mourning in Shiite Islam.

Once across the bridge and within the Shiite quarter we went briefly from house to house, visiting the private chapels set up for Muharram by Hyder's friends in the courtyards of their homes. Here *tazias,* gilded wood models of the tombs of the martyred Imams, were erected, flanked by *alams,* the battle-standards carried in the Ashura procession.

Then we came to our evening's goal, the shrine of Hazrat Abbas, where Hyder was scheduled to preach. My host settled me comfortably in the shrine's portico among a small group of black-clad men and boys; then he sat before the *alam* of Abbas and, head down, intoned an opening prayer. This completed, he looked out at us and began his sermon, reminding everyone once more of the old tale, of how Husain came to die at Karbala.

THE HISTORICAL BACKGROUND: BATTLE AND DEATH AT KARBALA

Essential to any understanding of Shiite Islam is an acquaintance with the events of A.D. 680 (the year 61 in the *hijri* or Islamic calendar) and the battle of Karbala. What follows is only a sketch, focusing on the actions and historical figures that play a prominent role in Shiite devotions today.

Left unsettled at the death of the Prophet Muhammad in A.D. 632 was the question of succession (*al-khilafah,* the "caliphate") to leadership of the growing Islamic community: to whom should power now devolve, and how should a ruler's qualifications be determined? One party favored the process of election by a circle of councillors and community leaders; the other espoused the cause of Ali ibn Abi Talib, cousin and son-in-law of the Prophet, who had married the Prophet's own daughter Fatima. The latter group referred to themselves as *Shi' at Ali* ("Alid partisans/supporters of Ali") or simply as *al-Shi' ah.* They maintained that the Prophet himself, guided by divine inspiration, had designated Ali as his successor; moreover, Ali's ties by marriage and blood bound him more closely than anyone else to the family of Muhammad. Both factions agreed that the caliphate should be restricted to members of the Quraysh, the tribe to which the Prophet belonged; but the Shiites limited candidacy to the immediate family of Muhammad and his descendants, the *Ahl al-Bayt (Ahl-e Bayt,* in Persian and Urdu: the "people of the household"). Despite his qualifications, Ali was blocked repeatedly from power: first the Prophet's companion Abu Bakr became caliph, then Umar, then Uthman. Ali did not contest their election, apparently out of a desire to avoid civil war. Finally, he did obtain the caliphate and ruled for some five years, only to be murdered in 661. Thereafter the caliphate passed to Muawiya ibn Abi Sufyan, governor of Damascus and Syria. Muawiya was a Qurayshi but also a member of the wealthy Umayyad clan, notorious for its late conversion to Islam and its obstinate hostility to Muhammad in the early days before the Prophet's final success in Mecca.

The Shiites' hopes now focused on Hasan and Husain, the two sons of Ali and Fatima. At stake was a growing Islamic empire which already had conquered much of the Near East, North Africa, and Iran. Muawiya coerced the elder son Hasan into yielding him the caliphate; Hasan was then forced into a pensioned retirement in Medina (where, according to Shiite sources, he was subsequently poisoned at the caliph's order). Although he was deprived of the caliphate, Hasan is nevertheless revered today as the second Imam after Ali. In Shiism the term Imam indicates those members of *Ahl-e Bayt* who are the true spiritual leaders of the Muslim community, regardless of any political recognition or lack thereof extended by the Muslim world at large.[1]

In the year 680 Muawiya died and was succeeded by his son Yazid. The latter is reviled today as a tyrant who felt no shame at making a public display of his drinking and his immoral life-style. At Muawiya's death Alid partisans in the Iraqi city of Kufa, long a Shiite stronghold, sent messengers to Mecca to Ali's surviving son Husain (now known as the third Imam), urging him to come to Kufa, lead a Shiite revolt against Yazid, and claim the caliphate that was rightfully his by virtue of descent from the Prophet. Husain accepted the call and set out from Mecca with only a small band of followers, including his personal bodyguard and the women and children of his household.

But Ali's son never made it to Kufa. At Karbala, near the River Euphrates, southwest of what is today Baghdad, he was intercepted and surrounded by forces loyal to Yazid. Meanwhile the Umayyad governor of Kufa had quelled the incipient rebellion there and by intimidation had prevented any Shiite attempts to rescue their leader at Karbala. From the second to the tenth day of the month of Muharram the Imam Husain and his followers withstood siege by Yazid's army, which hoped to force the small band to surrender. Husain chose death instead. Throughout the siege the defenders suffered from hunger and thirst. Anguished by the cries of Husain's children, Abu al-Fadl al-Abbas, half brother and personal attendant of the Imam, galloped to the Euphrates in an attempt to bring water. He perished in the attempt, dying in his brother's arms. Shortly thereafter, on Ashura, the tenth of Muharram, Husain's camp was overrun by the enemy. Husain himself was killed (an Umayyad soldier known as Shemr, portrayed in later accounts as a personification of evil, dealt the deathblow), his household taken captive. The train of prisoners, including Zaynab, Husain's sister, was marched through the desert to Damascus. Here Yazid gloated over the severed head of his rival, which had been brought from the battlefield for the caliph to dishonor with blows from a cane. Here too, within the very palace of Yazid, Zaynab held the first *majlis,* or lamentation assembly, to mourn for her brother. During this period of imprisonment Husain's four-year-old daughter Sakina died (in Hyderabadi iconography she is often represented by jasmine garlands intertwined with chains).

Given this history, it is not surprising that Damascus today has a number of shrines associated with the battle of Karbala, including one on the city's southern outskirts consecrated to Sayyidah Zaynab, another in the cemetery of Bab al-Saghir honoring sixteen of the warriors killed in the battle, and a third known as Mashhad Ra's al-Husayn, "the shrine of Husain's head." The latter site is of particular interest, located as it is in the northeast corner of the Great Umayyad Mosque. The site occupied by the mosque has been the focus of veneration since the ninth century B.C., as a shrine to the Syrian storm-god Hadad, as a Roman temple of Jupiter, and as a Christian basilica of John the Baptist. Because of the Husain chapel located within, the Umayyad Mosque is the object of Shiite visitation today, as are Bab al-Saghir and the shrine of Zaynab. I encountered numerous Iranian pilgrims at all three sites in a visit to Damascus in 1990.

THE IMAMATE AND THE HIERARCHY
OF RELIGIOUS SCHOLARS

What has been described above is no more than an outline of the events of Karbala known to every devout Shiite. According to the Ithna-Ashari or "Twelver" denomination of Shiism (the most widely espoused form of Shiism today, prevalent in Iran and Iraq as well as among the Shiites of India), since the time of Muhammad there has been a succession of twelve Imams in Islamic history. Each in turn was persecuted by the reigning caliph, each deprived of his rightful worldly rank and (with the exception of the twelfth) eventually murdered. It is believed that as a child, in the year 874, the twelfth Imam was taken into occultation by God: as a safeguard against murder he was divinely concealed from his enemies. According to Twelver theologians, this "Hidden Imam" has not been seen in the world since 941, when he entered the "Great Occultation." Yet he remains alive and will ultimately return as the Mahdi, "the one guided by God," who will usher in the end of time and final Judgment.

True worldly authority, then, rests with the Hidden Imam, but in his absence leadership of the Shiite community has devolved upon the *ulama* (plural of the Arabic term *alim*, "learned one," in the Iranian world sometimes referred to as mullahs). These are scholars trained in Islamic law, which has as its foundations Quranic scripture and the voluminous biographical traditions concerning the attested actions and sayings of the Prophet and the

Imams. A scholar who is recognized by his peers as sufficiently learned in the law bears the title of *mujtahid,* one qualified to engage in *ijtihad,* or the exercise of independent reasoning in applying the law to specific issues at hand, whether personal or public. Few Shiites are considered educated enough in the legal and scriptural tradition to attempt *ijtihad;* anyone lacking such expertise—the vast majority of believers—is commanded to select a recognized living *mujtahid* as his *marja' al-taqlid* or "reference model for imitation" and to follow such a cleric's example in ordering the moral affairs of his life. Until his death in 1989 Ruhollah Khomeini served as the *marja' al-taqlid* for many Shiites throughout the world; since then Abu al-Qasim al-Khui (a long-time resident of Najaf who was placed under house arrest by Saddam Hussein during the 1991 Persian Gulf crisis and Iraqi Shiite uprising against Saddam) has become one of the most celebrated *maraji'.* Numerous Shiites in Hyderabad today take al-Khui as their exemplar. In the Shiite world the *ulama* are characterized by a series of ranks and titles including *hujjat al-islam,* "argument in defense of Islam," *ayat Allah,* "the sign of God," and *ayat Allah al-uzma,* "the mightiest sign of God."

The *ulama* play an important role too in Sunni Islam, although the Sunnis lack as stratified a hierarchy of religious-legal authorities. From a comparative historical perspective, if the Shiites can be described as partisans of Ali and his descendants (the Imams), the Sunnis in turn can be regarded as those Muslims (the vast majority) who upheld the legitimacy of the reigning caliphs, not (the Sunnis would say) out of lack of reverence for *Ahl-e Bayt,* but out of a pragmatic wish to avoid the chaos and social strife that would have ensued in any attempt to install the Imams by force. (The above is of course no more than a rough shorthand distinction.) Acting on this principle, Sunnis extended recognition even to Umayyad rulers whom they knew to be brutal and corrupt.

At this point, however, it may be of interest to compare the attitudes of Sunni and Shiite *ulama* toward their own ideal role in society (as it should be) and toward the political rulers who govern the world as it is. The generalizations involved are considerable but still useful.

The collective self-image of the Sunni *ulama* can be said to have evolved in response to the fact that these scholars had an active and cooperative role to play in supporting the governing caliphs and in helping administer the Islamic state. True, that role was always limited and at times narrowly subordinated to the wishes of the regime in power. This especially holds for those scholars who were on the government payroll; at worst, such employees would be expected by their masters to scan Scripture for evidence to back the latest government edict, issuing *fatwas* (learned religious opinions) which lent Islamic legitimization to patently corrupt rulers. But from a Sunni perspective such compromises have seemed justifiable: stable government engenders a stable social order, in which the *ulama,* securely salaried and supported by the government, oversee the religious education and guidance of the Muslim population at large. The same pattern continues today: even with the abolition of the caliphate in 1924, the *ulama*-government entente can be seen at work in a staunchly Sunni country such as Egypt. Accustomed as they were to some share of authority and to the experience of the world's inevitable imperfection, Sunni *ulama* never insisted on the necessity of the moral superiority or spiritual infallibility of the caliph. If his administration made possible the practice of Islam, that sufficed. As for worldly perfection: this resided if anywhere in the principle of *ijma',* "the consensus of the community." When moral and doctrinal issues arise, the *ulama,* as learned representatives of the community, have the responsibility of publicly debating the proper course to be taken. The consensus they eventually arrive at will be shielded from error because of divine guidance. Infallibility then in Sunni Islam is collective and is found in the Muslim community as a whole.

The question of human sinlessness and infallibility (*ismah*) is one of the principal doctrinal issues distinguishing Shiism from Sunnism. The twelfth-century Sunni author al-Shahrastani, in his survey of religious sects entitled *Kitab al-milal wa-al-nihal,* "The book of religious communities and creeds," said the following of the Shiites:

> The Shiites are those who with exclusive devotion have become partisans of Ali (may God be pleased with him). They state their belief in his claim to both the imamate and caliphate, by right of designation and inheritance—whether this came about in secret or by public proclamation. They believe that Ali's descendants retain the right to be leaders of the community; and if in fact they are not presently rulers, this is because of tyrannous injustice (*zulm*) on the part of someone else, or because of necessary dissimulation (*taqiyah*) on the part of the Imams. And they say that the imamate is not an administrative issue which may be dependent on choice by the common masses, nor may the Imam be appointed by their election. Rather the imamate is an issue of ancient lineage, and it is a pillar of the faith . . . The Shiites agree on the necessity of stipulation and designation, and the certainty of the sinless infallibility (*ismah*) of the prophets and of the Imams.[2]

This passage neatly summarizes Shiite notions of communal leadership. Unlike the Sunni caliph, the Shiite Imam is (at least in theory) not only a worldly ruler but the highest spiritual authority. He is characterized by *ismah*—sinlessness and infallibility—a claim never put forward by the Sunni *ulama* for the caliph; hence the Imam is catapulted in rank above the caliph. The Imam's appointment takes place not through any process of collective election, but through *nass*, "designation" by his spiritual predecessor alone; and this designation can only be conferred on one who is a sinless descendant of the Prophet. The concepts of *nass* and *ismah* betray a mistrust of the "common masses"—the people and their representatives—who might err in the selection of a Muslim leader just as they once erred in their early neglect of the *Ahl-e Bayt*'s political claims.

These concepts of the imamate evolved within a community which saw itself as persecuted and excluded from power. If an Imam was denied his rightful place in the political realm, this was either because of "tyrannous injustice" (*zulm*) of the kind which befell Husain at the hands of Yazid, or because of "necessary dissimulation" (*taqiyah*), as was the case with Ali, the first Imam: he made a show of initially accepting his exclusion from the throne and pretended to support the first three caliphs because of the necessity of avoiding civil war. The *ulama* retrospectively assigned *taqiyah* as a motive to Ali and then elevated it into a guiding principle for any Shiite living under a tyrannous government too powerful to be safely resisted: one may give an external show of acquiescence while preserving silent resistance in one's interior, in one's heart. This concept affects both the Shiite *ulama*'s self-image and how they have defined their relations with worldly powers. Any government other than that of the twelfth Imam, the living sinless descendant of the Prophet, is necessarily flawed and unjust in its denial of the rightful claims of *Ahl-e Bayt*; but a mullah may cooperate with such a government to the extent necessary for survival, while treasuring resistance in his heart. The hidden sovereignty of the occulted Imam, although not mirrored in any worldly government, is manifested in the Imam's deputies, the *ulama*, who see themselves as custodians of his spiritual legacy; and his elevated moral rank is reflected in some fashion onto those religious leaders whom he guides.[3]

Such a quietist stance—silent opposition to worldly powers, coupled with spiritual authority among a persecuted and excluded minority—has suited the Shiite *ulama* well when they have been out of power. A problem arises, however, when the *ulama* suddenly find themselves to be the overt and manifest wielders of governmental authority. Such has been the case since the 1979 Iranian Revolution and the establishment of the Islamic Republic of Iran. In these circumstances the Shiite *ulama* have felt themselves challenged to preserve their traditional worldview of persecution and exclusion; this they have achieved by portraying the Iranian nation as a righteous minority menaced by powerful external enemies who seek to deprive it of its proper place in the world. Once more, then, as in the past, the Prophet's family and its defenders are threatened with violence and expropriation: thus the paradigm is preserved.[4]

2

Essentials of Islam Common to the Shiite and Sunni Traditions

TAWHID: GOD'S ONENESS. *TAWHID* EXAMINED IN THE LIGHT OF ANCIENT ARAB BELIEFS

Having reviewed some of the distinguishing events central to Shiite sacred history, it may be good for us to pause here and examine aspects of the Islamic faith adhered to by Shiite and Sunni Muslims alike. For although the historical events of the seventh century—Ali's caliphate, Karbala, the imamate of Husain—generated a Shiite theology which differs from Sunnism in important ways, nevertheless the two traditions share in common numerous religious beliefs and essential insights concerning the nature of divinity and God's relations with humanity.

All Muslims subscribe to a common *shahadah* (testimony of faith): "No god is there save God, and Muhammad is the messenger of God." (Shiites, however, subjoin an additional assertion, "And Ali is the beloved friend of God," a statement reflecting the exalted status of the Prophet's household and the Imams in Shiite popular piety. More will be said in a later section concerning Shiite devotion to the Imams). To begin, let us examine the first part of the *shahadah*, which summarizes the universal Islamic belief in *tawhid* or God's absolute Oneness.

The message of *tawhid* enunciated by the Prophet can best be appreciated by glancing at the audience to whom it was first directed, the Arab tribes living in and around Mecca. The religion of the Arab Jahiliyah ("the period of ignorance," as Muslim historians term the pre-Islamic era) can be characterized as animist: spirits (*jinn* or "genies") were believed to reside in and around rock formations, trees, and ruins in the desert wastes. Reverence was paid as well to numerous astral deities, including a creator-God, Allah, and "the daughters of Allah," a triad of goddesses associated with the planet Venus, with cave-sanctuaries and with sacred stones, who held power over fertility and the agricultural cycle, illness and healing, and personal destiny. Jahiliyah Arabs also felt themselves subject to the overwhelming force of *al-Dahr,* "Time," which sets the limit to human efforts and determines the end of human life. It is *al-Dahr* that inflicts death on the individual; the heroic code of living among the pagan Arabs — Meccans and Bedouin alike — included a fatalistic acceptance of this impersonal force.[1]

In the time of Muhammad's youth (the late sixth century A.D.) numerous sanctuaries to Jahiliyah deities existed throughout the Arabian peninsula. Some of these, such as the pagan shrine of the Kaaba in Muhammad's birthplace of Mecca, had for centuries been the object of *hajj* or pilgrimage; trade fairs and periods of truce among the warring tribes would be organized to coincide with the *hajj* season at urban pilgrimage centers such as Mecca. And in these cities, through contact with travelling merchants, Jahiliyah Arabs learned something of Judaism and Christianity: no formal expositions of dogma, but rather the vivid oral narratives that travel well along caravan routes — legends of the childhood of Jesus, of Moses in Egypt, of Noah and the Flood. Thus when Muhammad came to preach in Mecca he could assume that his audience knew of these figures; the Quran's concision in its summary references to Adam and Eve, Noah, Lot, and so on, is evidence that the Arab Meccans already had some acquaintance with the sacred tales of the Jewish and Christian traditions.

Of particular importance to the history of Islam were the Jahiliyah beliefs concerning death and the fate of the soul. The afterlife was imagined as a cheerless shadow-existence reminiscent of the grey underworld in the ancient Mesopotamian *Gilgamesh* epic. In this work the dying Enkidu has a dream which he relates to his friend Gilgamesh:

> I stood alone before an awful being; his face was sombre like the black bird of the storm. He fell upon me with the talons of an eagle and he held me fast, pinioned with his claw, till I smothered; then he transformed me so that my arms became wings covered with feathers. He turned his stare towards me, and he led me away to the palace of Irkalla, the Queen of Darkness, to the house from which none who enters ever returns, down the road from which there is no coming back.
>
> There is the house whose people sit in darkness; dust is their food and clay their meat. They are clothed like birds with wings for covering, they see no light, they sit in darkness. I entered the house of dust and I saw the kings of the earth, their crowns put away forever; rulers and princes, all those who once wore kingly crowns and ruled the world in the days of old.[2]

In comparing representations of the underworld in Mesopotamian and Jahiliyah literature, Emil Homerin notes that as in *Gilgamesh* the pagan Arabs likened the spirits of the dead to spectral birds: Arab poets frequently described the human soul after death as an owl which haunts the grave.[3] In the following verses the Jahiliyah composer Qurad ibn Ghuwayyah envisions his own death and burial:

> If only I knew what Mukhariq will say
> when my owl answers the screeching owls,
> And I am lowered into a deep shaft, its dust pouring
> upon me, in whose moist earth I'm long to stay.[4]

Though some sort of strengthless survival for the soul is occasionally pictured in Jahiliyah poetry, the Arabs of Mecca had no faith in any final Judgment or presiding deity who would reward or punish the dead with heaven and hell. The only immortality worth savoring was the reputation which lingers after one's death. Urwah ibn al-Ward captures the attitude well:

> Leave me and my soul alone . . . indeed I will
> buy with it—before I no longer possess the price—
> heroic tales which remain, and the brave is not immortal
> when he becomes an owl above the tomb
> answering the stones of the enclosure and complaining
> to everyone it sees, acquaintance or stranger.[5]

The Quranic message as preached to his fellow Meccans by Muhammad (after receiving it from the angel Gabriel, God's messenger) constituted a modification of the existing belief system rather than a clean sweep of Arab religious culture. Much of the religious vocabulary was retained but given a new meaning: as before, Muslims were to undertake the *hajj*, and the Kaaba was still the goal of pilgrimage; but now the Kaaba was understood as the first shrine ever erected in the history of the world, with the patriarch Abraham and his son Ismail (the Biblical Ishmael) credited as its builders. The "Black Stone" (a meteorite fragment venerated by the ancient Arabs) which formed part of the pagan Kaaba was also islamicized and retained in Muslim devotion, with the explanation that this had been a gift to Abraham brought down by Gabriel from heaven.

The Quran also mandated veneration of Allah—a deity familiar to every Meccan as a supreme creator-god; this command would have posed no serious problem to Muhammad's traditionally minded hearers. What did trigger angry resistance, however (and this is where the Quran makes a definitive break with pagan tradition), was the proclamation of *tawhid*, the assertion that there exists no god save Allah.

Why does the Quran lay such stress on God's unity, and what implications did *tawhid* have for the religious systems of seventh-century pagan Arabia? Belief in divinity in general, even belief in Allah, was not the issue; at stake rather was the question of how one should behave in this life, given the nature of divinity and the quality of the afterlife. What I mean here may be made clearer if we read Quran 25.1-3:

> Praise the One who has sent down the Criterion to His servant that it might be a warning to the worlds; He who has sovereignty over the heavens and the earth, who has not begotten a son, nor does He share power with any associate. He has created all things and has precisely determined their proportions.
>
> Despite this they take in preference to Him other gods, who create nothing, themselves having been created. Nor do these gods possess power over harm or benefit to themselves; they do not control death or life or resurrection.

Here we find a simultaneous assertion of *tawhid* and of the creation of a moral order, a "criterion" by which humans can distinguish right from wrong; in the same breath comes a withering blast against the polytheists. The old gods are not to be left standing; this deity does not share sovereignty. For the old system, with its diffuse network of gods, involved multiple areas of divine sovereignty, with competing claims to sacrifice and cult worship. The numerous gods distracted attention from the one God, from the one Criterion with its exactly measured exposition of right and wrong. *Tawhid* allowed the believer to focus on the single set of demands stipulated by a sole God, in whom sovereignty and beneficent power were concentrated.

Perhaps even more shocking to the Prophet's audience than the concept of *tawhid* were the Quranic doctrines linked thereto: resurrection, judgment and an afterlife of punishments and rewards. The Meccan reaction to these revelations is recorded in the following passage from the Quran (45.21-25):

> Or do those who commit evil calculate that God will treat them, in their life and in their death, in the same way as He treats those who believe and do good works? They are wrong in their calculations! God has created the heavens and the earth with proportioned fairness, in order that every soul may be rewarded in accordance with what it has earned; nor will they be treated unjustly . . . And yet they [Muhammad's Meccan adversaries] say: "There is nothing except our lower-worldly life. We die and we live, and nothing destroys us except *al-Dahr* [Time]" . . . And when God's clear signs are recited to them in words, the only argument

they have is: "If what you're saying is right, then bring back our forefathers from the dead!"

Contemptuous disbelief marks the crowd of onlookers. Muhammad's message flies in the face of Meccan common sense: Time crushes us all, and that is an end to things. What survives death is not worth a sermon. This passage captures the heckler's cry from the throng: Work a miracle on the spot, then; resurrect our ancestors.

The Quranic passage continues with instructions to Muhammad as to how to respond to this challenge (Quran 45.26-28):

Tell them: "God makes you live and makes you die. Thereafter He will gather you together on the Day of Resurrection . . ." For on Judgment Day those who speak idle lies will be the losers. And you will see each community of people on its knees, each of them summoned to account. On that day you will receive your reward for whatever you have done.

According to the Quranic vision of the resurrection of the dead, we will be somehow reunited with our physical bodies, bodies upon which will be visited either torments or pleasures (Quran 56.10-18, 41-43, 47-48):

Those who excel: these will be the ones brought near to God, in gardens of restful ease . . . reclining on couches studded with precious stones, seated facing one another. Immortal youths will go from couch to couch, offering cups and beakers and chalices filled from a fountain . . .

But as for those placed on the left: they will be in scorching wind and boiling water under the shadow of thick black smoke . . . They, who used to say: "So! When we die and have turned to dust and bones, after all that we will really be raised from the dead? And our long-dead forefathers along with us?"

By abolishing competing claims from all other deities, and by positing one sole existent God, *tawhid* focuses our awareness of divine demands and consequent human responsibilities. The concomitant doctrine of the Resurrection implies that we are answerable after death for what we do here on earth: instead of the Jahiliyah's netherworld with its wraithlike shadow-trance and grave-haunting wing-clad souls, the afterlife has now become something to strive for. And the corporeality of the Quranic resurrection makes it possible to imagine rewards and punishments in a way that is tangible and thrillingly immediate. The human and social impact of the doctrine of *tawhid* can be characterized thusly: heightened moral accountability.

Meccan response to the Quranic message was hardly encouraging. From the time that Muhammad first began receiving revelations, in the year 610, he preached to a largely hostile audience. Many men, including prominent members of his own Quraysh clan, jeered at him as a charlatan. Nor was the response better when the Prophet ventured to nearby Taif: village boys pelted him with stones. Only in 622, when he withdrew northward to Medina with a band of loyal followers, did Muhammad's worldly fortunes change: there the population welcomed him as a leader. As a consequence 622, termed the year of the *hijrah* or exodus, is now taken as the year from which dates are reckoned in Islamic chronology, for the *hijrah* to Medina generated the foundation of the Muslim community. In Medina Muhammad combined within himself the roles of religious, political, and military leader, successfully warding off several Quraysh attacks. Finally, two years before his own death, the Prophet returned south to take Mecca in a (mostly) bloodless conquest.

In the course of Muhammad's public career, first as an embattled visionary, later as a triumphant ruler, the doctrine of *tawhid* became more fully articulated. Again and again, with only slight variations of emphasis, the Quran describes a deity "who has not begotten a son, nor does He share power with any associate" (25.2). Such passages warned Muslims against the sin of *shirk*: attempting to associate divine partners with God. The early Muslim community understood the Quranic verses just quoted as a criticism of Christianity; notions of Sonship and Trinity detracted from the unique status of Allah as the sole author of power in our world. The Quran's articulation of *tawhid* likewise involved a denial of divine incarnation: the enfleshment of God would blur the distinction between Him and His creatures. From a Quranic perspective the Christian doctrine of the Incarnation arrogated to a mere human a rank reserved for the Divine alone. And in the Quran (5.116-118) Jesus himself is made to say that he never intended that others worship him as a god.

Tawhid further implies that no beings of any sort, divine or fleshly, have power to intercede with God on behalf of humans and soften His execution of just punishment. "God is the One who created heaven and earth . . . and then seated Himself on His throne," the Quran admonishes. "You have no patron or intercessor other than Him. Will you not bear this in mind?" (32.4) Heavenly intercessors would inevitably become the objects of human prayer and again would detract from God's authority as sole judge and overseer of retribution. For this reason the Quran swept away from the Daughters of Allah their traditionally acknowledged rank as intermediaries between the divine and human realms, an action bitterly resented by the Quraysh of

Mecca. The ninth-century historian Ibn Saad records that one of the Quraysh elders said to Muhammad in explanation: "We know that Allah killeth and giveth life, createth and preserveth, but these our goddesses pray to Him for us."[6] Protests notwithstanding, the Daughters of Allah were to find no place in Islamic cosmology.

For similar reasons the Quranic message did not countenance the idea of a priesthood, with consecrated leaders uniquely empowered to perform rites on behalf of a community. So too with the veneration of saints: priests and saints alike were seen as deflecting the individual's attention from the one divine Source. *Tawhid* mandates that no one—deity, priest, or saint—should mediate or influence the Muslim's direct experience of God, with all the personal accountability implied thereby.

Such at least is the Quranic theory. In practice, however, the principle of *tawhid* in its strictest sense is violated in the Sunni and Shiite traditions alike. Throughout the Islamic world the worship of saints and veneration of saints' relics is widespread; and the action of *ziyarah*, visits to the tombs of holy men and women, has long been combatted by reform-minded Muslims such as the Wahhabis of Saudi Arabia. In Sunni Islam saint worship is often incorporated into the liturgies organized by the enormously popular Sufi *tariqahs*, the associations which seek in their rituals to trigger the individual's experience of the mystical proximity of the divine (more will be said about Sufism below). Saints' tombs are often selected as sites where Sufi orders perform their public liturgies; this ensures widespread attendance at the services. In some instances the venerated founder of a *tariqah* will be buried within the precincts of a Sufi monastery; the monastery itself then becomes the object of pilgrimage, and the public comes both to pray to the entombed saint and to participate in the order's liturgies. In such instances a great deal of charismatic prestige accrues to the *shaykh*, the current living master of the order, who is perceived as the spiritual heir of the deceased founder. For after all, the *tariqah* leader controls access to the shrine and hence to the saint who may be contacted within. Thus the Sufi shaykhs become a palpable link in the chain of intercession, which extends from the living to the holy dead and thence to God. Such *tariqah* masters have often wielded great authority in the community at large; small wonder then that the noted Muslim scholar Fazlur Rahman, in a discussion of Sufi brotherhoods and saint worship, criticized popular Sufism as a "religion within a religion" and "veritable spiritual jugglery . . . Islam . . . at the mercy of spiritual delinquents."[7]

At Sufi pilgrimage sites the prayers addressed to the saint involve petitions and insoluble problems of every sort, including marital disputes, illness, infertility, and threatened failure in school or civil service examinations. The saint perceives the suppliant's piety and intercedes with God on the individual's behalf; thereafter the saint becomes a conduit through which *barakah*—divine blessing—flows. For if God reveals Himself in Scripture as sole judge, He is also characterized repeatedly in the Quran as *rahman* and *rahim*: compassionate and merciful. In popular devotion it is believed that His compassion will extend to giving ear to a plea mediated by one of His holy men and women.

As will be seen below, Sufism also has a place in the Shiite tradition, but the influence of the *tariqahs* today is much slighter in Shiism than it is in Sunnism. After the establishment of a Shiite state in Iran with the founding of the Safavid dynasty in 1501, the Iranian Sufi brotherhoods were subjected to outbursts of sporadic but occasionally very violent persecution. This was in part because the *shaykhs* exerted charismatic leadership of a kind claimed by the early Safavid shahs themselves. More important even than this difficulty, however, was the fact that Shiite *ulama* saw Sufi devotionalism as competition which interfered with the cult of the Imams. Each *tariqah* had its own carefully elaborated hierarchy, supervised by a spiritual master who exacted oaths of obedience from his novices. As noted above, at death some of these masters could well be ranked as saints with intercessory powers. Brotherhoods held their own liturgies in their own monasteries; the initiate's religious life would be dominated by the order to which he belonged. An urban monastery might house in its precincts a soup kitchen, inn, library, or medical clinic; thus its influence would radiate outward into nearby neighborhoods. Furthermore, the *tariqahs* encouraged their members to pay the *zakat* (the charitable alms-tax mandated by the Quran) to the master of the brotherhood rather than to the Shiite *ulama,* who felt themselves entitled to receive and administer the donations.[8]

The *ulama*'s resentment of the Sufi *tariqahs* came at a time when Iranian religious leaders were encouraging the development of specifically Shiite forms of popular devotion, partly as an attempt to develop a coherent ideological response to the powerful Sunni dynasty of the Ottoman Turks, opponents who warred against the Safavids in a number of sixteenth-century battles. In the face of Ottoman control over the Arabian peninsula and the cities of Mecca and Medina, Shiite *ulama* encouraged *ziyarah* to the tombs of the Imams, especially Najaf, Karbala, and Mashhad; Shiite pilgrims claimed the honorific titles of Karbala'i and Mashhadi, a custom analogous to the title *hajji* borne by veterans of the Mecca pilgrimage. The *ulama* developed a hierarchy of devotion, in which common believers might feel themselves linked spiritually to the Hidden Imam through a chain of mullahs, *mujtahids,* and *maraji'*.[9]

Prominent religious scholars lent their support to the observance of Shiite commemorations, such as Muharram, and to the belief that weeping in grief for Husain's death may gain one merit in the afterlife. Prestigious clerics such as Muhammad Baqir Majlisi (d.1699) promulgated the concept of the intercessory powers of the fourteen *Ma'sumin* or "Immaculate Ones": the Prophet, Fatima, and the twelve Imams.[10] In Shiite folklore the Lady Fatima is said to be invisibly present at every *majlis* or lamentation liturgy held in honor of her slain son; tears shed on Husain's behalf during the liturgy move her in turn to intercede with God to forgive the sins of the mourners. (We will see illustrations of this belief in my description of Muharram rituals in Hyderabad.) Thus in the course of Islamic history a specifically Shiite ideology can be said to have evolved, one which advocated the intercessory powers of the *Ma'sumin* even at the expense of *tawhid.*

I think one may argue that the Sunni and Shiite traditions diverge from each other in practice far more than in theory. They agree on essentials such as divine unity, but the working-out of this doctrine over time has been conditioned by human imperfection and human inability to transcend limitations unaided—hence the cry for intercession. Sunnism responded with the saints and the mediating Sufi masters; Shiism with the "Immaculate Ones" and the mediating *ulama.* Purists thunder that intercessors should go the way of the Daughters of Allah; but the more forgiving may see saints and Imams alike as the quality of *rahmah,* God's mercy, articulating itself through history.

PROPHETHOOD AND QURANIC VIEWS OF HUMAN NATURE

God, so the Quran tells us, creates humans, sustains them, and showers them with favors before gathering them back to Himself. In exchange God asks that we acknowledge Him as the sole author of these blessings. Such acknowledgment constitutes the act of *islam,* the Arabic term designating an individual's submission to God. But the problem—and chapter 96 of the Quran makes this explicit—is that people are weak and forgetful, with a tendency to rebel against their Lord. This rebellion manifests itself as a mistaken belief in self-sufficiency, that humans have no need of God. Yet because God is merciful, again and again He sends reminders of the need for *islam.* These reminders are conveyed by prophets (also referred to in Scripture as "warners" and "messengers") who bear the admonitory revelation of divine Lordship. Such Quranic figures are consonant with the ancient Jewish scriptural tradition of prophethood, in which individuals raise their voices to warn their own people of moral decay and imminent punishment.

Prophetic messages constitute God's means of establishing relationships with human societies across time. To deny the need for such revelation is to claim that humans are independently capable of perfection. Such arrogance amounts to the sin of *shirk,* for only God possesses the qualities of absolute self-sufficiency and self-subsistence; and any person who grasps at such independence is cloaking himself with divine attributes reserved for God alone.

The nature of divine intervention in human history is presented clearly in chapter 7 of the Quran, an early Meccan revelation which descended on Muhammad during his long period of rejection endured at the hands of the Quraysh. The chapter catalogues in summary fashion legendary events and sacred tales that must have been long familiar to the Prophet's audience (to judge from the concision with which these tales are presented). The Quran reminds listeners briefly of these accounts and then organizes these events meaningfully so as to highlight the playing-out of recurrent themes across time. Again and again, Scripture argues, divine favor is bestowed on a given people, who are raised up to become a great civilization, prosperous and secure. Generations pass, and the favored society gradually forgets the source of its prosperity. People lose knowledge of the one deity who observes all behavior and to whom all accounts must be rendered; as a result any sense of an integrated moral system begins to fray. Idols are venerated as competing and distracting gods, appetites are indulged, justice abused. At this point Allah in His mercy selects a "warner" to show the civilization the decline into which it has entered and to remind it of the need for submission to God. For ease of comprehension the man chosen as prophet will be selected from among the people to whom the message must be preached.

Unfortunately the most typical response is rejection. Present customs have become consecrated; people have no inclination to reappraise their enshrined innovations or to accept the warning message as a call to the truer and original path of submission. The prophet finds himself mocked as a liar and imposter. Punishment is not long in coming—flood, earthquake, a rain of stones from the sky—and the arrogant civilization is effaced. Only the warner and the minority who accepted his message are saved. Then another people is raised up, shown favor, and given the opportunity for *islam,* for submission to God's sovereignty.

Chapter 7 presents a number of Biblical narratives: Noah, the Ark, and the Great Flood; Lot and Sodom and Gomorrah; Moses, Pharaoh, and the Israelite captivity in Egypt. When compared with the Hebrew scriptural accounts in *Genesis* and *Exodus,* it can be seen that the Quran has retold the tales to fit the outline noted above: favor, decline, warning, rejection, and punishment. But the Quranic retelling also demonstrates that this glum progression of events is not inexorable. After having been graced with deliverance from Egyptian captivity, the Israelites show their forgetfulness of Allah by creating a golden calf for worship; yet they repent in time and are spared the destruction visited on Noah's people and Sodom and Gomorrah.

Native Arab legends are recalled as well in chapter 7's pageant of moral history. Two non-Biblical Arab prophets, Hud and Saleh, are despatched to the peoples of Ad and Thamud. Each civilization rejects the messenger sent to it and is consequently destroyed. According to Islamic tradition, the people of Ad lived some centuries before the age of Muhammad; they occupied the southern coast of the Arabian peninsula, what is today Oman and Yemen. Muslim commentators explain that their level of material civilization was far advanced; they were great builders and irrigated the desert with networks of canals. By Muhammad's day this people had vanished, and only ruins remained to attest their presence. Quranic scholar Abdullah Yusuf Ali says of the Thamud people that "their seat was in the northwest corner of Arabia (Arabia Petraea), between Medina and Syria." Thus their territory included some of the most important Levantine trade routes. Despite past prosperity, by the seventh century A.D. and the age of Muhammad their civilization had vanished. Yusuf Ali suggests that Petra (in present-day Jordan) and other abandoned cities in the region may possibly be attributed to the legendary people of Thamud. Certainly the Quran's description (7.74) of them as dwellers who "sculpt the mountains into homes" recalls the tunnelled vaults and cliffside stone courts visible today at the site of Petra. Yusuf Ali notes, too, a biographical account to the effect that Muhammad, after his acceptance as ruler of Medina, led a military expedition northward to counter a Byzantine attack from Syria; on this march he traversed the ancient territory of the Thamud and encountered the remains of their cities.[11]

As with Noah and Lot, the Quran's references to Ad and Thamud are terse; Muhammad's audience was apparently already familiar with these tales. We may assume the existence of pre-Islamic legends concerning these lost cities. Such accounts would have arisen as the result of Arab discoveries of abandoned ruins: travellers might well create stories comprising imaginative speculations on the fate of a vanished civilization. The genius of the Quran is to have taken these Arab legends and fitted them into an integrated moral framework along with accounts of lost cities and natural catastrophes from the Biblical tradition: Sodom and Gomorrah, the Great Flood, the drowning of Pharaoh's army. All these legends, when arranged as they are in the Quran, join to reveal a pattern and recurrent theme: past history as warning for the future. Muhammad's Meccan audience, prone as they were to make mock, were thus cautioned: let them consider their own legendary traditions afresh and learn a new lesson therefrom. Near the end of chapter 7 the point is made clear: "Haven't they looked closely at all, thinking about the realm of the heavens and the earth and everything which God has created? Haven't they considered the possibility that perhaps their own moment of fate has drawn near?" (7.185)

Worth noting too in this context is that the moral themes presented in chapter 7 of the Quran recur in later popular Arabic literature of the medieval era. This is particularly true with regard to the pietistic "lost city" motif which recurs in narratives from the *Alf laylah wa-laylah* (The "Thousand and One" or "Arabian" Nights) such as *The City of Brass*. This tale takes as its historical kernel an actual expedition led by Musa ibn Nusayr, the eighth-century Muslim general who traversed northwest Africa in a series of conquests which added to the territories of the expanding Islamic empire. Later medieval geographers and chroniclers recounted legends to the effect that Musa in his travels came upon a mysterious abandoned city in the Sahara. The *Arabian Nights* tale takes the legend of Musa as its base and elaborates therefrom an admonitory tale on the evanescence of worldly pleasures. In the *Nights* fiction, Musa and his men find a splendid but eerily depopulated black palace; on one of its gates is inscribed a poem with the following verse: "So do not let the world deceive you with its adornment," an echo of Quran 31.33, "So do not let the lower-worldly life deceive you, and do not let the Deceiver deceive you away from God." The pious *shaykh* accompanying the expedition contemplates the palace and announces, "It is a warning to whoso would be warned"; within, the travellers discover a desolate tomb with the inscription "O you who arrive at this place, take warning from what you see." Again, echoes from Scripture: Quran 59.2 reads, "So take warning, you who have sight"; the Quran's story of Joseph and his brothers closes with the sober reminder that "in their story was a warning for those with understanding" (12.111). Quranic vocabulary and scriptural thematic motifs likewise recur at each stage of Musa's journey. A genie imprisoned in a stone pillar tells the travellers how it had refused submission to God and His prophet and was then punished for all eternity. Statues pivot and silently point the travellers to the City of Brass, where the men find storerooms of heaped-up wealth presided over by the perfectly preserved corpses of the city's former inhabitants. The travellers learn from inscriptions within the City of Brass that the inhabitants' overabundant wealth helped them not at all in warding off death; God has preserved the corpses and the vestiges of wealth as a warning to all travellers who pass by. As with the Quranic accounts of Ad and Thamud, listeners to this *Arabian Nights* tale would be expected to learn a lesson from the monuments and surviving ruins of past history and apply it to their own lives.[12]

THE QURANIC UNDERSTANDING OF JUDAISM AND CHRISTIANITY: SHIITE VIEWS OF PROPHETHOOD IN THE JEWISH AND CHRISTIAN TRADITIONS

As we have seen in the preceding discussion, Jahiliyah Arabs had some familiarity with Judaism and Christianity; Muhammad could take this familiarity for granted as he preached in the streets of Mecca. Jahiliyah knowledge of Jewish and Christian doctrine was slight, however, and there was probably little acquaintance with written Biblical texts; it is more likely that the most vivid narratives from the Bible—the Flood, Sodom and Gomorrah, and so on—were transmitted orally as tales.

The opportunities were many for contact with conveyers of this tradition. In Muhammad's youth there existed a large settlement of Jewish artisans and traders in Medina. Jewish emigration to the western coast of Arabia may date back to the first and second centuries A.D., when refugees fled the Roman conquests of Jerusalem. Cultural and religious influence was also exerted by Christian Syria, a province of the Byzantine empire. Arab merchants frequently ventured as far north as Damascus; Muhammad is said to have joined such caravans as a young man before receiving the call to prophethood. Bedouin and other wanderers were particularly impressed with Christian monks and the lives of solitary devotion they led in desert hermitage cells. A ninth-century historian records that a Syrian monk named Buhaira welcomed the young Muhammad and other Quraysh to a feast as they were resting on their travels through the north. In turn Christian wine merchants joined caravans to the south and carried on trade in the Arab cities of the peninsula. Thus it is not surprising that Jahiliyah religion was highly syncretistic: 360 pagan idols encircled the sanctuary of the Kaaba, but on its walls were painted portraits of Jesus and the Virgin Mary.[13]

When Muhammad began to receive Quranic revelations he interpreted these in light of the religious traditions with which he was familiar. His announcement that a divine voice had addressed him led many Meccans to conclude that he was *majnun,* possessed by a *jinn* or genie. Such spirits were said to seize and inspire tribal poets who pronounced incantatory verse for the protection of their clan and the binding of their enemies. The charge of *jinn*-possession is understandable: many of the early Quranic revelations were delivered in *saj'* or prose-rhyme, the same form of verse employed by ecstatic poets of the Jahiliyah. The Meccans simply labeled Muhammad in accordance with the categories they already knew. But he rejected the titles of poet and *majnun* alike; again and again (as in 7.183 and 23.70) the Quran asserts that this messenger is possessed by no *jinn*. Instead Muhammad understood the voice which spoke to him as that of the angel Gabriel, conveying a message from God.

This conviction and the reference to Gabriel suggest that Muhammad identified his revelations with the Jewish and Christian traditions rather than with the tribal religions of ancient Arabia. But this does not mean that he rejected the ambient Jahiliyah heritage altogether. True, he assumed the title of prophet rather than poet; but his achievement was to synthesize the Arabian legacy with Judaism and Christianity: thus (as we have already seen) the Kaaba was retained as a place of worship but was henceforth identified as a site built by Abraham.

From a Quranic perspective Judaism and Christianity can be regarded as "Abrahamic," that is, as later historical manifestations of the same original Abrahamic faith of Islam. Recall that the term *islam* indicates a monotheistic submission to Allah as sole god; Islam as a religion thus has existed since Adam—for as long as there have been humans to enter into relationship with God by offering Him their submission. As we have seen, there exists a "chain of prophets" (*silsilat al-anbiya'*) who throughout history have issued the same call to *islam* whenever such a reminder was needed; the Quran depicts Abraham as one of the earliest of these prophets. Chapter 6.74-79 offers a poignant vignette showing Abraham arguing with his father Azar, an idol-carver and star-worshipper. One evening they studied the night sky together, and Azar pointed out Venus, saying, "This is my master." Together they watched till the planet set, and Abraham replied, "I do not love things that are subject to decline." The Quran commentator al-Suyuti in his *Tafsir al-jalalayn* remarks of this passage, "For it is not proper that the Lord undergo change and transition."[14] Abraham broke with his father's religion in order to restore humankind to *islam*; thus have all prophets done, the Quran argues, risking the disapproval of those about them for the sake of the message.

Judaism and Christianity are rated highly in the Quran because their prophets were bearers of the true monotheistic confession. Muhammad's mission, however, was necessitated by the recurrence of spiritual entropy: the Islamic message preached by Abraham and Moses and Jesus had become gradually distorted by the followers of these prophets. The Torah revealed to Moses had sought to return humans to the path of submission; subsequent moral decline among the Jews led to the revelation of the Gospels entrusted to Jesus (the Quran treats the Gospels not as writings about Christ but as a message entrusted to him). The Christians in turn had betrayed the scriptural commission assigned them, thus necessitating the revelation of the Quran.

More specifically Jews and Christians are charged with having engaged in *tahrif*, the willful perversion of God's word. That is to say, they altered the text of the authentic Scriptures entrusted to them, excising any predictions they could find of the advent of Muhammad and likewise corrupting the Torah and Gospels so that these Scriptures no longer corresponded to the message preached in the Quran. Hence the curious status of Judaism and Christianity in Islamic countries: on the one hand they are ranked as superior to pagan religions and to Hinduism, Buddhism, and other faiths regarded as idolatrous; Jews and Christians living under Islamic governments in the past have enjoyed a protected legal status (even if such status in many ways resembled that of second-class citizens). The genealogy of these two faiths is, after all, Islamic, descended as they are from the ancestor—Abraham—whom they claim just as Muslims do. But on the other hand Judaism and Christianity are also treated to a certain extent as fossil religions—imperfect survivals from the past—superfluous now that they have been superseded by the perfect and uncorrupted Islamic message of the Quran.

Shiite Islam in its understanding of Judaism and Christianity attaches an additional and entirely distinctive set of significances to the prophets of the Abrahamic traditions. As noted earlier, Ali ibn Abi Talib was appointed by Muhammad, according to Shiite belief, to be undisputed ruler over the Muslim community upon the Prophet's death. Ali is thought to have served a kind of spiritual apprenticeship under Muhammad before assuming the role of caliph and Imam: he accompanied the Prophet everywhere and was initiated into the secrets of the Quran (more will be said about this last point when we discuss *ta'wil*). Shiites retroject this relationship as paradigm into the Biblical past: each prophet is said to have been accompanied by a lieutenant who ultimately succeeded his master to become Imam of the community. The model has been followed throughout sacred history: Abraham was aided by Ishmael, Moses by Aaron, Jesus by Simon Peter.[15] The prophet receives divine revelation and promulgates it; the Imam sees to the conservation of the message so that it will be safeguarded for future generations. The majority of disciples have access only to the public and outer form of the revelation, but before death each prophet privately interprets the revelation for his lieutenant and teaches him, phrase by phrase, the hidden inner meaning of God's message. According to Shiite belief, this teaching makes the Imam uniquely qualified to be the prophet's successor; the Imam in turn will draw about him an elite circle of the faithful whom he will initiate into the secret significances of the revelation.

3

Shiite *Ta'wil*: The Esoteric Dimension of Quranic Scripture

QURAN INTERPRETATION AND THE ORDERING OF MUSLIM SOCIETY

In Sunnism and Shiism alike the Quran enjoys an authority not fully comparable with that of the Bible in Judaism and Christianity. The latter religions ascribe the Bible to human authors (albeit divinely inspired) and consider the component texts comprising Scripture to be the product of human history, the record of the Creator's interaction with His people. From a Muslim perspective the author of the Quran is not Muhammad nor any other human but rather God Himself; the sacred text predates human history and was revealed at the predestined moment in time to Muhammad through the agency of the angel Gabriel. Muhammad did no more than recite the words dictated to him by Gabriel (and "Quran" in fact is the Arabic term for "recitation"); hence the frequency throughout the text of the imperative "say (the following) . . . !"

The centrality of Quranic scripture in Islamic society stems also from the fact that the Quran reflects the two stages of Muhammad's public career—persecuted prophet and triumphant administrator. The early Meccan revelations give warning of judgment and punishment and establish the principles of the faith: *tawhid,* prophethood, resurrection. The chronologically later Medinan chapters adjudicate the many issues arising in a pressing and adventitious fashion that Muhammad confronted in his role as civic and military administrator: marriage, money-lending, inheritance and bequests, slavery, treatment of orphans and prisoners of war, truces and the division of plunder from battles. Thus the Quran reflects the pragmatics of political and civil administration; its authority as prescriptive text reaches into every corner of public and private life, secular and devotional alike. Jesus gazed at the coin with Caesar's head thereon and acknowledged a dichotomy between earthly and spiritual power, but Muhammad's kingdom was very much of this world (although he had God's word to guide him in patterning it after heavenly models).

To appreciate the breadth of the Quran's jurisdiction, imagine for a moment a different ending to the biography of Christ as recorded in Scripture: Jesus fleeing from the Garden of Gethsemane and losing his pursuers in the olive groves; a *hijrah* north back to Galilee, where he becomes a recognized community leader and defeats Roman legionary detachments sent against him; then a return in triumph eight years later as the head of an armed force, with which he expels the Romans from Jerusalem and restores Judaism to an earlier purity, one predating the corrupting influence of Hellenistic paganism. Simon Peter would have rejoiced to be allowed finally to wield his sword in defense of Christ; and the Gospels would then have recorded the administrative decisions made by Jesus as he faced the problems of governance and warfare in the Near East. Instead, Jesus surrendered himself to crucifixion, and a new religion emerged, out of his disciples' meditation on his choice of surrender and death and what came after.

But to return from speculation to history: the Muslim successors of Muhammad as rulers of the growing Islamic empire were expected to follow his example of administering society in accordance with Quranic revelation. The sacred text naturally formed the basis of the religious legislation that structured Islamic society. But as the empire grew along with the complexities of administration, a problem began to make itself felt. Although Islamic scripture is acknowledged as all-embracing in its sovereignty as a guide to life, only a relatively small proportion of the Quran is explicitly legislative. In some instances later revelations appear to contradict earlier ones; other passages offer generalities instead of prescriptive details. This is in fact a strength, an index of the Quran's flexibility in application to current issues; but a widespread feeling developed that more data was needed to aid authorities in decision making. The only real legislator is God, who has encoded His immutable law (termed *shari'ah*) in the Quran; but for the decoding and adoption of this law in the form of earthly legislation further aids are needed. This led to the compilation of *hadith,* accounts concerning the life of the Prophet: his personal habits and life-style, his response to problems and situations unrecorded in the Quran, and his private remarks to friends concerning matters great and small (these utterances were carefully distinguished from the Quranic revelations dictated by Gabriel and publicly recited by Muhammad as God's word). The *hadith* and Quran together thus became the major sources of Islamic law (though it should be noted that Shiites broaden the definition of *hadith* to include the sayings of the Imams).

The customary behavior and practices of Muhammad were referred to as his *sunnah* (an Arabic term referring originally to the traditionally accepted practices followed by Bedouin tribes); thus the *hadith* comprise the record of the Prophet's *sunnah*. The Quran refers repeatedly to the *sunnat Allah*, "God's ancient custom," as in 48.23: "This is God's *sunnah*, which has been in existence since early times; you will find no alteration in God's *sunnah*." The term thus carries resonances from Scripture, the law, and immemorial Arab tradition. Supporters of the caliphate and the dominant social order after Karbala referred to themselves as *ahl al-sunnah*, "people of the *sunnah*," whence the appellation Sunni.[1]

There are four major forms or "schools" of law recognized in Sunnism: the Hanafi, Shafii, Hanbali, and Maliki; while Shiite law is often referred to as Ja'fari, in honor of the sixth Imam, the learned teacher Ja'far al-Sadiq. In the Sunni and Shiite creeds alike the study of Islamic law is the special province of the *ulama*, the scholars or jurisconsults who make their specialty a mastery of the Quran, the *hadith* collections, and the genre of literature known as *tafsir* (commentaries on Scripture). When sought for guidance, whether in a matter of state or in a private family concern, the jurisconsult checks first to see if the current issue is addressed directly by a Quranic verse or some incident recorded in the *hadith*. Failing this, he applies the technique of *qiyas*: reasoning by analogy from Scripture to the case at hand, choosing for comparison that part of the tradition which most nearly resembles the problem before him.

Matters of public concern may generate controversy among the *ulama*. In such instances (as I have noted above) Sunni legists will debate each other as they seek *ijma'*, the consensus of the community on the given issue. The consensus arrived at is said to be guarded from error.

Shiite *ulama* likewise debate each other when there is disagreement over public legal/moral issues, but they ascribe infallibility to the Hidden Imam rather than to the community (unsurprising, considering that the majority consensus had kept descendants of Ali from the caliphal throne). The rare scholar who is particularly outstanding for his piety, charisma, and knowledge of Quran and *hadith* may then sometimes be referred to as *na'ib al-Imam*, "the deputy of the Hidden Imam." Such a cleric will have considerable advantage over other *ulama* in winning acceptance for his application of divine law; for although the *na'ib* himself is not infallible, in some sense (at the popular level at least) he is perceived as enjoying the spiritual protection of the infallible Imam whom he serves as deputy.[2]

It can readily be seen from the above that the sciences of Quran commentary and Quranic law are central to the ordering of any Muslim society. As a way of safeguarding the normative status of Quranic scripture and the legal systems derived therefrom, both Sunni and Twelver Shiite *ulama* agreed that the phrase "seal of the prophets" that is applied to Muhammad in Quran 33.40 should be construed as a doctrinal assertion that he is the last of the messengers to be sent by God to humankind. Otherwise there would be no certain legal or religious sanction against Muslims who might suddenly announce themselves as new "warners" in the Abrahamic tradition, bearing freshly revealed scriptures entrusted to them by God. Such a scenario would banish the Quran to the shelf of superseded revelations along with the Torah and the Gospels, thereby threatening the whole structure of laws and religious hierarchy grounded in the Quran. And the *ulama* were not frightening themselves with idle worries: early Islamic history records a number of pretenders who claimed to be successors of Muhammad in the tradition of Abrahamic prophethood. The most famous of these claimants was the poet Abu al-Tayyib Ahmad ibn al-Husain (d. A.D. 965), better known to his contemporaries as al-Mutanabbi, "the would-be prophet." He wandered the Syrian desert reciting verses that he claimed were prophetic revelations from God. Bedouin tribesmen from various clans accepted him as a prophet and committed to memory his pronouncements. Some few of Mutanabbi's prophetic recitations survive:

> By the travelling star, and the revolving sphere, and night and day, verily the unbeliever is in a risky way. Proceed on thy road, and follow the track which the Muslims before thee trod. For by thee will Allah suppress the error of those who have perverted His faith, and erred from His path.[3]

The style is a conscious imitation of the Quran; so too the content: listeners are cautioned to adhere to the original path of ancient Islam; unbelievers are chastised for corrupting the faith. This preaching continued until the governor of Homs sortied with a military force, scattered the Bedouin, and captured the pretended "warner." Mutanabbi suffered imprisonment for two years until influential admirers secured his release, upon his promise to the governor that his poetry would bear no more claims of prophecy. Mutanabbi went on to become one of the most celebrated poets of the Arab world, but for years afterward rival courtiers would tease him in public about his nickname and heterodox youth.

Other claimants did not get off so lightly. In the eighth century a number of Alid partisans announced themselves as prophets in attempts to gain Shiite support against the reigning Islamic dynasty; the caliphs had them put to death. The tenth-century chronicler Mas'udi records vivid anecdotes of the Abbasid ruler Ma'mun holding interviews in his palace with a series of men who had been imprisoned for claiming prophethood. In fact, for centuries thereafter the figure of the would-be prophet survived as a stock character in Arabic literature: popular tales describe the caliph Harun al-Rashid visiting madhouses for amusement, where he interrogates inmates who maintain they have been contacted by Gabriel with a message of warning for humankind.[4]

METHODS OF READING THE QURAN: THE EXTERNAL AND INTERNAL DIMENSIONS

Claims of prophethood in the medieval era seem to have been especially characteristic of heterodoxy within Shiism, associated as they often were with revolts against the Sunni caliphate. Another source of controversy linked to the Quranic message was the exercise of *ta'wil*: the esoteric interpretation of Scripture. This comprises a method of textual study in which the reader scans the *zahir*, the exterior—the literal meaning of the work—in order to penetrate through to the *batin* or interior purport. The approach often becomes atomistic: individual phrases are grasped and squeezed for meaning, their context not always taken into account. In *ta'wil* what is readily apparent is no more than the bolt-ring on a trapdoor that the knowing may tug open to reveal a hidden world of significances.

Ta'wil is a particularly Shiite form of exegesis, one which arose in part because of dissatisfaction with the mere *zahir* of the sacred text. For the Quran lacks references to specifically Shiite issues—Ali's rightful succession to the caliphate, the status of the Imams, or events central to Shiite history such as the battle of Karbala. Yet Scripture must of necessity have insights to yield on matters of such importance; the question was simply one of learning how to read the text properly. Underlying the attraction of *ta'wil* for Shiites was a larger dissatisfaction, a restlessness with things as they are, with a world order in which the tyrannous ruled and insults to the Prophet's family stood unavenged. One may speculate that this perception of disorder in the world led Alid partisans to probe beneath the surface of the one text revered by Sunnis and Shiites alike as the repository of absolute significances; here if anywhere would be disclosed the patterns which show God's purposes in human history.

In this science of correspondences, Quranic images of luminosity are held to indicate the Prophet's family and the Imams, as in 64.8: "So believe in

Allah and His messenger and the light which We have caused to descend."
According to Shiite esotericist *ta'wil*, at the beginning of time God initiated
the process of creation by allowing some of His own light to emanate from
Himself. These emanations were the spiritual essences of the *Ahl-e Bayt*, who
in turn illuminate the world. Thus the conjuration which opens chapter
91—"By the sun and its radiance of early morning, by the moon when it
follows after the sun . . . "—is understood as a mystical reference to
Muhammad and his successor Ali. The moon—successor or nightly heir, if
you will, of the sun—receives solar light and reflects it to the earth after the
sun disappears; Ali received the spiritual light of Muhammad and transmitted
it to the Muslim community upon the Prophet's death. Because God is
merciful, He has placed on the earth signs (*ayat*) of His presence; the Quranic
phrase *ayat Allah*, "sign(s) of God" (whence the honorific title Ayatollah
among the Shiite *ulama*), is taken to indicate the Imams. Two examples from
Scripture will illustrate this concept: "As for those who refuse to believe in
the signs of God: in truth God will be quick to settle accounts with them"
(3.19); "We will display to them Our signs, on the horizons and within
themselves" (41.53). These "signs," understood in *ta'wil* to be the immaculate Imams, make accessible to sinful humans the guidance encrypted by God
in Scripture; failure to acknowledge the Imams as God's signs means one
will never fully savor the hidden meanings of the Quran. Worth noting too
is Quran 5.56: "Indeed the party of God (*hizb Allah*) will be the ones who
conquer." The Prophet's family, their descendants the Imams, and their
Shiite supporters are said to be referred to here in the words *hizb Allah,* a
phrase echoed in the title of today's militant Shiite organization in Lebanon,
the Hezbollah.[5]

THE "GREAT SACRIFICE":
SHIITE MEDITATIONS ON ABRAHAM AND ISHMAEL

I will limit myself here to only one more example of *ta'wil* (we will encounter
more when I discuss Quranic verses associated with Muharram liturgies in
Hyderabad). The passage I have in mind is Quran 37.100-110 and Abraham's
sacrifice of Ishmael (Arabic Ismail; in Islamic belief Ishmael—ancestor of
the Arabs—is commonly held to have been the object of Abraham's sacrifice
rather than his brother Isaac). As in *Genesis* death is averted at the last
moment: Abraham and Ishmael both submit to God's will (the verb *aslama*
is used in the text, from the same root as *islam*), the father as slayer, the son
as victim; but their Lord calls out and declares the test of submission
successful:

When they had both submitted, and Abraham had laid him face down, We called out, "Abraham! You have already fulfilled the vision." In truth it is in this way that We reward those who do good. This indeed has been the clear and evident test. And we ransomed him with a great sacrifice (*wa-fadaynahu bi-dhibh azim*).

To restate the final sentence: God allowed Ishmael's life to be spared, but it was redeemed at the cost of *dhibh azim,* "a great sacrifice." What is meant by this last phrase? In a popular collection of legendary traditions known as *Qisas al-anbiya'* ("Tales of the Prophets") the eleventh-century author al-Tha'labi reports that the victim substituted for Ishmael was a ram brought by Gabriel from paradise (an explanation reminiscent of Genesis 22.13 in which a ram is provided for Abraham after he passes the test of obedience). Tha'labi adds that this animal was the very creature once accepted by God as Abel's sacrifice. The Sunni al-Suyuti in his commentary on Quran 37.107 similarly notes that the ransom was effected with a ram and he explains that the substitute sacrifice is termed "great" (*azim*) because it was brought from heaven: like Tha'labi, he describes it as the beast once offered by Abel.[6]

Shiite exegesis also accepts the equation *dhibh*=ram, as is evidenced in the discussion by Muhammad Husain al-Tabataba'i in his work *al-Mizan fi tafsir al-Quran,* where he describes the ransoming victim as "a ram brought by Gabriel from the presence of God." But to rest content with this explanation alone would be to remain at the level of *tafsir,* commentary on the *zahir* or apparent exterior of the text. The process of *ta'wil* reveals that 37.107 in its *batin* or interior sense is a prefiguration of Husain's death at Karbala. The mullah Muhammad Baqir Majlisi offers an interpretation imparted by the sixth Imam, Ja'far al-Sadiq (this is in keeping with portraits of the Imams as masters who initiate believers into the secrets of *ta'wil*): Abraham, granted foreknowledge of Husain's martyrdom, wept bitterly, declaring that the Imam's future death grieved him more than the imminent slaying of his own son. God responded to these tears, saying, "O Abraham, I have through your grief for Husain and his martyrdom ransomed your grief for your own son as though you had slain him with your own hand"; that is, Abraham's sorrow for Husain moves God so greatly that He accepts this grief as a "ransom" which redeems the life of Ishmael. Another text, authored by adherents of either the Ismaili or Nusairi Shiite sect, asserts that the ram symbolizes Husain himself; the implication is that as Ishmael was spared by the slaughter of the sacrificial animal, so too the entire Muslim community was granted the possibility of salvation by the death of Husain in battle (the theological aspects of this interpretation will be further discussed below).[7]

Hyderabadi Shiites with whom I discussed Quran 37.107 offered the following argument in defense of a *batini* reading of this text (I compile here the gist of several conversations): Can a mere ram (even one brought from paradise) truly be considered "great" and an adequate substitute for a human, especially a boy as noble as Abraham's son? Obviously not, if one contemplates the text carefully. Therefore the cryptic declaration "We ransomed him with a great sacrifice" is meant to lead the reader to a careful consideration of the true identity of the victim in the profoundest sense intended by Scripture. Yes, Abraham slaughtered a ram, but this was no more than a typological rehearsal for a greater and more terrible slaughter yet to come. The redemption of Ishmael by means of a sacrificial animal was necessarily incomplete; the redeeming sacrifice was adequately completed only centuries later at Karbala, when a prophet's son was ransomed by the life of another prophet's grandson.

It should not be imagined that esoteric understanding of Quran passages such as the above is restricted to only a handful of clerics in the Shiite community. The popularity of certain *ta'wil* readings is attested by a verse from an Urdu lamentation poem entitled *Karbala la ilah illa Allah* ("Karbala: no god is there save God"); the poem is chanted by one of the most popular men's guilds in Hyderabad during their public Muharram liturgies:

> Karbala is the place of the Great Sacrifice
> The place where truth and falsehood were apportioned
> On the afternoon of Ashura this decree was made—
> Karbala: no god is there save God.[8]

The first line of this Urdu verse—*Karbala hay maqam-e dhibh-e azim*—repeats the Arabic phrasing found in Quran 37.107, *dhibh azim,* "a great sacrifice." In this poem the battlefield is imagined as an altar where the sacrificial victim Husain is slaughtered; the repetition of Quranic phrasing links this sacrifice with the ancient one of Ishmael.

SHIITE COSMOGONY: THE WORLD'S ORIGIN
AND DIVINE PATTERNS OF SUFFERING AND SALVATION

The term *ta'wil* literally signifies "to return a thing to its point of origin," so it is only logical that much esoteric commentary links the Imams and the family of the Prophet with events at the dawn of creation. The orientalist scholar Ignaz Goldziher cites a medieval Shiite Quran commentary which records a tradition concerning the first man, Adam. While still in paradise

Adam was commanded by God to gaze at the heavenly throne. He looked and beheld radiant images reflected in the throne: the forms of Muhammad, Ali, Fatima, Hasan and Husain, "just as a person's face is reflected in an untroubled mirror." Adam might well be the first man, but even he enjoys no seniority over the Prophet's family and the Imams. This passage confirms the preexistence and hence the spiritual eminence of the *Ahl-e Bayt* over all other human beings. Goldziher notes too how this text bears witness to the incorporation of Jewish legendary traditions into Islam: for a haggadic account recorded in the Talmud tells of angels descending and ascending the heavenly ladder, gazing first at Jacob asleep in the wilderness, then at the image of the patriarch preserved since the beginning of time on the throne of God.[9]

Ta'wil serves, then, to justify Shiite reverence for the Prophet's family by subordinating incidents and personages from the Quran to events in the lives of the Imams; the former can be fully understood only in the light of the latter. In their exegesis, however, orthodox Twelver *ulama* took care to respect *tawhid* and avoid statements which might be construed as deification of the Imams. Doctrinal caution went hand in hand with political developments. In the period from the ninth through the eleventh centuries, Twelver Shiites effected a kind of rapprochement with the reigning caliphal dynasty: they adopted a quietist posture, shunning agitation against Sunni rulers; in turn some prominent Twelver families found patronage at the court in Baghdad and employment in the government bureaucracy. Orthodox Twelver jurisconsults sometimes even joined with Sunni *ulama* in condemning heterodox Shiites and other Muslims who seemed to threaten the social order (the state-sponsored crucifixion of the Sufi mystic Hallaj, publicly executed in Baghdad in A.D. 922, is a case in point).[10]

Other Shiites were less cautious with their dogma than the Twelvers and found themselves labeled *ghulat*, "heretics," "doctrinal extremists" (from the word *ghuluww*, "doctrinal extremism"). Sunnis and Twelvers recognized each other as Muslims, but both denominations spurned as unacceptable deviants those Shiites found guilty of *ghuluww*. Many kinds of belief were grouped under this pejorative heading, often involving some infringement of the principles of unity and prophethood set forth in the *shahadah*. Shahrastani's twelfth-century heresiography offers the following introduction to the *ghulat*:

These are the ones who have gone to extremes in pressing the claims of the Imams, to such an extent that they have set the Imams beyond the limits assigned to created beings and ascribed to them powers pertaining to divinity. In some instances they liken one of the Imams to God; in others they liken God to His creatures. In the first case they overstate the powers of the Imams; in the second they try to limit those of God. Their dubious and error-filled doctrines arose from various sects: the *hululiyah* [those who believe in the possibility of the descent of God's divine spirit to take up residence in select human beings], the *tanasukhiyah* [those who believe in the transmigration of souls], the Jews, and the Christians. I mention the Jews and the Christians because Jews liken the Creator to His creatures, and Christians liken created beings to the Creator; and these false doctrines have penetrated deeply into the minds of those Shiites who have become heretics, so that now they ascribe divine powers to certain of the Imams.[11]

Shahrastani and other heresiographers record the names of dozens of Shiite *ghulat* sects, many of which preached revolt against the Sunni caliphate while seeking a charismatic leader among the descendants of Muhammad. Often, the disenfranchised from various strata of Islamic society were attracted to these groups. Bloodshed and violent failure terminated most such uprisings; what remains of the sects today are descriptions by medieval authors hostile to the *ghulat* and fearful of the disorder they threatened. A number of the *ghulat* groups articulated theological systems that registered in some way their adherents' anger at the injustice visited on the world by the exclusion from power of the Prophet's bloodline; the righting of this injustice would lead to a new age of prosperity, with tyrants punished and loyal supporters of *Ahl-e Bayt* vindicated.

Among the *ghulat* described by the heresiographers is a sect known as the Mughiriyah, followers of al-Mughirah ibn Said of Kufa (d. A.D. 736). Originally a supporter of the fifth Imam, Muhammad al-Baqir, Mughirah abandoned his allegiance to al-Baqir, announcing instead that he himself was an Imam and indeed a prophet who had been visited by the angel Gabriel. Arrested and brought before the Umayyad governor of Iraq, Mughirah called on the governor to submit to his prophetic message. The governor had him crucified instead.[12]

Of the information that survives pertaining to the Mughiriyah, perhaps the most remarkable material is a sort of creation narrative attributed to the sect's founder. Shahrastani describes this narrative with undisguised scorn but with considerable detail:

Al-Mughirah . . . went to such extremes concerning the rightful claims and status of Ali that no rational person could give credence to him. But he went even further than this, in his ascription of anthropomorphic traits to God. He claimed that God most high consists of a form and a body, possessing limbs in the likeness of the letters of the alphabet. His shape is that of a man formed of light. Upon His head is a crown of light. He possesses a heart from which wisdom wells forth.

And he claimed that when God most high wished to create the world He pronounced the most exalted Name, which flew forth and settled on His head in the shape of a crown. Al-Mughirah said: And this refers to God's utterance: "Give glory to the most exalted name of your Lord, who has created and arranged in order" [cf. Quran 87.1-2].

Then He apprised Himself of the future deeds of humankind and wrote them on the palm of His hand. He grew angry at the future sins of humankind and broke into a sweat. Two oceans gathered and formed from His sweat: one of them salt, the other sweet, the first dark, the second luminous.

Thereupon God gazed at the luminous sea and saw His own shadow. He plucked out the eyes of His shadow-figure and from them created the sun and the moon; and then He annihilated what was left over of His shadow, saying: "It is not right that there be any god save Myself" [cf. Quran 19.92].

Al-Mughirah said: Then He created all of creation from the two oceans. Believers were created from the luminous sea, unbelievers from the dark. First He created the shadow-forms of people; and of them the first which He created was the shadow of Muhammad—upon him be prayers and peace!—and the shadow of Ali. These He created before creating the shadow-forms of the cosmos.

Next He proposed to the heavens and the earth and the mountains that they undertake the "necessary burden" [cf. Quran 33.72], namely that they prevent Ali ibn Abi Talib from attaining the office of leadership of the community; but they refused. Then he proposed this task to humankind. Thereupon Umar ibn al-Khattab ordered Abu Bakr to accept the task of keeping Ali from the office of leadership. Umar promised Abu Bakr that he would have Abu Bakr appointed caliph, by treachery and betrayal, if Abu Bakr in turn would agree to have Umar succeed him as caliph. Abu Bakr accepted this plan and, acting in concert with each other, they undertook to prevent Ali from attaining his office.

All this, in accordance with the word of God most high: "And man took the necessary burden upon himself; truly he was unjust and ignorant" [Quran 33.72].

And al-Mughirah claimed that God most high revealed the following with regard to the case of Umar: "Like Satan, whenever he says to humans: 'Become unbelievers!' Then when in fact they become unbelievers, he says to them: 'I wash my hands of you!'" [cf. Quran 59.16].[13]

Note first of all how this story is studded with borrowings from Scripture: Mughirah has strung together a series of disparate Quran verses in such a way as to form a narrative. But in their new context the verses bear a freight of significance that has little to do with their literal meaning. Mughirah's text can be regarded as a classic exercise in *ta'wil*: excerpted scriptural phrases are grouped by the exegete in such a way as to reveal previously unsuspected meanings. What emerges is a creation myth articulated with Islamic vocabulary but reflecting the thought systems of older civilizations and pagan religious survivals. This is part of the fascination of Shiite esotericism: Quran verses became conduits through which flowed ideational motifs of the ancient Mediterranean and Near East, forming a reservoir of freshly islamicized imagery accessible to Muslim thinkers.

Mughirah's portrayal of God as a luminous being has some slight base of justification in the Quran: chapter 24.35 terms Him "the Light of the heavens and the earth." Slighter still is the Quranic rationale for the hypostasizing of God's "most exalted Name." Popular Islamic devotion posited the existence of ninety-nine known names of God, each based on a divine attribute cited in the Quran; invocation of these names provided help in times of need. The "most exalted Name" is hidden and hence a source of power for any mystic who can learn it. But Mughirah's representation of this Name as a crown atop God's head and of His limbs "in the likeness of the letters of the alphabet" suggests affinities too with the Kabbalah and Jewish meditations on the inner significance of the Torah, wherein knowledge of the divine names yields one access to the bearer of these names and to that Being's power.[14]

The heterodox portrait of God as "a man formed of light" also attests possible Jewish influence, but there may be overtones here as well of the dualist Manichaean belief systems once popular in Babylonia and Iran: at the beginning of time a luminous "Primal Man" is armored in the "five elements of Light" and wars against the "King of Darkness." Mughirah's entire account savors of Gnosticism. He sketches a step-wise progression to creation (deeds—sweat—oceans—shadow) which puts great boundaries of distance between God and His creation. This is characteristic of Gnostic philosophies. Gnostic also is Mughirah's depiction of humans as the adventitious products of passion (formed from the sweat of God's sudden anger) rather than as the result of a proportioned plan and magisterial divine intention. So too in the Valentinian gnosis of second-century Egypt: a spirit known as the "lower Sophia" undergoes anguish at her estrangement from God; her sufferings become reified and form the raw substance out of which is shaped our material world. Mughirah injects the motif of *tawhid* when he has God annihilate the remnants of His shadow—"It is not right that there be any god save Myself"—but the Islamic veneer is thin. Small wonder that the Mughiriyah were cast out among the *ghulat*.[15]

The priority given to Muhammad and Ali in the creation of humankind is a motif which we have already seen in another Shiite account describing the heavenly throne. To appreciate Mughirah's references to Abu Bakr and Umar, however, it is necessary to review briefly events from early Islamic history. Muhammad's aged companion Abu Bakr became the first caliph upon the Prophet's death in 632; Umar ibn al-Khattab succeeded Abu Bakr when the latter died a mere two years later. It is known that in the quarrels over the succession Umar had lent his support to Abu Bakr's candidacy as first caliph. In Shiite eyes the caliphate of both men was illegitimate, as Ali's claim to the title was thereby neglected. In Mughirah's doctrine the exegete advocates a conspiracy theory—Umar must have pledged his support in exchange for a promise that he would inherit power in turn—and then retrojects the conspiracy to the very origins of the world.

Why then does Mughirah represent God as the instigator of the plot to bar Ali from the caliphate? Mughirah's scriptural warrant for this notion is a *batini* reading of Quran 33.72, where the Creator asks the heavens, earth, and mountains to accept the *amanah,* the "trust" or "necessary burden"; they refused, but humankind accepted. *Tafsir* explications of this passage describe *amanah* as the burden of free will and moral responsibilities, the capacity to choose between good and evil. The inanimate material world refused the *amanah*; humans audaciously accepted. The Quran goes on to suggest that the burden is more than humans alone can bear unaided—"truly he was unjust and ignorant"—because of man's weak and rebellious nature. Thus far goes the *tafsir.* Mughirah's *ta'wil,* however, offers an interpretation that has little to do with the literal meaning of the Quranic text: the *amanah* now becomes the burden of undertaking to prevent Ali from attaining his rightful role of leadership. Mughirah's scenario reprises the scriptural order of events: the physical world recoils from the very idea of undertaking such a hateful task; the offer is then made to humankind, and from among them two men step forward and accept. Abu Bakr and Umar are seen as evil, yet the deed they commit is somehow necessary. Shahrastani's summary nowhere explicates the theodicy underlying this narrative, but Mughirah seems implicitly to wish us to see Umar and Abu Bakr's betrayal as the instrument of God's will.

Relevant to this issue of the divine intention are several conversations I had with Hyderabadi Shiites in 1989 and 1991 concerning God's role in the battle of Karbala. When asked why God had permitted Husain and his entourage to suffer and die, my informants cited what they perceived as two benefits stemming from Karbala. At the public and societal level, the Imam's sacrifice awakened Muslims to the corruption into which the entire realm was sinking thanks to its brutal and tyrannous rulers. At the level of the individual Muslim, Karbala makes more likely the possibility of personal salvation in the afterlife: the Shiite who remembers Karbala every year at Muharram and weeps for the martyrs will be rewarded by the intercession of the Ma'sumin on his or her behalf in paradise. Iranian Shiite villagers interviewed in the 1970s by the anthropologist Reinhold Loeffler expressed similar ideas in their stories of the "Cup of Suffering": before our world was created, Husain elected freely to drink to the bottom the Cup of Suffering offered him by God, thereby committing the Imam to undergo his passion at Karbala; in exchange Husain was promised intercessory powers on behalf of all who lament him.[16]

The treachery of the first two caliphs, then, as portrayed by the Mughiriyah, may be likened to the Christian concept of the *felix culpa*: without Adam's sin humankind would not have been blessed with the entrance of Jesus into human life. So too in Shiite history: the conspirators' treachery was heinous but necessary, leading inexorably to Karbala and the salvific benefits which would flow therefrom.

Although rejected as heterodox for its anthropomorphic description of the Creator, Mughirah's doctrine is nevertheless true to the Shiite understanding of the workings of the world. Ali's exclusion from power, the defeat at Karbala, the sufferings of *Ahl-e Bayt*: these were not accidents, chance failures because of poor leadership among the Shiites. These events were predestined and were merely played out as the fulfillment of a cosmogonic drama enacted at the very beginning of time. Seen then from the perspective of eternity, the sorrows of the seventh century disclose a divine patterning, and Shiites become part of this divine economy as they experience for themselves the sorrows of Karbala in the annual Muharram liturgies.

DIVERSITY WITHIN SHIITE ISLAM: THE TWELVER, ISMAILI, AND NUSAIRI-ALAWITE TRADITIONS

The Mughiriyah cosmogony is a good example of how towering an imaginative superstructure could be erected on the smallest of Quranic foundations. It is understandable that many orthodox Muslims profoundly distrusted the *ghulat* and the exercise of *ta'wil*; for in the hands of the undisciplined, *ta'wil* seemed to give free rein to extravagant and self-indulgent speculations while encouraging disregard for the letter of Scripture and its ritual and moral injunctions. Such disregard constituted a threat that could not be ignored, for Quranic injunctions furnished the basis of the legal system which held Islamic society together.

As part of their effort to maintain a rapprochement with the dominant caliphal powers, the *ulama* of Twelver Shiism upheld the validity of the *zahir* and the regulations of *shari'ah* as manifested in the Quran. These are to remain in effect until Judgment Day and the Resurrection, when the Occulted Imam returns as the Mahdi to administer and enforce the law directly and fill the earth with justice. At the same time Twelver jurisconsults held to the reality of the Quranic *batin*, knowledge of which had been conveyed by the Prophet to Ali. Through a chain of initiation each Imam in turn had privately instructed his successor in the science of *ta'wil*, so that today the twelfth and last Imam is the living heir of the esoteric knowledge underlying each chapter of Scripture. Access to this wisdom is controlled by the Imam's representatives, the *ulama*, who become qualified to undertake *ta'wil* through their study of *shari'ah* and the Imams' teachings, coupled with the intense veneration they cultivate for *Ahl-e Bayt*. The *ulama* in turn impart as much of this knowledge as they deem good in their dealings with common believers. The result in Twelver Shiite theology was an equilibrium between the *zahir* and *batin*, in which the *ulama* as religious leaders preserved good relations with Muslim society at large while maintaining a hierarchy of initiation and spiritual privilege within the Shiite community.

The balance struck between the exegetical *batin* and *zahir* is one of the traits which distinguishes Twelver Shiism from the other major Shiite denomination surviving today, the Ismailis or Seveners. Numerically Ismailis comprise only a small minority of the world Shiite population, but they have had a disproportionately large role to play in Islamic history.

This community arose as the result of an eighth-century dispute within Shiite ranks over the succession to the sixth Imam, Ja'far al-Sadiq. Apparently Ja'far had originally designated his elder son Ismail to succeed him; when Ismail predeceased his father, however, Ja'far then selected Ismail's younger brother Musa al-Kazim as spiritual heir. This transfer of designation created much controversy among Shiites. The majority accepted Ja'far's younger son Musa as the rightful successor; this group (later to be termed Twelvers) believed that the imamate passed to Musa's descendants and terminated with the Twelfth Imam, who is alive but in occultation till the Day of Judgment. A minority, however, contended that since Ja'far had originally designated his elder son Ismail as successor, the imamate was now hereditary among Ismail's offspring.

The latter contention was no more than a starting point for the formation of a distinctive Shiite theology. Over the next few centuries Ismailis quarreled repeatedly with each other over issues of communal leadership and the claims of various individuals to be the rightful designated successor to the line of Imams, so that the Seveners proliferated into numerous subsects. From the ninth to the thirteenth centuries, during a period when Twelver *ulama* defined Shiite doctrine in a way that made possible a peaceful entente with the Sunni majority, Ismailism in its various branches, like the "doctrinal extremists" of the *ghulat* (with whom the Ismailis shared certain affinities in worldview), attracted the discontented outlaws and would-be revolutionaries who, unhappy with the caliphal order, hoped for a more equitable society. Given the heterogeneity within its own ranks, Ismailism in the medieval era never experienced a consensual standardization of dogma to the degree achieved by the Twelvers; nevertheless, certain generalizations can be made about Ismaili doctrine.

Early Ismaili speculation described Ismail's son Muhammad as a prophet; with his advent and the imminent approach of Judgment Day, the *shari'ah* binding common Muslims no longer held priority. The *batin* underlying the law is eternal and changeless; but the legal codes derived from the mere *zahir* are mutable, varying from one age of humankind to the next. Within Ismailism the belief gradually developed that there will always exist among us a succession of visible and manifest Imams, descended from the Prophet's family and Ismail's progeny, to guide the Shiite community. This concept is in opposition to the Twelver belief in an occulted Imam who has been kept alive but hidden from human view in God's custody since the ninth century. For Ismailis today the line of Imams has continued in the person of leaders endowed with the honorific title of Aga Khan. Absolute obedience is to be given to the Ismaili Imams, each of whom is known as a "Speaking Quran": it is the Imam who makes available to believers the *batin* concealed within the scriptural text. For such Muslims it becomes possible to attain direct knowledge of the divine will by contact with the Speaking Quran. As a consequence, the written text of Scripture, the *hadith,* and the law are relegated to a subordinate status; nor need one necessarily consult the *ulama* who act as guardians of the scriptural tradition. Ismailism has thus earned the hostility of Sunni and Twelver jurisconsults alike.[17]

In the Middle Ages the Ismailis were feared for their militant defiance of the dominant caliphal establishment. The Ismaili onslaught worked at two levels. First, the sect's leaders dispatched *da'is* ("callers" or "summoners," a word derived from the Quranic term *da'wah*—"summons"—used to describe Muhammad's prophetic mission) to tunnel away at the foundations of Sunni society from within. Disguised as a merchant or Sufi dervish, a *da'i* would wander from town to town, loitering at mosques and bazaar stalls to engage men in conversation. Those he judged susceptible he would question concerning obscure verses from Scripture until he succeeded in sowing doubts as to the proper understanding of the Quran. Gradually then he would initiate chosen novices into an alternative understanding of the Quran. During the height of orthodox fear of the Ismailis, any *da'i* caught at such covert missionizing risked immediate imprisonment or death. Interestingly the treatises written by an Ismaili confraternity known as the Ikhwan al-Safa' (Brethren of Purity) describe the life of Jesus in such a way as to make him look very much like an Ismaili *da'i*: Christ is said to have known that he could not manifest himself openly to humans, given their state of ignorance, imprisoned as they are in Nature and the material world. Hence he took the disguise of a physician and healer and wandered from town to town, preaching, mingling with men, and piquing their curiosity with parables so as to stimulate a new understanding of Scripture.[18]

The second approach favored by medieval Ismaili leaders was direct action in the form of violence. The militant Ismailis were often referred to collectively as the Batiniyah, "adherents of the hidden dimension." Two sects in particular were notorious, the Qarmatians and the Nizaris. The Qarmatians declared all Muslims who did not heed their *da'wah* to be *kafirs*, unbelievers, with their lives and property not to be respected. Acts of public worship undertaken by the orthodox were seen as attempts at resistance against the esoteric message. Armed with this ideological justification, Qarmatian *da'is* gained adherents among several Bedouin tribes; together they raided caravans of pilgrims journeying on the *hajj*. In the year 930 they attacked Mecca itself—bastion of the old worship now superseded by the new *da'wah*—killed pilgrims on the streets of the city, and pried loose from the wall of the Kaaba the venerated Black Stone. They kept the Stone for twenty-one years, finally extorting a large sum from the caliph in exchange for its return to Mecca.

More dreaded even than the Qarmatians were the Nizari Ismailis, known pejoratively to their opponents as the Hashishiyin (hashish-users), better known in the West as the Assassins. The Nizaris were far more selective than the Qarmatians in their violence, targeting orthodox *ulama* and Sunni government officials for political murder. The assassinations were carried out by Nizari initiates called *fedayeen* (plural of *fedayee/fida'i*, "one who offers his own life as a sacrificial ransom"). The *fedayeen* were dispatched from inaccessible mountain fortresses in northern Iran (where they held a castle in the Elburz Mountains known as Alamut or the "Eagle's Nest") and in Syria. The master of the Assassin Order was nicknamed *shaykh al-jabal*, the "Old Man of the Mountain," word of whom reached Europe via the Crusaders and travellers such as Marco Polo. Saladin, the great champion of orthodox Islam during the Crusades, waged war against the Nizaris, besieging their

Syrian fastnesses and in turn eluding several *fedayeen* attempts at assassination.

It was at Alamut during Ramadan of the year 1164 that the master of the Nizaris proclaimed the "Great Resurrection": the new age was at hand, the *zahir* abrogated, the *batin* made manifest for initiates. In token of the old law's passing, wine was served from the fortress pulpit and the Ramadan fast solemnly violated. Orthodox chronicles of the time registered horror.[19]

The terror of the Nizaris receded only in 1256 with the Mongol invasions, when the warlord Hulagu Khan overthrew the Eagle's Nest and scattered the Assassins. Within a generation the orthodox Mamluk sultan Baybars likewise subdued the Syrian fortresses of the Order. The ruins of Assassin citadels survive in a number of remote sites in the mountain highlands of Syria, including Masyaf, where a Nizari castle dominates the heights above a village populated today by Ismailis. The Ismaili watchman who unlocks the fortress gate will tell you stories without prompting of the Assassins and of sultan Saladin's unsuccessful attempts to take their Syrian strongholds.

Ismaili violence is a thing of the medieval past. Under the progressive-minded leadership of the Aga Khans, the Ismailis in the twentieth century have become the most forward-looking of all Muslim denominations, sponsoring numerous humanitarian and educational projects. As in the past, both *shari'ah* and Quranic scripture are subject to the interpretation of the living and present Imam, who still commands devoted obedience among his followers. Thus Ismailism today retains its emphasis on the primacy of the *batin*. Ismailis are everywhere a minority; in Pakistan they have frequently been harassed by Sunni fundamentalists. The latter accuse the Ismailis of heterodoxy and of unpatriotic disloyalty to the *shari'ah* which has shaped the legal codes of Pakistan as an Islamic nation. In response the Ismailia Association of Pakistan issued a document entitled "Fundamentals of Ismaili Faith" which attempts to align Ismaili doctrine with Twelver Shiism (the latter is acknowledged as orthodox in Pakistan). Thus, for example, the Ismailia Association asserts unequivocally that "the Holy Prophet Muhammad is the last and final Prophet."[20] Nevertheless some Muslim scholars judge Ismailism today only on the basis of its medieval past. The eminent Twelver Shiite author Muhammad Husain Tabataba'i states that "the difference between Twelve-Imam Shiism and Ismailism lies in that for the latter the imamate revolves around the number seven and prophecy does not terminate with the Holy Prophet Muhammad."[21] Fazlur Rahman in his textbook survey of Islam is harsh with the Ismailis:

The Ismaili interpretation offers itself not merely as authoritative but as absolutely authoritarian, emanating from the infallible Imam. Add to this the subterranean character of the movement, the resort to terrorism, subversion, and assassination by the Qarmatians and the Assassins and the strict taboos on social intercourse with non-Ismailis and the picture of historic Ismailism is complete.[22]

Rahman passes over in silence Ismailism's reorientation in modern times and its commitment to humanitarian efforts under the Aga Khans.

The case of the Ismailis illustrates a trend at work in late twentieth-century Islam. With secularism on the defensive in many Muslim countries, Islamic credentials have increasingly become revalidated as a means to political power and as a litmus test of popular credibility. In this atmosphere religious minority groups of dubious status have attempted to establish their orthodoxy. As with the Ismailis in Pakistan, so too with the Nusairis in Syria, a sect whose veneration of the first Imam is so extreme that they have been spurned as *ghulat* by Sunnis and Twelver Shiites alike, on the grounds that they deify the Imam Ali. Their name is derived from Muhammad ibn Nusair (d. A.D. 883), who (according to the heresiographers) claimed divine lordship for Ali and the rank of prophet for himself. Nusairis themselves today prefer the title "Alawite" in order to emphasize their devotion to Ali rather than their historical derivation from a doctrinal extremist. Their belief in *tanasukh* (transmigration of souls) is linked to a moral system of reward and punishment: the evil are reincarnated as dogs and snakes; the souls of the good are lifted up to the heavens and granted a place among the stars. Syrian Alawites whom I met in Tartous and Hosn Suleiman in 1990 described God as "unknowable and invisible, a great secret"; they added that "Ali is the means by which God manifests Himself to us." My informants acknowledged, too, in conversation with me that their liturgies include the ritual drinking of wine. So it is understandable if the Alawites' status within Islam has been problematic. Even Mustafa Ghalib, a Muslim scholar whose writings display a sympathetic interest in *batini* thought, criticizes the Alawites for their citation of traditions concerning miracles wrought by Ali and the other Imams as proof of the divine rank of the *Ma'sumin*:

> If we translate the Nusairi technical vocabulary and doctrinal symbols we will find that their intention is to demonstrate that for every action and every word there is a special *ta'wil* which none know save those shaykhs who have been instructed by the Imams. This *batini ta'wil* is that which distinguishes them from their brothers the Shiites, for the Nusairis go beyond the permissible limits of doctrine in their *ta'wil*. Their extremism lies in their attribution of special virtues and exalted sacred attributes to the Imam Ali ibn Abi Talib (may God be pleased

with him!) . . . We do not disavow the miracles and wonder-working with which Nusairi books are filled, but we do object to the abusive exploitation of these deeds as proof of the Imams' occupying the rank of gods.[23]

For their part the Alawites have fought for acceptance as Muslims within the Twelver Shiite tradition. The modern Alawite author Muhammad Amin Ghalib al-Tawil (d. 1932) concludes his *Ta'rikh al-alawiyin* (History of the Alawites) with an essay entitled "Means for achieving the advancement of the Alawites":

> Despite what some people think, the Alawites constitute neither a separate distinctive religion nor a separate distinctive denomination. Rather, the Alawites are Ja'fari Shiite Muslims . . . Alawites believe that the twelve Imams are *ma'sum,* preserved from sin and error, and that the words of the Imams serve as definitive authoritative guides. Alawites also believe that it is impossible for the Imam to contradict the Quran and the *hadith* . . .
>
> Thus there remains no distinction whatsoever among Muslims in this part of the world except for the recognition of equality between Sunnis and Shiites. This is not too much to ask of enlightened people in this day and age, when reason prevails, which is the best determinant of the public interest. The tie of nationalism is the greatest and strongest of ties.[24]

The question of Alawite recognition has an important political dimension today as well, for the president of Syria, Hafez al-Assad, and the government officials and military officers on whom he relies to maintain power are from Syria's Alawite minority. It is understandable that al-Assad, as a member of a community rejected by other Muslims as heterodox, embraced Baathist ideology, with its emphasis on pan-Arab secularism rather than Islamic identity as a means of achieving national unity. Nevertheless al-Assad has remained conscious of the stigma of *ghuluww* that still adheres to the Alawites. Hence in 1973 he requested a *fatwa* from Musa al-Sadr, a prestigious Twelver mullah and the head of Lebanon's Higher Shiite Council, concerning the denominational status of the Alawites. Musa al-Sadr replied with a *fatwa* to the effect that the Alawites do in fact constitute an orthodox community within Shiite Islam. Much was at stake in this ruling: religious legitimacy within Syria for al-Assad, Syrian military and political support for Twelver Shiites in Lebanon's civil strife. Recognition benefited both parties.[25]

4

Variations on the Esoteric Tradition in Poetry and Theosophy: Examples from Attar, Hafez, and Suhrawardi of Aleppo

Twelver Shiite dogma, it has already been noted, affirms a precise balance between the external and internal dimensions of Scripture. For the good of society as a whole, an individual's spiritual insights into the hidden purport of sacred writ cannot take precedence over the law articulated in the literal text. *Batin* and *zahir* share equal validity.

And yet, again and again a strangely antinomian note is sounded in the Islamic literature favored by even the most orthodox Shiites. Mystical poetry frequently pictures observant and pious Muslims who are suddenly blessed with a glimpse of the Divine; so enraptured do they become that they forget themselves and all routine acts of prescribed worship. Such persons have been elevated, even if only momentarily, beyond the earthly realm, hence beyond the law which regulates earthly life. These ecstatics now perceive the inner order which informs the universe; their rank, it is implied, is higher than that of the conventionally pious who see the *zahir* and nothing more.

This theme is expressed in the tale of Shaykh Sam'an found in *The Conference of the Birds,* a thirteenth-century poem composed by the Iranian mystic Farid al-Din Attar.[1] Sam'an is introduced as an orthodox Muslim and veteran *hajji,* a custodian of the Kaaba who observes all the canonical fasts and has learned the Quran by heart. But all this is swept away when he becomes afflicted with the love of a young Christian girl. Enslaved by her beauty, the old man does whatever she orders, becoming a swineherd (thus mingling with animals declared unclean by Scripture) and drinking with her the wine forbidden by Quranic precept. Sam'an's pious friends are shocked and try to persuade him to resume the Quranically mandated ritual prayers which once informed his daily life. Perform the *ghusl,* they urge him (this is

the purificatory ablution with water which is required before prayer if one
has just experienced sexual intercourse or has otherwise incurred ritual
impurity); Sam'an replies that his ablutions henceforth will be in blood
(normally a substance ranked as *najis* or ritually polluting but now transformed into an acceptable purifying fluid because the "bloodshed" involved
is Sam'an's annihilating martyrdom under the spell of love). When reminded
to pray, he cries that his new *mihrab* is the face of his beloved (the *mihrab*
is the prayer niche in a mosque indicating the direction of Mecca, the sacred
site towards which orthodox Muslims are enjoined to orient themselves in
prayer). Exasperated, another friend shouts at him to perform the *sajdah* (the
ritual prostration before God in prayer); Sam'an announces that he will
comply, but that from now on he will bow only to this girl and her beauty.
Conventional ritual and conventional understandings have been transcended;
the old man knows a rapture such as he has never before experienced.

In the end Sam'an does return to orthodoxy: the Christian girl is moved
by God to convert and dies a Muslim; the shaykh gives up wine and the
company of pigs and resumes his worship, to the relief of his friends. But
(the author implies) familiar actions will now be different: henceforth when
he performs Quranic rituals there will be a new depth of feeling; the moment
of rapture has left its imprint on all future acts of worship.

Attar's verse can thus be read as a poetic exercise in *ta'wil*: the external
prescriptions of Scripture are ultimately upheld, while the inner significance
of these regulations is explored. But in Twelver Shiism a prestige attaches
to the *batin* which is lacking in the *zahir*: all Muslims are bound to the
observance of *shari'ah*, but not all will perceive its hidden meaning. For the
spiritual elite the understandable temptation is to assert one's deeper comprehension, to be observant of the law for the good of the many yet to imply
that one is inwardly free of mere prescriptions because one perceives the
transcendent order hidden within the law. Hence the attraction of ecstatic
and antinomian literature.

Consider this fourteenth-century Persian poem by Hafez, who remains
one of the most widely read poets in Iran today:

> Hair a mess, sweaty, smiling, and drunk
> shirt torn, reciting love-poems, a wine-cup in his hand:
> His eyes made clear he wanted to stir things up;
> he breathed one sigh after another.Late last night he sat himself by my pillow,
> then laid his head to my ear and in a sad voice said:
> Hey, old-time lover of mine, are you asleep?
> Any lover to whom such nighttime-wine is given

is no more than a *kafir* refusing to believe in Love
unless he becomes an idolater worshipping Wine.
Get out!, you with your abstemious asceticism,
and don't find fault with dreg-drinkers,
Because we were given nothing save this one gift
on the day before Creation when God asked us,
"Am I not your Lord?"
That which he poured into our cup, we drank it down,
regardless of whether it was wine of Paradise,
or wine of drunkenness, we drank it down.
Laughter of the wine-chalice and a sweetheart's curly hair:
O how many vows of penitence have such things shattered,
just as has happened to all the vows of penitence made by Hafez![2]

These stanzas reflect Hafez's characteristic delight in apparent paradox. The
work opens as a love poem: the beloved steals to the narrator's bed to rebuke
him for lack of devotion. But the beloved's rebuke plays with the categories
of religious vocabulary, inverting their conventional meaning. The narrator
is scolded for being a *zahid* (an ascetic focused on devotional austerities),
which one might otherwise think a praiseworthy occupation. Instead he is
urged to become a *badeh-parast* (literally a "wine-worshipper," a phrase
carrying a scandalous suggestion of the sin of *shirk* and violation of *tawhid*).
Otherwise the narrator will be no more than a *kafir-e ishq* ("an infidel
refusing to believe in Love"; *kafir* of course is a Quranic term repeatedly
used in Scripture to denounce those who refuse to acknowledge God's
sovereignty).

The poem's dramatic high point comes with the imperative *bo-ro* ("Get
out!"), where we may imagine the sleepy narrator chased from his comfortable bed. The beloved's authority to cast out *zahids* is derived from his
remembered vision of the *ruz-e a-last*, the day when God proclaimed "Am
I not your Lord?" This is a reference to Quran 7.172, where God is described
as having assembled all of Adam's future descendants in heaven before the
creation of the world in order to obtain their recognition of Him as Creator.
In Sufi meditations the *ruz-e a-last* is imagined as that time preceding fleshly
creation when our souls enjoyed intimate company with God, before we were
separated from Him and sent down to the earthly realm and forced to endure
the isolating limitations of human bodies. In Hafez's version of this cosmogonic drama the gift of wine was conferred on the beloved and the whole
sodality of "dreg-drinkers"; and the phrase *khamr-e behesht* ("wine of
heaven") recalls chapters 52 and 56 of the Quran, with their description of

the drink to be served the faithful in paradise by youthful cupbearers. For a moment one remembers the Assassins of Alamut and the Great Resurrection proclaimed from their Eagle's Nest: the law is now abrogated, paradisal pleasures may be enjoyed in this world. But Hafez savors ambiguity too much to make so definitive a proclamation, and he retreats at once to obscurity: the drink poured out for us, was it truly wine of paradise or simply wine of earthly drunkenness? No matter. Both stimulate ecstasy; we drank it down.

Left unresolved of course is the question of whether this wine should be understood literally or figuratively. And that is how it should be. The law must be sustained; but Hafez conveys, too, the momentary reckless joy felt by those who perceive a hidden world beyond the apparent order.

The ambiguity-laden mysticism of such poems retains its attraction in Iran today. Confirmation of this genre's attractiveness came from a surprising quarter in 1989, after the death of Ayatollah Ruhollah Khomeini. The Ayatollah's son released the text of a mystical poem authored by his father that was very much in the Hafezian tradition. Khomeini employed numerous stock images from the vocabulary of Persian mystical poetry: the poem's speaker announces he is giving up the mosque and the role of *zahid* in order to haunt the wine tavern and worship the wine-servers therein. This, from an outstanding member of the Twelver Shiite *ulama,* the Islamic Republic's fiercest guardian of Quranic precepts, the unbending enforcer of the law for all Iranians under his jurisdiction. But one may speculate that it is precisely because Khomeini observed the *zahir* so stringently that he felt free to explore the *batin,* an inner world where, like Shaykh Sam'an, he could be delivered briefly from the law and its constraints.[3]

Khomeini's thought was also influenced (via his study of *hikmat-e ilahi* or "divine wisdom") by the writings of the theosopher Shihab al-Din Yahya al-Suhrawardi (d.1191). Born in northwest Iran, Suhrawardi wandered through Turkey and Syria as a young man, studying law and the Quranic sciences, staying in Sufi hospices, seeking spiritual learning. Finally he came to Aleppo, where he was befriended by Saladin's son, the prince al-Malik al-Zahir. But the outspoken Suhrawardi antagonized the *ulama* of Aleppo in public disputations, and they denounced him to Saladin on a charge of heterodoxy. The *ulama* alleged that Suhrawardi refused to accept the finality of Muhammad's prophethood and that he believed that God might raise up new prophets at any point in history subsequent to Muhammad. Hermann Landolt speculates that Suhrawardi "was suspected of crypto-Ismailism"; certainly his wandering from town to town, and the dervish garb he affected, fit the profile of an Ismaili *da'i.*[4] This was a dangerous time in history to be tagged an Ismaili: Saladin was waging his jihad against Richard Lion-Heart and the Crusaders and had no patience for internal security problems (recall that the Ismaili Assassins had dispatched squads of *fedayeen* on more than one occasion against Saladin). On Saladin's orders Suhrawardi was imprisoned and executed.

The theosophy developed by Suhrawardi, one which was to have a profound influence on subsequent generations of Iranian Shiite thinkers, is termed *hikmat al-ishraq,* "the wisdom of illumination." Suhrawardi posits an origin for humankind reminiscent of ancient Gnosticism: separated from our Creator by imprisonment in flesh, we have forgotten our divine origin and subsist in an exile of perpetual darkness (Suhrawardi cites Quran 59.19 to justify this cosmology: " . . . those who have forgotten God, so that in turn He has made them forget their own selves"). If we wish to recapture the memory of our origin and prepare ourselves in this life for reunion with the Creator in the next, then we must undertake a combination of spiritual ascesis and philosophical training. In response God may choose to illuminate us with a burst of His divine light (in support of this notion the theosopher cites Quran 50.22, "You had been inattentive to this; but We have unveiled from you that which covered you. Thus today your vision is piercing!"). At such a moment we glimpse briefly our first homeland and discern the spiritual patterns governing the universe.[5]

Suhrawardi's cosmology borrowed from Ismailism, which in turn derived in part from the Greco-Roman Ptolemaic model of the universe; but the vocabulary he used to describe his world system was largely Islamic (and Suhrawardi himself saw his work as a union of Platonist wisdom and ancient Iranian Zoroastrian religion in an Islamic context).[6] In a treatise entitled "The Sound of Gabriel's Wing," the narrator, a young man, ventures by night to a Sufi monastery; once inside, he goes to a doorway leading to a garden.[7] There he finds seated ten white-haired *shaykhs* of radiant appearance. Only one, however, the nearest of the ten, will speak to the quester; this *shaykh* is Gabriel, who explains in symbolic language the significance of what the young man beholds. Each of the elders is a celestial Intellect or angel, charged with suzerainty over one of the crystalline spheres encircling the earth. Only the Intellect presiding over the nearest of the spheres to earth, that of the moon, can hold communion with humans.[8] For the moon partakes of the qualities of both the sublunar and extralunar realms—mutability (as proven by its waxing and waning phases) and timeless eternity; the spheres beyond the moon defy human access. Suhrawardi further islamicizes his schema by identifying the archon of the lunar realm as the angel Gabriel. His outspread right wing (that which is arched toward the outer spheres and the

Creator) is of pure light; his left wing (that which is closer to our earth) is flecked with darkness. Only through Gabriel do humans experience the celestial realms and find traces of their Creator, and just as Gabriel once illuminated Muhammad with God's divine light, so too may the angel touch any other theosophist-questers who have prepared themselves adequately.

Blasphemous? Perhaps; it is easy to see whence the Aleppine *ulama* derived their fatal accusation that Suhrawardi denied the finality of Muhammad's prophethood. But in fairness to Suhrawardi one should note that he never seemed to show much interest in claiming prophetic rank for himself or the privileges associated therewith (nor did he stir up trouble among the Bedouin tribes with a pretended Quran as had Mutanabbi); in any case in his writings he explicitly described Muhammad as the seal of the prophets.[9] Rather he wished to assert the possibility of ascending to an ecstatic *batini* vision of the world's hidden order through a willed program of philosophic studies and spiritual ascesis. What excited Suhrawardi was the thought that in response to this discipline an angel would descend and meet him halfway.

5

The Patterns that Inform History: Shiite Worldviews and the Understanding of Past and Future

THE ZAYDI TRADITION IN SHIISM

Shiism evolved originally as a political rather than as a religious movement, one focused on the question of leadership within the Islamic community. Evidence to support this assertion can be found in events of the seventh and eighth centuries subsequent to the death of Husain at Karbala. Husain's direct descendants, those men now sanctified as Imams in Twelver belief, retreated into quietism, refusing to condone or lead open military revolts against the Sunni caliphate. They chose instead political obscurity and contented themselves with a role as spiritual teachers of the Shiite minority. But many Alid partisans grew dissatisfied with the quietism of Muhammad's direct descendants and sought out other more distantly related members of the Prophet's household who might be willing to lead an anticaliphal insurgency. One after another ephemeral Shiite sects arose, led by Alid rebels who claimed lineage from the Prophet. Each sect briefly became a focal point of political dissatisfaction and revolt, only to be cut down by caliphal forces. Through all this the Twelver Imams sat aloof, immersed in private teaching; thus the line survived.

One of the most famous Alid rebels of this period was Zayd ibn Ali, grandson of Husain and half brother of Muhammad al-Baqir (the latter is recognized in Twelver Shiism as the fifth Imam). Zayd attracted the support of militants impatient with al-Baqir's political passivity; he led an uprising against the reigning Umayyad government in Kufa, only to be killed in the street fighting there in 740. But Zayd's conception of political authority survived after his death among his followers. The Zaydis asserted that the imamate is open to any descendant of Fatima and Ali, not simply the direct descendants of the Household designated in the Twelver line of Imams. But to qualify for the title of Imam one must come forward publicly and claim the leadership of the Muslim community; quietism and avoidance of political responsibility disqualify a claimant. It follows from this too that Zaydis reject any notion of a Hidden Imam or occultation, since manifest worldly authority is a primary attribute of the Imam. Likewise the number of Imams is not limited to twelve but is ongoing, a part of human history. Finally, the Zaydis reject the attribution of any supernatural powers to the Imams; in this they opposed the deifying tendencies prevalent among the *ghulat*. Although a small minority within Shiism, the Zaydis survived on into the twentieth century in remoter parts of the Islamic world such as the highlands of Yemen.

TYPOLOGY AND THE FORESHADOWING OF HUSAIN'S MARTYRDOM

It may be argued then that Zaydism represents a survival of the earliest and most purely political form of Shiite Islam. Much more gradual, over a number of generations, was the emergence of Shiism as a religious movement closely related to, but distinctive from, the sensibility of the Muslim majority. The theology surrounding religious (as opposed to exclusively political) Shiism was articulated in the intellectual circles of the Twelvers, the Ismailis, and the *ghulat*.

Shiite theology busied itself especially with the retrospective assignment of meaningful causes to the salient events of sacred history: Karbala, the sufferings of the martyrs, the exclusion of *Ahl-e Bayt* from power. The orientalist Louis Massignon hypothesizes that these injustices led Shiite thinkers to struggle with the problem of evil in the world: they asked themselves why God permitted such sorrows to be inflicted on the Prophet's family and his descendants.[1]

What resulted in Shiite thought was a belief that these events had been divinely predetermined in accordance with a cosmic pattern of necessity. From the beginning of time God had known of humankind's future sins; because He is merciful and compassionate (two of the most frequently asserted divine attributes in the Quran) He permitted the sufferings of immaculate and guiltless victims, who by their acceptance of these trials would gain merit with God and hence the power to intercede on behalf of sinful humanity. To gain access to this intercession sinners must acknowledge the deprivations and injustice endured by *Ahl-e Bayt*; anyone who withholds this acknowledgment is in effect denying the full reality of the sacrifice made by the *Ma' sumin*. Therefore in every age God tests men and women by challenging them to honor the Prophet's family as fully as possible and to lament the tragedy of Karbala.

Central to the Shiite worldview is the belief that earlier ages of human history foreshadowed Karbala. "For the name 'Shiism'," asserted the medieval Alid author Nawbakhti, "is an ancient one; there were the Shiites of Abraham (*shi' at Ibrahim*), and of Moses and of Jesus and of all the prophets, God's prayers and blessings upon them all."[2] That is to say, each of the ancient prophets underwent rejection and persecution by his own people (a motif made explicit in the Quran itself, as noted earlier); each of them attracted a *shi' ah*, a band of devoted partisans, who endured his persecution along with him. Joseph in the well, Moses before Pharaoh, Jesus driven to the cross: all become typological models foreshadowing the martyred Husain. Karbala casts a shadow forward in time as well: those today who choose to come together as a *shi'ah* to honor the Imams will be tested and suffer persecution for their loyalty just as were the companions of Husain. Thus God underscores the pivotal importance of Karbala by patterning world events in every age—past, present, and future—so as to conform with events of the seventh century. The discerning have only to study past history to sense both God's recurrent presence in human affairs and the free will which He permits humans as they either disregard or respond to the signs of His presence.

Shiites with whom I discussed the significance of Karbala emphasized Husain's foreknowledge of the siege and death he would undergo. His defeat in battle was not the result of a fluke or some lapse on his part as a military leader; had he wanted, he could have avoided entrapment outside Kufa. The point of this assertion is that Husain's sacrifice was voluntary; and it is the willed nature of his loss that made his death meritorious and salvific for others.[3]

A visitor to the shrine of Husain's head in Damascus will see within the inner sanctum a large prayer-placard bordered by illustrations of white flowers. Pilgrims sit before the sign quietly reciting the Arabic invocations printed thereon. Among these verses is the prayer: "Peace be upon Husain, the martyr, the thirsting one slaughtered as a sacrificial victim (*al-madhbuh*), the one slain unjustly (*zulman*)." This sentence affirms two principles important to the present discussion. The word *madhbuh* ("slaughtered as a sacrificial victim," with its echo of Quran 37.107 and the phrase *dhibh azim*) gives a formal and planned liturgical air to the death of Husain, who submitted like Ishmael to the divine will as he came to the "altar" of Karbala. The term *zulman* ("unjustly") is important too for our understanding of

Karbala; for the slaying of Husain was an injustice tainting all forms of worldly government thenceforth, for as long as the Prophet's descendants and defenders are denied their rightful power. And because proper governance is viewed in Islam as a religious matter intimately linked with the practice of the faith and the welfare of society as a whole, the wrong inflicted at Karbala will have repercussions generation after generation in all aspects of human life until the injustice is finally righted. This will come about only when the last direct descendant of Husain, the occulted twelfth Imam, returns to usher in the Day of Judgment, a time viewed in Shiism as the correction of the injustice inflicted on *Ahl-e Bayt* and as the correction of all the wrongs which flowed therefrom.

Given the magnitude of the evil done at Karbala and the strength of the tyrannous forces unleashed thereby, it is unsurprising that history subsequent to the seventh century keeps repeating a pattern familiar from the lives of the early prophets: the persecution of a righteous leader and of his small band of loyal followers, who are kept from power but look forward to their ultimate vindication through the help of God. One may object that in Islamic history Shiites have not always been excluded from political power, that in fact a number of Shiite governments have held dominion—Buyids and Ismaili Fatimids in the tenth century, Safavids in the sixteenth, and of course the Islamic Republic of Iran in the twentieth—but these facts have not carried significance in the face of the overriding paradigm of persecution, exclusion, and suffering. As in the articulation of any worldview, history which does not fit the paradigm is discarded.

SACRED HISTORY AND THE SHIITE LITURGICAL CALENDAR

The injustice visited upon *Ahl-e Bayt* at Karbala is remembered annually in Shiite communities throughout the world during the season of Muharram. In Hyderabad the Guruh-e Ja'fari, one of the many men's guilds which perform *matam* (breast-beating and other acts of self-mortification, to be described in part II of this book), chants the cry *Ya mazlum Ya sayyidi,* "O wronged one, O my lord," over and over as they pound their chests in lamentation. Thus the memory of the ancient injustice is actualized, made a part of the present.

But Muharram involves more than just commemoration of the past. Hyderabadi informants recounted for me the story of how the Kufan Shiites failed to come to Husain's rescue; each year in the present brings with it a chance to make up for the Kufan failure, to undertake a kind of collective penitence and show that if today's Shiite community had been present at

Karbala it would have stood and died with Husain. Generation after Shiite generation bears witness that it accepts the responsibility of undertaking this active penitential lamentation; just as Muslims universally recognize the existence of the *silsilat al-anbiya'*, the "chain of the prophets" extending across history up to the time of Muhammad and the seventh century, so too by analogy we may conceive of a *silsileh-ye matamdaran*, a "chain of breast-beating mourners" extending across Shiite history from the seventh century to the present and beyond till the advent of the Mahdi.

Muharram activities extend to acts of communal charity and generosity as well as mourning. Families who can afford to construct a *sabil*, booths where water and other refreshments are served to congregants as they make their way from one shrine to another in an almost incessant series of liturgies during the foremost sacred days of Muharram. Offering water to passersby is of course a pragmatic act of charity; but it also in some way breaks the barrier of time: if one could have, one shows, one would have offered water from the Euphrates to the besieged of Karbala in their thirst.

In part II of my study I focus on the most intense period of the mourning season, the first ten days of Muharram, but in fact the period of tears extends throughout all of Muharram and beyond into the following month of Safar. And more: in a sense Muharram casts its shadow over the entire year. The wrong committed at Karbala is too great ever to be set aside completely. During my two summers in Hyderabad I attended *jeshns*, feast days and festive occasions in the Shiite liturgical calendar, in the month of Dhul hijjah, the month preceding Muharram. Lights and colored tinsel were strung from chapel ceilings, garlands draped round the necks of poets and other celebrants, candy distributed to the children. Yet beneath the gaiety was an undertone of foreboding. The Id al-Ghadir celebrates what Shiites understand as Muhammad's public designation of Ali as his successor; but again and again the preacher reverted to the usurpation of the caliphate by Abu Bakr and Umar and thundered at the wrong to be inflicted on Ali so soon after the joyous honor bestowed upon him. In the Christian faith Palm Sunday commemorates Jesus's welcome by the crowds of Jerusalem, but Good Friday follows too closely thereafter to permit unalloyed joy. So too in the Shiite calendar; but in Shiism the Resurrection remains hidden in the future, awaiting the end of history and the return of the last Imam.

6

Shiism in India: Historical Background and Cultural Influences

The eleventh-century Afghan warlord Mahmud of Ghazna was celebrated for his numerous raiding expeditions into India. A telling anecdote survives concerning one of these quests in search of plunder, in which he conquered the city of Somnat. Victory secured, Mahmud ordered Somnat's Hindu temple destroyed. Thereupon temple priests came forward to save the shrine's chief idol, offering the sultan gold as ransom if he would spare the statue. His officers were inclined to accept, but Mahmud prided himself on his orthodoxy. He had the idol thrown onto a fire; while the flames jumped up he declaimed virtuously that the meritorious fight against idolatry weighed more with him than gold. Yet as the statue burnt it cracked open from the heat, revealing a cache of jewels that spilled forth at Mahmud's feet. So then, the onlookers knew, one could fulfill the religious obligation of combatting paganism and still be rewarded here in this life for the effort.[1]

This legend illustrates an early Islamic view of India, as a land of *kafirs* and as a source of lawful plunder. The reality of Muslim-Hindu relations in the medieval period, of course, was more complex. Commerce flourished, as did peaceful Muslim settlement. For Shiites, moreover, India from very early on represented something further: a place of refuge from Sunni caliphal persecution. This is reflected in a legend to the effect that the besieged Husain at Karbala made the offer, by way of compromise with his Umayyad enemies, to exile himself to India.

The city of Hyderabad is located in the south-central region known as the Deccan. This area fell under Muslim domination in the fourteenth century with the founding of the Bahmani kingdom by Hasan Gangu. Originally an officer from the northern realm of the Muslim Delhi sultanate, Hasan took advantage of internal weakness in the northern state to consolidate the Deccan conquests initiated by the Delhi sultan Muhammad ibn Tughlaq.

The folklore surrounding Hasan Gangu and the naming of the Bahmani kingdom is important for what it reveals of the cultural forces at work in southern India. In one legend Hasan is described as a man of noble Iranian ancestry but of impoverished circumstance, forced to make his way in the world as best he could. One day he fell asleep outdoors beneath a tree and was seen by a passing priest of the Hindu Brahman caste. The Brahman halted in astonishment at the figure he glimpsed behind the sleeping Hasan: a great cobra, coiled and alert, keeping watch to safeguard the wayfarer. This tableau recalls the iconography of the sleeping Vishnu (a Hindu god revered as sustainer and preserver of the universe), who is depicted as reclining beneath the outspread hood of a watchful cobra.

Knowing the snake's action to be a portent, the priest waited till Hasan awoke, then told him what he had witnessed and offered to become the poor man's servant, on the condition that Hasan add the priest's title to his name. Hasan agreed, and when fortune favored him with rule over a kingdom the new sultan conferred on it the name Bahmani (supposedly a corruption of the word *Brahman*).[2]

Another account states that Hasan claimed descent from the ancient Sassanid ruler of Iran, Bahman ibn Isfandiyar; for this reason he took the title Bahman Shah and named his kingdom Bahmani.[3]

These stories reflect two of the enduring cultural and religious influences on Hyderabad, the Persian and the Hindu. The Bahmanis recruited courtiers and soldiers from Iran as well as central Asia; the Iranian Nimatullahi *tariqah,* a Sufi brotherhood of Shiite orientation, sent dervishes to preach in the Deccan. Nimatullah Wali, master of the order, dispatched to one of the Bahmani sultans a gift consisting of an emerald twelve-pointed crown (symbolizing the spiritual lordship of the twelve Imams).[4]

In the early sixteenth century the Bahmani realm disintegrated into independent princedoms, one of which, the Qutb Shahi dynasty of Golconda, founded the city of Hyderabad in 1591. The Qutb Shahis sponsored public Muharram processions and built a number of Shiite shrines in Hyderabad. The Shiite Safavid government of Iran cultivated good relations with the Qutb Shahis, apparently in an attempt to combine forces against the powerful (and largely Sunni) Mughal kingdom of northern India.

In fact diplomatic relations between the two Shiite states gave the Mughals an excuse to invade the Deccan. In the seventeenth century the Mughal ruler Aurangzeb complained of the Qutb Shahi sultan as "an oppressor against whom the people were invoking the heavens, a heretic who had perverted all his subjects from the pure Sunni faith, and lastly an ally and financial supporter of the king of Persia. Not to punish such a heretical ruler would be failure of duty on the part of an orthodox Islamic emperor." One of the demands made by Aurangzeb was that henceforth the Qutb Shahis should omit the name of the Iranian shah in all public prayers within their realm.[5]

In 1687 Aurangzeb conquered the Qutb Shahis, and a new dynasty, the Asaf Jahi, was established in their place. Originally viceroys of the Mughals, the Asaf Jahis too asserted their independence. During the time of the British Raj, the Asaf Jahi realm centered on Hyderabad was recognized as a sovereign Native State; it retained its independence until forcibly incorporated into postcolonial India when invaded from the north in 1948. The Asaf Jahi nizams or rulers were Sunnis (with the possible exception of the last nizam, about whom more will be said later), but they retained numerous Shiite ministers and continued the Qutb Shahi practice of sponsoring public Muharram liturgies, while ruling over a population the majority of which continued to be Hindu.

Even today, long after the dissolution of Hyderabad state as an independent kingdom, traces of Iranian cultural influence from the past can still be felt. A branch of the Nimatullahi brotherhood exists in Hyderabad; its adherents (well-educated and prosperous Shiites) meet several times a week in a small chapel not far from the well-known shrine of Yousufain. In 1991 I was invited to one of their evening *halqahs* or gatherings. After performing together the *namaz* (the ritual prayer Quranically prescribed for all Muslims), members took turns chanting poems in Persian authored by Hafez and the Sufi saint Jalal al-Din Rumi. Occasionally, early on a Friday morning, members go to pray at the tomb of Mir Mahmud Deccani, a Nimatullahi shaykh whose shrine is on the outskirts of Hyderabad.[6]

Given the Safavid-Qutb Shahi entente from the past, it is natural to inquire whether the Islamic Republic of Iran today cultivates relations with Hyderabad's Shiite community. The short answer is yes, it does; but I will save discussion of this interesting topic for part II of my study.

In reading my descriptions of Muharram liturgies throughout the rest of this book, students of Indian religion will doubtless be struck by the obvious influence of Hindu ritual on Hyderabadi Shiite observances. This is understandable given the overwhelmingly Hindu milieu in which Hyderabad's Shiites have survived. Reform-minded Muslims sometimes complain of this persistent influence. On one occasion a self-described Wahhabi grumbled to me that the Old City Shiites, with their garland-draped relics and incense burners, might as well be bowing before a row of Ganesh elephant-idols.

Shiites whom I questioned, however, described this syncretism as a kind of strength: the external borrowing from Hinduism, they said, helped attract the many Hindus who visit Hyderabad's Shiite shrines and offer homage to Husain during the month of Muharram.

7

Representations of Muharram in British Fiction and Memoirs from the Raj

Sir Arthur Lothian, one-time British Resident at Hyderabad representing the Empire's interests in that Native State, recalled in his autobiography his first arrival in India in 1911. Fresh from Oxford and newly landed at Calcutta as a member of the Indian Civil Service (ICS), the young Lothian received somewhat of a jolt when he tried to leave Calcutta to begin his first assignment:

> After a day or two spent in collecting the necessary kit for my life up country I set off by train for Jessore in the evening. The great Moslem festival of Mohurrum was then being celebrated, and the route to the station lay through Sealdah Square, which the police had made the turning-place for rival processions that reached that nodal point from all directions. Unfortunately the police arrangements had broken down somehow, and the various processions had got mixed up and started fighting. When I arrived at the square in an old ticca gharry [a hired closed cab], it was a seething mob of men belabouring each other with swords and lathies [weighted bamboo cudgels]. They did not attack me, but the gharry was badly jostled, and it was a very scared driver and bewildered young civilian that got through to the relatively quiet oasis of the station. The sea of dark excited faces, without a white one visible amongst them, brought home to me, as nothing which I had read had done, how relatively few white people there were in India, and the narrowness of the margin on which law and order depended.[1]

From early on the British government in India seems to have viewed public Shiite Muharram observances primarily as a security risk harboring a great potential for violence. William Sleeman (an administrator famous for his suppression of the notorious Thuggee cult in the 1830s) described the riots that often erupted when Hindu festivities coincided with Shiite lamentation liturgies. He characterized the public Shiite rituals as "the mournful procession of the Muharram, when the Muhammadans are inflamed to madness by the recollection of the really affecting incidents of the massacre of the grandchildren of their prophet . . . the Muhammadans, clothed in their green mourning, with gloomy downcast looks, beating their breasts, [are] ready to kill themselves, and too anxious for an excuse to kill anybody else." But Sleeman judged that the Raj stood to gain from such conflicts:

> Many of my countrymen, full of virtuous indignation at the outrages which often occur during the processions of the Muharram, particularly when these happen to take place at the same time with some religious procession of the Hindoos, are very anxious that our Government should interpose its authority to put down both. But these processions and occasional outrages are really sources of great strength to us; they show at once the necessity for the interposition of an impartial tribunal, and a disposition on the part of the rulers to interpose impartially.[2]

A distasteful spectacle, this: an English official calculating the benefits accruing to the government from Hindu-Muslim confrontations. It might be tempting to construe a conspiracy from such statements and allege that British authors falsely fabricated an image of Shiite liturgies as violent in order to justify imperialist arguments for British dominion in India. A tempting allegation, but facile and wrong-headed; for in fairness to the Raj it must be pointed out that Muharram in many Indian cities often was and still today often is an occasion for violence, whether Hindu-Muslim or Sunni-Shiite. Given the recurrent possibility of bloodshed, it is only natural that administrators viewed Muharram primarily as a security risk. I would argue, too, that India's postindependence national government today views Muharram much as did the colonial Raj—as a volatile religious season which must be closely monitored, but which if successfully channeled and contained may demonstrate the benefits of centralized external authority. Readers may judge the strength of my argument on the basis of evidence I present in part II of this book. Here I wish only to note that British authors writing on Muharram commonly noted the threat of violence but were varied rather than uniform in their response to this threat. Philip Woodruff, a former member of the ICS, published a description in 1954 of how District Officers tried to keep the peace at Muharram. The challenge can be outlined as follows: Shiites vied with each other as to who could make the largest and most impressive *tazias* (gilded wooden models of the tombs of the slain Imams, carried in procession on Ashura); magistrates issued codes (for reasons made clear below) limiting the height and width of these *tazias,* but the regulations were often disregarded. Hindus for their part kept zealous watch during the *tazia* procession to ensure that the model tombs did not touch (and hence desecrate) the numerous Hindu shrines located along the Muharram procession route. The Muslims in turn resisted as an insult the notion of altering their traditional route one whit so as to avoid possible confrontation (this resistance is still a point of pride and source of confrontation in Muharram disputes today).

Woodruff illustrates the problem by describing altercations that arose in certain villages because of pipal trees lining the procession route. Hindu villagers treated the trees as sacred and created small shrines there; the ICS officer sketches a confrontation that often arose on the day of the Muharram procession:

> Either the gilded tower or the pipal tree has grown since last year; the image will not pass unless a branch is cut. The Hindus of the village with their six-foot bamboo quarter-staffs have collected and wait grimly for the first insult to the sacred tree. The Muslim escort of the image will not agree to deviation by a yard from the usual route, still less that the tower should bow its head or be carried aslant.[3]

Woodruff makes clear what was the mark of a really good government administrator: "never letting things come to such a pass—or rather, impasse." Some officials arranged in advance for diggers to excavate and deepen the roadway where it passed beneath the trees' canopy of leaves, so that the *tazias* could pass the sacred pipals without so much as brushing the overhead branches. Other magistrates recorded the maximum height allowed for each *tazia* and permitted the procession to begin only if each model met the stipulated measurements. Woodruff notes one particularly ingenious solution:

> E.H.H. Edye . . . arranged between festivals for two elephants to graze near an offending pipal tree; elephants are not exactly sacred but are under the special patronage of Ganesh and no one would grudge them a branch or two from a pipal. And next year, to everyone's surprise, the tomb passed easily where before it had stuck.[4]

But what is important to note is the rationale that the ICS officer believes underlay all these strategies: "This skilful management was needed because there was very little force available . . . In most districts there were no British soldiers; in very many there were no soldiers at all, British or Indian."[5]

What emerges from Woodruff's account is that the ICS took a professional pride in averting confrontations that might have exploded in violence. Hindu-Muslim bloodshed indicated the government's lack of skill in conciliatory administration; the use of soldiers to put down Muharram violence was a further admission of failure.

But from a writer's point of view violence averted did not always make for the most exciting copy, whether in the form of newspaper articles or short stories. Shiite liturgies caught the attention of Rudyard Kipling (1865-1936), one of the most widely known authors of Victorian England and the British Raj; however, the concerns he brought to Muharram differed considerably from those of the Indian Civil Service.

During the 1880s, at the very beginning of his career, the young Kipling lived in the city of Lahore in the Punjab. While there he wrote two newspaper articles (for the *Civil and Military Gazette,* where he worked as a reporter and subeditor) and one short story on the city's Shiite processions. The pieces appeared within a few years of each other (1885, 1887, and 1888), and the later pieces borrow from the earlier, so one can get some sense of the unfolding of Kipling's ideas.

The earliest piece is a newspaper article published in October 1885 for the *Gazette.*[6] The text begins as coverage of a Muharram riot in Lahore; but Kipling goes on to note dismissively that there really hadn't been much fighting after all:

> "Certain fellows of the baser sort"—whether incited thereto by excess of strong drink or fanaticism is of no importance—had undoubtedly fallen to on Thursday night and broken each others' heads. It would be gross flattery to style the Hindu-Mussalman fracas a riot; but it was at least something that needed repression—albeit a scuffle on the part of the very scum and riff-raff of the City of the Two Creeds; when religious feeling runs high and strong, arms and potent liquors are not wanting.

Immediately thereafter the young reporter displays a fascination with the apparatus of civic control:

> There is something impressively methodical about the manner in which a district officer anxious for the good name of the city he governs, sets to work at keeping it in order. Behind his own personal influence; behind the machinery he sets in motion of First Instance, Revision, and Appeal, lies—if not the business-end of the rifle at least the butt, which can be brought down firmly on the toes of vagrom man . . . Lahore on Friday night was held by the local authorities to stand in need of a warning, if not a lesson. Two companies of the 5th Fusiliers, a hundred and

fifty men of the 24th Punjab Lancers, and an indefinite number of armed policemen, therefore, were detailed to keep watch.

What impressed Kipling was the sureness of touch with which the District Officer wielded precisely the amount of force needed to keep order—neither the bullet nor the bayonet in this instance, merely the rifle butts of the Punjab Lancers applied smartly to the bare feet of any rioters.

Not content, however, with recording merely that Lahore's Muharram celebration had passed in a largely uneventful and carefully supervised fashion, Kipling set out from the military garrison (where the article's opening is set) to wander the Old City alone in search of firsthand impressions of the procession—a mark of the curiosity that distinguished him as a good reporter and outstanding writer. Soon lost in the network of unlit alleys, the young Englishman found himself immobilized among towering tomb displays and fervently chanting Muslims. Instead of maltreating the lone European, however, those around him took pains not to jostle him; Kipling noted the "almost painful anxiety of the crowd not to offend." Seeing that Kipling was lost, a "respectable native gentleman" took the reporter under his wing with "Oriental courtesy":

> With a grace and a dignity which would bring a blush even to the most hardened British cheek, that native gentleman took charge of the alien, and for the time being made him his guest. Did he wish to examine a *taboot* [alternate designation of the *tazia* or replica of Husain's tomb]? Forthwith the *taboot* was lowered, and the circulation along the street stopped until the Sahib was satisfied. Would he care for some really good sword play? Two *ghatkas* [fencers] appeared at once; circulation was stopped as before and with four men to see that he was not inconveniently crowded, the Sahib watched the game.

And when Kipling announced himself to be tired, the "native gentleman" found him a guide and carriage to see him safely back to the fort and the European cantonment.

In this early essay Kipling shows the interest in native life and customs which was to become a hallmark of his later fiction; but he is also honest enough to report his confusion and dependence on charitable Indians. One senses that Kipling wrote up frankly his first impressions—fear, then gratitude—while these were still fresh in his mind. Remarkable, given the paternal condescension that marks the introduction of this same article, with its admiration for the display of European force to keep order.

The ambivalence is even more marked in a second Muharram piece that Kipling published two years later in the *Gazette*.[7] He starts by recalling the disturbances of 1885:

> Two years ago, Lahore at the end of the hot weather was enlivened by a small Mohurrum fight in the City, and the outcries of many *bunniahs* [shopkeepers]. A British regiment, to the extent of four companies, was dug out of its bed at Mian Mir, the 14th Bengal Lancers smote with their lance-butts on the toes of the peace-breakers and Lahore Fort was crowded with riotous subalterns . . . In the dearth of other news, down-country papers called the scuffle 'riots'.

He contrasts this minor excitement with the uneventfulness of the current season: "This year's Mohurrum has passed with a peace that was almost dullness." As in his first article Kipling notes the Deputy Commissioner's watchful presence and the colorfulness of the *tazia* procession; but his tone now is jaded:

> Seen from the safe shelter of a well-curb the movement was picturesque; but after a few years the eye of the dweller in this country becomes scarred and his heart hardens, so that the finest effects of red light and black shadow, seas of turbans, upturned faces and arms tossed aloft, fail to impress him as anything new or startling . . .
>
> With the best will in the world, and all possible desire to recover 'the first fine careless rapture' of the griffin who gazes on the gaudier aspects of the East, the attention wandered from the crowd to the watch, and interest was swallowed up in a yawn. There had been no trouble, the City was quiet and another Mohurrum had been safely tided over. Beyond the city walls lay civilization in the shape of iced drinks and spacious roads.

Lacking violence Muharram seemed now scarcely worth reporting. The word "griffin" is telling, an Anglo-Indian term used for an English newcomer or greenhorn just landed in India. Kipling makes it clear he is now one of the seasoned veterans; hence the studied nonchalance.

But he retains his eye for detail:

> In the broader streets, surrounded by the faithful, sat *Maulvis* [mullahs] reading the story of the death of the Blessed Imams. Their *mimbars* [pulpits] were of the rudest, but the walls behind them were in most cases gay, with glass lamps, cuckoo-clocks, vile 'export' trinketry, wax flowers, and kindred atrocities. A Normandy shrine could hardly have been in worse taste, but, looking at the men who listened, one forgot the surroundings. They seemed so desperately in earnest, as they rocked to and fro, and lamented.

The passage registers both fascination and distaste (as well as a slap at French Catholicism and Shiism alike in one sentence). Here Kipling drops for a moment the pose of distanced urbanity: in spite of himself he is touched by the intensity of religious devotion he witnesses. Viewed from this distance in time, there is one passage in this article that strikes the reader as prescient:

> Properly exploited, our City, from the Taksali to the Delhi Gate, and from the wrestling-ground to the Badami Bagh would yield a store of novels . . . However, until someone lifts its name into the light of a new fame Lahore is only a fraction of a Deputy Commissioner's charge, to be watched, drained, coaxed and scolded as such.

It is clear where Kipling's larger interests lay; and he was soon to put his Muharram reportage to use in a different context. The year following the appearance of this article, in 1888, he published a short story entitled *On the City Wall* in which the action is set during Muharram celebrations in the Old City quarter of Lahore.[8] Here in his fiction Kipling imagined a full-scale Muharram riot of the kind that eluded him in his newspaper reporting in 1885 and 1887.

In the introductory pages of this story, before the action gets fully underway, Kipling delivers an editorial blast against the notion of native Indian self-government:

> No one, not even the Supreme Government, knows everything about the administration of the Empire. Year by year England sends out fresh drafts for the first fighting-line, which is officially called the Indian Civil Service. These die, or kill themselves by overwork, or are worried to death or broken in health and hope in order that the land may be protected from death and sickness, famine and war, and may eventually become capable of standing alone. It will never stand alone, but the idea is a pretty one . . . If an advance be made all credit is given to the native, while the Englishmen stand back and wipe their foreheads. If a failure occurs the Englishmen step forward and take the blame. Overmuch tenderness of this kind has bred a strong belief among many natives that the native is capable of administering the country.

But to the plot: Czarist agents in Lahore hatch a scheme to free a Sikh warlord who has been imprisoned by Her Majesty's government for leading insurgencies against the Raj. The escape is timed to coincide with Lahore's Muharram riots; while the police and military are trying to quell disturbances, the agents will take advantage of the confusion, to spirit away the chieftain. Thus the processionists in the Old City's Shiite liturgies become pawns in the Great Game played out between Britain and Russia for control of India and its frontier lands. And by extension the disorders associated with Muharram become a threat to the security of the Indian Empire itself.

Among the plotters is one Wali Dad, "a young Muhammadan who was suffering acutely from education of the English variety and knew it. His father had sent him to a Mission-school . . . When his father died, Wali Dad was independent and spent two years experimenting with the creeds of the Earth and reading books that are of no use to anybody." A self-proclaimed agnostic and freethinker, resentful of the British and scornful of his own background, Wali Dad fits into neither Muslim nor English society.

Wali Dad accompanies the British narrator through the Old City on the night of the tazia processions. Lahore is described as a place of pandemonium: "The drums were beating afresh, the crowds were howling 'Ya Hasan! Ya Hussain!' and beating their breasts, the brass bands were playing their loudest." Wali Dad's initial response is one of disdain: "It is a most disgraceful exhibition. Where is the pleasure of saying 'Ya Hasan, Ya Hussain,' twenty thousand times in a night?"

But as they move cautiously along the streets, where Hindu and Muslim are striking each other with fist, stick, and club, Wali Dad undergoes a transformation:

> "It is a lucky thing that they are fighting with natural weapons," I said to Wali Dad, "else we should have half the City killed."
>
> I turned as I spoke and looked at his face. His nostrils were distended, his eyes were fixed, and he was smiting himself softly on the breast. The crowd poured by with renewed riot—a gang of Musalmans hard-pressed by some hundred Hindu fanatics. Wali Dad left my side with an oath, and shouting: "Ya Hasan! Ya Hussain!" plunged into the thick of the fight where I lost sight of him.

Late in the evening, the riot quelled, the narrator discovers his friend:

> On returning to Lalun's door I stumbled over a man at the threshold. He was sobbing hysterically and his arms flapped like the wings of a goose. It was Wali Dad, Agnostic and Unbeliever, shoeless, turbanless, and frothing at the mouth, the flesh on his chest bruised and bleeding from the vehemence with which he had smitten himself. A broken torch-handle lay by his side, and his quivering lips murmured, "Ya Hasan! Ya Hussain!" as I stooped over him. I pushed him a few steps up the staircase, threw a pebble at Lalun's City window, and hurried home.

Thus in Kipling's rendering Muharram reduces the half-Europeanized Indian Muslim to his irrational native self. Or perhaps to something even lower: the simile "like the wings of a goose" shows Wali Dad leveled to the status of animal, a very silly and helpless one at that. And the first symptom of this transformation had been the breast-beating: *matam* and Muharram lamentation are now associated with loss of self-control.

These passages point to the difference in tone between Kipling's earlier newspaper pieces and *City Wall*. Gone now are the half-grudging acknowledgments of his fascination with Muharram, the wry affection with which he noted religious devotion at the shrines, the recollection of courtesy shown him when he was lost and bewildered in a crowded procession. Like any good short story writer, Kipling in *City Wall* focuses on one big theme. His theme of choice for the tale: the fitness of the English to rule over India, given the Indian propensity for irrationality as manifested at Muharram. The topic's importance is reinforced by the Russian scheme to take advantage of disorders resulting from Muharram. Excluded from the narrative are any human-interest details which do not contribute to this argument. This is not to say that our author had lost his gift of sympathetic insight into native life—any reader of *Kim* knows Kipling better than that—but simply that such sympathies were shelved for the making of this tale.

Certain details from the newspaper articles are in fact selectively retained in *City Wall*: "The troops were banging the bare toes of the mob with their gun-butts . . . Never was religious enthusiasm more systematically squashed." What Kipling brings forward from his earlier writing are notes on methods of coercion by which the British impose peace. So too in *City Wall* he enlarges on his brief newspaper references to district officers and policemen:

> Hugonin, the Assistant District Superintendant of Police, a boy of twenty, had got together thirty constables and was forcing the crowd through the streets. His old gray Police-horse showed no sign of uneasiness as it was spurred breast-on into the crowd, and the long dog-whip with which he had armed himself was never still.
>
> "They know we haven't enough Police to hold 'em," he cried as he passed me, mopping a cut on his face . . . The dog-whip cracked across the writhing backs, and the constables smote afresh with baton and gun-butt.

The English district officer cited in Kipling's earlier work has now grown into a figure of heroic dimensions, imposing order with a crack of the whip, herding the crowd before him. The ICS in reality prided itself on its finesse in handling Muharram; Kipling, however, glories in confrontation and the imagined use of force.

His story received an enthusiastic reception in some quarters at least. The collection in which *City Wall* appeared, entitled *In Black and White*, was reviewed in the July 1890 issue of the popular London literary journal *The Athenaeum*:

> His little book of studies . . . sets before us in contrast the native and the master—the crafty subservience of the one, the contemptuous self-reliance of the other; and as the stay-at-home Englishman peruses its pages he falls to marvelling afresh at that standing miracle, the maintenance of the British raj. Mr. Kipling knows his natives, as he knows his soldiers, at first hand. He has eaten bread and salt with them . . .
>
> For skilful presentment in a few bold strokes of a strange and moving scene it would be hard to beat the escape from the flooded mine in 'At Twenty-Two' or the fanatical riot of 'On the City Wall' . . . The latter, with its account of the . . . sudden outbreak of those racial and religious passions which the paramount power alone controls, is admirably told.[9]

A rather different British perspective on Muharram emerges from the writings of John Campbell Oman, a professor of natural sciences at the Government College of Lahore, who in 1907 published a popular-format study entitled *The Brahmans, Theists and Muslims of India*. Included in this work is a careful description of Muharram in Lahore based on his personal experiences while residing there.[10] The book particularly merits attention as it appeared within a generation of *On the City Wall*, and like Kipling's tale it is set in Lahore. With other English authors he notes the risk of sectarian combat triggered by the Shiite processions: "On these occasions the resources of the guardians of the public peace are, in the large cities, often taxed to the utmost, for the spirit of fanaticism is in the air."[11] But Oman's interests extend much further. While Lothian and Woodruff limit themselves to a mention of security precautions and the need for public order, the professor evinced enthusiasm for everything, the rosewater sprinkled over the mourners, the sermons, the torch-juggling, and the crowded food-stalls. Throughout he shows a good eye for detail, as in this catalogue of *tazias*:

> One of these *tazias* might be merely a tower of four or five storeys built on a light bamboo framework. Another more elaborate and bizarre in form would have the appearance of a strange composite being, with a woman's face and the body of a peacock, bearing a house on its back. Some *tazias* were supported upon winged horses with long ostrich-like necks, surmounted with human faces of

feminine type. One was borne on the head of a winged angel who, by means of a simple contrivance manipulated from behind, was made to beat his breast in a rather ridiculous fashion. No doubt this huge mechanical toy brought forcibly, perhaps touchingly, to the minds of Shiah spectators that even the denizens of other worlds mourned the martyrdom of their Imam.[12]

Condescending at times, yes; but Oman's hauteur is repeatedly overwhelmed by a fascination with all aspects of the procession—and in any case he seems to have pegged things exactly right in interpreting the mechanical angels as symbols of mourning by "denizens of other worlds" for the slaughtered Husain (I will have more to say about other-worldly mourning for Husain in part II).

Recurrent in Oman's portraits is the attempt to analyze religious sentiment:

While the *tazias* stood in their appointed places on the roadside, devout women were fanning them with palm leaves and horse-hair *chauris* (fly-flappers), and even with their own *chaddars* (veils). Some were Hindu women, probably unfortunate mothers, who thus paid respect to these effigies of the martyrs' tombs, in the fond hope that Imam Husain would graciously extend his protection to their surviving children and grant them long life . . . In one instance I noticed a woman pinning on to a *tazia* with her own hands a paper on which her *arzi* (petition) to the martyr was written, and it need not be doubted that she did so in trembling hope of a favourable response . . . So there before my eyes were exhibited in action those simple and touching sentiments which lie at the root of religion—solicitude for loved ones, and a trustful appeal for help to any unseen spiritual power that might possibly be won over by gifts or flattering attentions to hear and answer prayers.[13]

Similarly, in his account of *matam* the author remarks on the evident sincerity and genuine earnestness with which boys and young men pounded their chests. What animates and unites his otherwise diffuse descriptions is an implicit desire to understand the feelings that motivate Muharram participants—piety, competitiveness, desperation, opportunism.

At the end of his section on Muharram processions Oman does glance once more at the motif of violence and public disorder, but he does so with an impishness that hints that he may be playing with the reader's expectations and with the stock scenes an English audience might have looked for in an exotic Indian setting:

Immediately behind the horse [which represented Duldul or Dhul janah, the riderless horse of the slain Imam] came the police guard, forming a cordon about the animal and its attendants. There were women also in the procession slapping their breasts in lamentation for Husain's martyrdom, but I am not quite sure whether they came immediately before or after the horse. The latter I think.

Behind the force of constables, all of them on foot, rode the embodiment, for the nonce, of the British raj, a solitary Englishman with a resolute but bored expression on his face—the Assistant Superintendent of Police.[14]

My final example of British representations of Muharram in India is from a boy's adventure novel entitled *The Drum* by A.E.W. Mason, a popular author of the late nineteenth and early twentieth centuries. His most famous novel is probably *The Four Feathers* (published in 1902), set during the Mahdi revolt in the Sudan; *The Drum* came rather late in Mason's career, in 1937. The fact that this is a children's story is suggestive of how widely shared were certain British assumptions concerning the nature of Islam in general and Muharram in particular, insofar as the author may be imagined to have drawn on readily recognizable conventions requiring little explanation in creating his tale.

The plot can be summarized as follows: Political officer Frank Carruthers is posted as British representative to the Khanate of Tokot, a Muslim tribal kingdom said to be located on the mountainous northern frontier of India. The ruling Khan, Sher Afzal, and his gallant young son Shuja ul-Mulk are both loyal friends of the Empire and welcome Carruthers, his wife, and a small contingent of British soldiers to Tokot. Shuja ul-Mulk is befriended by an English drummer boy who teaches him a recognition signal as they practice together on a regimental drum; the prince then steals a musical instrument known as the "Yudeni drum" from the tower of his father's palace and uses it to perfect the tattoo. Mason explains to his readers that in Tokoti belief the Yudeni is a "fairy's drum" and that at intervals a ghostly "fairy drummer" visits the tower to beat this drum. At the very beginning of his story Mason shows that the British governor of Peshawar has heard legends of this instrument:

"By the way, you might find out the story of the Yudeni drum, and how much truth there is in it."

Carruthers was perplexed. The legends of the Hindu Khush were innumerable. The dwellers in those deep valleys between dark forests and glistening scarps of snow had other gods besides the Allah of their official creed—gods of the ice and the storm, and in a lower hierarchy the imps and the goblins whom witchcraft could appease. Carruthers had heard many a story about his camp-fire of their malevolence and the devices by which it might be diverted. But the Yudeni drum was new to him.

"The drum and the fairy drummer," the Governor repeated.

"I'll make enquiries," said Carruthers.[15]

By taking this ancient instrument, Shuja ul-Mulk appropriates for the sake of his British allies the power popularly associated with the Yudeni drum. But meanwhile treachery is afoot: the Khan's own mullah and vizier plot with enemies inside the kingdom and have him murdered. Shuja ul-Mulk barely escapes with his life. The intriguers plan next to storm the British Agency in Tokot in an attack timed to coincide with "the great carnival of Muharram." The king's son, however, takes the Yudeni drum and with it taps out a warning to his English friends of the impending attack.

At the beginning of his novel Mason acknowledges that he borrowed the concept of the Yudeni drum from Algernon Durand's memoir-cum-travelogue, *The Making of a Frontier* (published 1900), a work based on Durand's experiences in the Hindu Kush and the northern mountain territories in the regions around Gilgit. Mason quotes directly from Durand's chapter on "Folk-lore and Sport": "The Yudeni drum, or fairy's drum which was kept on the top of every Chief's castle, played a part in the ancient ceremonies."[16] Durand had noted the persistence of pagan belief and rituals in the mountains despite the recent incursions of Islam:

> The feasts . . . are beginning to fall into desuetude; Mahomedanism is gradually pushing them out, but they, and the observances which accompanied them, are still to be seen in some parts . . .
>
> Before us, backed by the silent terraced fields of a dead generation, lay the little altar of a dead faith. And yet one felt it was not dead; the great god Pan laid his hand upon one's heart, all nature was filled by his presence, and one felt the impulse which brought the women there to offer their humble sacrifice to the living god of the stream and the hillside rather than turn to the cold deity of Mahomedanism.[17]

Mason borrowed freely from Durand for the geographical setting of his novel, for descriptions of Islamo-pagan syncretistic practices, even for his characterizations of Muslim tribesmen. But the story is entirely Mason's, and it was Mason's idea to set the tale's denouement during Muharram. Here are Captain Carruthers and his wife as they receive their first warning of impending attack:

> Marjorie Carruthers . . . rang her hand-bell at tea-time and no one came. She went along to the kitchen. It was empty. She went out towards the servants'

quarters. That busy place was undisturbed by any sound or movement. A little disquieted, she sought out her husband in his office.

"Frank, all the servants have left."

Frank Carruthers got up from his chair. For a moment neither of them spoke. On another day Carruthers himself might have been less uneasy. But this was Muharram, when the passions of Islam would be aroused and fanatics have their way.[18]

Warned just in time by the pounding of the Yudeni drum, the Carruthers take refuge with Shuja ul-Mulk in a cavern close to the Agency compound. Nearby the old mullah leads a mob in a frenzied search throughout the Agency grounds and living quarters. He has promised to slaughter the husband and wife as token of his alliance with the neighboring chieftain Umra Beg:

"In the garden, then, seek, seek!" cried the Mullah ... They had between them promised the lives of the British Agent and his wife to the Tokotis, to Umra Beg, to all the peoples of the border. They were to be the great sacrifice on the day of Muharram, the signal which would set alight the frontier from Dir to Kashgar and Yarkand ... Umra Beg waited behind the hills across the river. Tokot must seal its pact with the blood of the English runaways, before he was going to move.[19]

Heart-pounding language. Like Kipling, Mason couples Muharram with anti-English treachery among the natives and makes the holyday part of a threat to the very borders of the Empire. Mason conjures a ghastly vision of Muharram as a season linked with human sacrifice and unholy covenants (a distorted reflection of the sacrificial imagery of the *dhibh azim* found in Quranic scripture and Shiite *ta'wil*). In his presentation Muharram is the time when such things would most naturally occur among Muslims, "when the passions of Islam would be aroused and fanatics have their way." One may speculate that Mason chose Muharram as his setting because this matched a set of presuppositions among his English audience, notions so widespread that even children could be expected to share in them.[20]

Part II

Ritual and Popular Devotion in a Shiite Community:
Muharram Liturgies of Hyderabad

8

Shiite Shrines of the Old City

The city of Hyderabad in southern India, in what is today the state of Andhra Pradesh, has for centuries been one of the major Shiite population centers in the subcontinent. This Shiite presence can be traced back (as I noted in part I) to the Deccani Bahmani kingdom and the sixteenth-century founding of Hyderabad by the Shiite Qutb Shahi dynasty of Golconda. But even under the Asaf Jahis, Sunni successors to the Qutb Shahis, ministers of state gave public support to the great Shiite shrines in the city and patronized the religious liturgies held in connection with Muharram.[1] Hyderabad, once the capital of an independent princely Native State in the time of the British Raj, dwindled in power after absorption into post-independence India in 1948; but even today it remains one of the best localities in India for observing Shiite rituals surrounding Muharram. Despite this, relatively little has been written on the subject of Muharram in Hyderabad and still less on the Shiite men's guilds of Hyderabad.[2] In Hyderabad the men's associations are identified by the terms *matami guruh* ("lamentation guild," plural *matami guruhan*) or *anjuman* ("association"). While residing in this city during the Muharram seasons of 1989 and 1991, I became acquainted with members of six *guruhan*; this led me to investigate how they help arrange the liturgies and rituals culminating in Ashura. Since in what follows I make some distinction among the types of worship found in various localities in Hyderabad, I will begin by discussing briefly the Shiite neighborhoods of the city. I then describe the *ashurkhanas* or shrines where liturgies are celebrated and thereafter focus on the men's associations themselves and their function in the observance of Muharram in Hyderabad.

My informants estimate that some 80 percent of Hyderabad's Shiite population live in the Old City, that is, the cluster of localities south of the Musi River grouped around the Charminar mosque.[3] The majority of the

Shiite population is Ithna-Ashari or Twelver; a few of the men I encountered told me they had been raised as Ismailis but had then attached themselves to the Twelver community in Hyderabad when they moved to the Deccan. Most Shiites living in the Old City reside in one of five neighborhoods: Dar al-Shifa', Purani Haveli, Mir Alam Mandi, Dabirpura, and Yaqutpura. These comprise some of the poorer quarters in Hyderabad. Most of the religious services I attended were here in the Old City; but I was also invited to *majalis* ("mourning assemblies," singular *majlis*) in the homes of very well-to-do Shiites living in Banjara Hills, the prosperous outlying area north of the Musi River near Husain Sagar. The basic form of the *majlis* was the same in every quarter I visited, but the Old City varied from Banjara Hills enormously with regard to style and length of liturgy.

Walking through the streets of the Old City, one is struck by the large number of *ashurkhanas* to be found in every Shiite quarter. The *ashurkhana* has a number of functions. It serves as an assembly-place where *majalis* are held during Muharram and *jeshns* or festive assemblies are held during other seasons of the year; it is used as a storehouse for the *alams* (copies of battle-standards or banners borne by the martyrs of Karbala) and the *tazias* that are carried in Muharram processions.[4] For most of the year the *alams* are hidden from public view, locked within a storage room in the *ashurkhana*. In the last few days of Dhul-hijjah, however, shortly before the onset of Muharram, those responsible for the place clean the *ashurkhana* thoroughly, then set up a platform and erect the *naizas* or lance-poles on which the *alams* will be erected for veneration. Thus during Muharram the *ashurkhana* is transformed into a shrine and becomes the object of *ziyarah*, "visitation" or "pilgrimage," by local residents.

In his book on the Qutb Shahi shrines of Hyderabad, Sadiq Naqvi describes fifteen of the oldest *ashurkhanas* in Hyderabad and its outlying areas.[5] The buildings he cites include a number of the most splendid in the city, replete with high exterior walls, spacious courtyards, and carpets, tilework, chandeliers, and glass lamps within donated by the nizams or former rulers of the region. Some of the older *ashurkhanas* in the city are maintained today as *waqfs* or charitable trusts.

But such structures are atypical. In Hyderabad the most common form of *ashurkhana* is simply a room in a private home (or sometimes only a space partitioned from the main room by a black curtain) where a family stores its collection of *alams*. These *alams* often are heirlooms that have been handed down within a family for generations. The standards are kept locked in a wooden box until the onset of Muharram, when the *ashurkhana* room will become a family shrine. Even the poorer families I visited claimed to have at least a few *alams*; I counted displays of some sixty to seventy-five in the wealthiest homes. "Every Shiite home in Hyderabad," Professor Naqvi asserted in conversation with me, "becomes an *ashurkhana* during Muharram."

Naqvi's generalization is largely supported by a survey undertaken by the social anthropologist Nadeem Hasnain from Lucknow University. Hasnain found that 92 percent of the Shiite families he interviewed in Andhra Pradesh maintained *ashurkhanas* in their homes.[6] Several Shiites whom I met in Hyderabad, however, pointed out to me that although many of the poorer families possess their own *alam,* they live in homes so small that they have no space to set aside as an *ashurkhana.* In these cases such a family brings its *alam* for Muharram to the home of a wealthier neighbor, who includes the standard in his own shrine display and then invites the poorer family to attend *majalis* there. In a dozen of the larger private homes I visited in the Old City, the *ashurkhana* was in the form of a roofed open platform facing an interior courtyard; the *tazias* and *alams* are protected on the roofed platforms. In the forepart of the platform is a *minbar* (a raised seat for the *zakir* or preacher) facing the courtyard; during *majalis* guests sit facing the platform in the courtyard, which is covered with white cloths for the liturgies.

Socioeconomic differences among Shiite households are reflected also in the *alams* they possess. The battle-standard in its most basic form is a metal crest that when displayed on its *naiza* or lance-pole is often draped with *dhattis* (banners in the form of velvet or brocaded cloth) and sometimes covered with sandalwood paste as a mark of devotion. Some of the older *alams* in shrines open to the public contain relics associated with the sufferings of Imam Husain and his companions. Wealthier families boast *alams* of bronze or heavy silver, crafted two or three centuries ago in Iran, Iraq, or Lucknow, according to my informants, and then brought to Hyderabad when the given Shiite family emigrated to the Deccan. The surface of each standard is usually inscribed with a dedication consecrating it to one of the *Ma'sumin* or to Hazrat Abbas, Ali Asghar, or another of the martyrs of Karbala. The top of the standard is often carved in the shape of a *panje* or mystic protective hand, with the names of the *Panjetan* (the Prophet, Ali, Fatima, Hasan, and Husain) inscribed thereon. The borders of some *alams* are shaped with representations of floral motifs, grape clusters or dragons' heads; others are surmounted by a carving of *Dhul-fiqar,* the sword of Ali ibn Abi Talib. Poorer families can buy cheap *alams* of "German silver" alloys from market-stalls around the Charminar mosque. Craftsmen in Purani Haveli and Dar al-Shifa' will also create *alams* to order according to any one of a number of traditional patterns.

From the above it seems clear that *alams* constitute both a major part of the iconography of Muharram and a focal point of popular devotion in Hyderabad. Many of the standards are adorned with symbols which conjure forth for the viewer—at least the viewer conversant with Shiite iconography—the events associated with the martyr to whom the given *alam* is consecrated. The standard of Abbas is ornamented with a *mashk,* a representation of a waterskin (remember that Abbas, half brother and bodyguard of Husain, was killed trying to bring water from the Euphrates to Husain's family tormented by thirst); the standard of Ali is frequently shown as surmounted by *Dhul-fiqar.* In two of the private *ashurkhanas* I visited, extra space was set aside for the standard of Ali Akbar, the eighteen-year-old son of Husain who was killed in combat with Yazid's forces at Karbala. The wall behind and to either side of the *alam* was spattered heavily with red paint; white sheets crumpled at the foot of the standard were also stained bright red—a token of the young man's blood shed in battle.

9
—

Shiite Men's Guilds of Hyderabad:
An Overview

GENERAL CONSIDERATIONS:
MEMBERSHIP AND MEETING-PLACES

Initially it was difficult for me to learn much about the *guruhan*; the first few people I consulted were well-to-do, educated Sunnis and Shiites, who dismissed these organizations as composed of ignorant uneducated men who knew nothing about the true nature of Islam or the forms of worship actually required by the religion. When I pressed such critics for their specific objections, they singled out the unnecessary emotion and violence with which—according to these critics—the associations perform acts of self-mortification in public. Of course many of the practices related to Muharram in general have repeatedly been criticized by some educated Shiites, and foreign visitors have occasionally encountered a reluctance to discuss Muharram ritual on the part of those Muslims who feel such practices have nothing to do with orthodox Islamic observances. Sir Richard Temple, British Resident at the court of the nizam of Hyderabad, made the following entry in his journal under the date of May 14, 1867:

> In the evening I went out driving to see the *tazia* processions by torchlight in Chadarghat. The usual crowds and detachments of the Nizam's troops were present. About midnight the torchlight procession of the "Na'l Sahib" took place. I wrote to the Minister to know if it was worth seeing, but he replied that it was attended only by the lowest class of the population.[1]

With regard specifically to the *guruhan* of Hyderabad, I should note that of the dozens of men whom I myself met from these organizations, many in fact were well-educated, successful in the business community, and very knowledgeable about Shiite traditions and history. Moreover, many of the guild members I encountered also belong to Shiite charitable organizations, such as the Imam-e Zamana Mission and the Elia Theological Association, organizations founded for the purpose of providing educational and vocational help to the Shiites of Andhra Pradesh.

Although Shiites belonging to the men's associations may live in any part of Hyderabad—and in fact many expatriate Hyderabadis still claim membership in their given group and return from abroad each year at the beginning of Muharram to join their guild in its liturgies—the heart of activity for these associations is the Old City. It is here that the groups have their headquarters and hold their assemblies and processions. According to my informants in the *guruhan,* there are some thirty-five to forty of these men's associations active in the city of Hyderabad. The primary purpose of these guilds, as defined by the members themselves, is the performance of *matam* (acts of mourning for the Karbala martyrs often involving self-mortification, discussed below in more detail) during the first ten days of Muharram.[2] Most of these *guruhan* are quite small, averaging perhaps twenty to twenty-five members, comprising residents of a given locality or quarter, who confine themselves to performing *matam* at *majalis* in private *ashurkhanas* in their own neighborhoods.[3] In most guilds the majority of members is composed of young men in their mid-teens to mid-twenties; nevertheless in such associations the assemblies are led by older men, usually in their thirties or forties. Furthermore, at most *majalis* I attended I noticed at least a few senior members in attendance, anywhere from fifty to seventy years in age. But the elder members of the *guruh* tend to stand at the fringe of the assembly during *matam;* having participated in the severer forms of *matam* when they themselves were younger, they now leave the most strenuous self-mortification to the teenagers and young men.

The five largest *guruhan* in Hyderabad are generally agreed to be: Anjuman-e Parwaneh Shabbir; Guruh-e Haydariyah; Guruh-e Ja'fari; Guruh-e Husaini; and the Anjuman-e Masoomeen.[4] These groups are said to average several hundred members each. Such numbers indicate simply the men who belong; it should be noted that other family members will often be involved in a *majlis:* wives and daughters watch from behind purdah, and young sons perform *matam* at the periphery of the assembly to the best of their ability.

Most guilds lack their own *ashurkhana;* two exceptions are Parwaneh Shabbir, which has an *ashurkhana* (built in 1986) in Mir Alam Mandi, and Masoomeen, which has a shrine and headquarters building in Panjetan Colony, between Nur Khan Bazaar and Dar al-Shifa' in the Old City. The largest *guruhan* solve the problem of finding assembly space in one of two ways: they will congregate in the private homes of members who have large *ashurkhanas* with spacious courtyards attached, or they will perform *ziyarah,* visiting the older shrines of the Old City which are open to the public. Some of these shrines are endowed as *waqfs* and hence are available to the community. The larger guilds differ from the smaller primarily in their degree of organization and scope of activity. Such associations as Parwaneh Shabbir and Ja'fari draw their membership from all over Hyderabad and sometimes beyond; they will arrange bus transportation for their members to facilitate visits to the major *ashurkhanas* throughout the city, and they are authorized by the custodians of the major shrines to perform *matam* at the end of the *majlis* on important holydays, such as the seventh and tenth of Muharram, when the courtyard of the given *ashurkhana* will be filled with hundreds of men who follow the lead of the *guruh* in performing *matam.* Thus the largest of the guilds have a highly public profile in the Shiite quarters of Hyderabad.

The history of Hyderabad's oldest *guruhan* goes back at least to the nineteenth century. According to my informants, however, the number of men's associations has multiplied in recent years, with most of the city's *guruhan* having arisen only in the last twenty to twenty-five years. This information led me to inquire about the factors that might contribute to the formation of new guilds in Hyderabad. Following are the reasons most frequently cited by members themselves.

Personality clashes within already existent groups are the most common cause for the creation of new guilds, according to my informants. Such conflicts are said to occur primarily among the officers of a *guruh.* The Guruh-e Haydariyah, one of the largest Shiite associations in Hyderabad, arose in this way, as a result of quarrels among the officers of Masoomeen only a year or two after the founding of Masoomeen. The two groups share virtually the same style of *matam,* a fact explained by Haydariyah's derivation from Masoomeen.[5] Both guilds are popular with teenagers; my impression is that the groups compete to some extent for new members. Older adherents of Guruh-e Ja'fari and Parwaneh Shabbir described quarrels within *guruhan* as a conflict between generations, between older and younger members. As one Parwaneh Shabbir member (a retiree in his late sixties) commented, "New groups form because of authority disputes. Some young man doesn't want to do what he's been told." My informant added tartly, "Every family has an unruly child, and every group has its unruly members. This leads to divisions, to new *guruhan.*"

Part of the dissatisfaction triggering such divisions is linked to issues of language. An important component of Muharram liturgies is the *nauha,* a lamentation chant that is recited while acts of *matam* are performed at the conclusion of many *majalis.* Older guilds, such as Ja'fari, pride themselves on their conservative retention of traditional *nauhas* composed in Persian and occasionally Arabic; the resultant problem is that many participants do not understand what they are reciting. The newer associations offer *nauhas* which are composed in the vernacular Urdu and hence are more widely comprehensible.

When interviewed, some Shiites claimed that the increase in *matami guruhan* over the last twenty years is linked to the gradual rise in Hyderabad's Shiite population, an increase that compensates partially for the extensive emigration by Muslims which occurred in the wake of the 1948 Police Action (whereby the newly independent national government of India overthrew the nizam's Muslim-dominated regime and forcibly incorporated Hyderabad State into post-independence India).[6] But Mir Sabir Ali Zawar, founder and secretary of Anjuman-e Masoomeen, asserted during an interview at Masoomeen headquarters in July 1991 that the proliferation of *guruhan* has been caused rather by the recently increased number of Muharram liturgies held in the Old City:

> Today everybody wants to have a *majlis* in their homes; there are more programs and more *majalis* than there ever used to be. *Majalis* used to be the exclusive province of a select few; now it seems that such a mark of eminence is within the reach of more people. As a result there is much more demand for groups to come and perform *matam* at the *ashurkhanas* in people's homes. The increase in *guruhan* is a response which fills this "market need."

Thus the *matami guruhan* are perceived as having an important role in the liturgies to which they are invited at family shrines in private homes. Ali Mohsin Khan, a businessman in his mid-forties who is president of a charitable foundation known as the Elia Theological Association, offered an elucidation of the role played by the men's guilds in Muharram liturgies. The interview was held in his home on July 8, 1991.

DP: Why does a family invite a *matami guruh* to come to its home for a *majlis?*

AMK: When a family holds a *majlis* in its home, then if they're wealthy enough to have a big *ashurkhana* with a lot of room, they'll give an invitation to one of the *guruhan* to attend. The *guruh* will lead the *matam* and *nauha*-chanting at the end of the *majlis*. Families give such invitations to make sure that they fill the *ashurkhana*, for each *guruh* will bring sixty to seventy men and boys.

DP: That many people?

AMK: Well, maybe twenty-five to thirty members. The rest might not be official members or pay dues, but they come because they like to do *matam* with this particular group. If the sponsor belongs to a *guruh* himself, naturally he'll invite his own *guruh* to his home; if he doesn't belong to any group then he'll try to get a popular group which will draw people with its *nauhas* and *matam*.

DP: You said the host families want to be sure to fill the *ashurkhana*?

AMK: Absolutely. If I'm the host, then my goal is that as many people as possible should come to my shrine. This time now, Muharram, is the only time of year you'll find a millionaire standing on a street corner asking everyone passing by, "Please come to my house." He'll invite even a rickshaw-puller, someone he won't even look at the rest of the year. That's why you see well-dressed old men walking around handing out printed announcements of their *majalis* to everyone they see; they're trying to get people to come to their homes for Muharram *majalis*.

DP: Why this emphasis on filling the *ashurkhana*?

AMK: We strongly believe that Hazrat Fatima, the mother of Husain, comes to every *majlis*. We seek to have as many people present as possible, so that when the *majlis* ends and Fatima returns to Paradise, she'll feel satisfied at seeing so many people honor her son. Our sole purpose in all this is to satisfy Husain's mother.

In my conversations I tried to determine what factors lead a man to seek membership in a particular *guruh*. Three factors in choosing a guild are cited by members whom I interviewed. An individual may be attracted to a *guruh*'s style of *matam* and *nauha*; he may find their location convenient, if they congregate at shrines within his own neighborhood; or it may be that relatives belong to a given group and encourage him to join. This last factor is particularly important. Very few *guruhan* actually define and limit their membership by lineage and kinship ties (one that does, the Guruh-e Husayniyah, is described below); but in practice all the men's associations I encountered tend to some extent to be family affairs. Anyone whose father belongs to a given *guruh* is expected to join that same group—a natural tendency, as one father in Parwaneh Shabbir explained to me, given that he himself had been bringing his own son to Parwaneh Shabbir's *majalis* since the boy was ten years old. "He's grown up in the *guruh*; he's used to it."

NOTES ON TWO OF THE MOST POPULAR
HYDERABADI GUILDS: THE MOTHS OF HUSAIN
AND THE IMMACULATE ONES

A visitor entering the Old City headquarters of the Anjuman-e Parwaneh Shabbir will note a *tazia* and preacher's pulpit at one end of the large hall; above these, displayed on the wall, is a banner illustrated with the *guruh*'s insignia: moths circling a candle flame. "Parwaneh Shabbir" is an Urdu title meaning "the moths of Husain"; the moth/flame imagery is drawn from Persian Sufi poetry, where the moth symbolizes the mystic's soul drawn in the frenzy of spiritual love to the annihilating light of divine Majesty.[7]

This association was founded in 1947 by two brothers, Seyyed Ahmed Ali and Mir Hussein Ali (who are currently the president and vice president, respectively). In conversations with me the officers described their organization first and foremost in terms of the *matam-nauha* style practiced in their liturgies. Seyyed Ahmed explained that he and his brother created a "modified Punjabi *matam*" (to be described below) in founding the guild. Hassan Abbas Rizvi, the association's foremost reciter, told me that he first joined Parwaneh Shabbir in 1975 at the age of twenty-four because he was attracted to its style of *nauha*: "I saw that this group selects chants which are chosen to make people weep. These chants convey Husain's sadness properly." And in the course of two Muharram seasons Parwaneh Shabbir's *nauhas* impressed me as particularly dirge-like, elegiac, and mournful, especially when compared with groups like Haydariyah and Masoomeen, which try to attract younger participants.

In 1947 Seyyed Ahmed chose a total of fourteen men as founding members (a number selected, so he told me, to correspond to the fourteen *Ma'sumin*); today the organization claims a membership of one thousand to twelve hundred in Hyderabad alone, with several hundred members in branch affiliates in the Persian Gulf countries and North America. Membership dues are collected annually at a business meeting at the beginning of Muharram; no fixed fee is required. Nevertheless, as the president pointed out, enough funds were collected in this way to permit the construction of the guild's large headquarters hall and *ashurkhana* in 1986.

Parwaneh Shabbir seems to appeal to successful professional men; here I met numerous businessmen, a librarian, a banker, a factory manager, and an accountant—in fact the largest single concentration of educated Shiites in any of the *matami guruhan* I encountered. Both in the liturgies and in the social gatherings to which I was invited, I noted an unspoken emphasis on *adab*: courtliness and quiet dignity of manner.[8] Teenagers and younger boys were present, too, but they were there with their fathers and unobtrusively shaped their conduct to imitate their elders.

During the 1991 Muharram season I was offered a copy of the application form (imprinted with the moth/flame insignia) for admission to the *guruh*. The conditions for admission stipulate: obedience to the association's president at all times; regular attendance at Muharram *majalis* and participation in *matam* (in fact, one is adjured henceforth to consider *matam* a "religious duty": *aur sineh zani apna farz samajhunga*); and proper behavior when attending Muharram liturgies (*adab-e majlis ka hamisheh khiyal rakhunga*: "I will at all times bear in mind the deportment appropriate to the *majlis*"). The admission form's emphasis on deference and proper conduct was reflected in the behavior I encountered in the dozen or so liturgies I attended with this group. New members with whom I spoke shared my impression: as one candidate put it, he was attracted by the sophistication and educational attainments of the members. Parwaneh Shabbir's collective self-image is that of a gentlemen's club.[9]

Several senior members have spacious *ashurkhanas* adorned with numerous *alams* in their homes. These members take turns hosting some of the guild's *majalis*. One such liturgy stands out in my mind as an illustration of the way in which *guruh* membership involves not only an individual but his family. It is the custom of Hassan Abbas Rizvi, one of Parwaneh Shabbir's reciters, to hold a *majlis* for Parwaneh Shabbir members at home in his private family shrine every year on the sixth of Muharram. This day is consecrated to Ali Asghar, the infant son of Husain who was slaughtered at Karbala. The focus of devotion at this liturgy is the *jhula* (cradle), a small silver model of an infant's cradle or child's swing, mounted on a tray and topped by an *alam* draped with jasmine garlands and red flowers. It is kept stored with the *alams* on a dais at one end of the *ashurkhana*. The *jhula* is meant to symbolize the innocent youthfulness of the slain child; such symbols stimulate the participants' desire to weep. As a conclusion to the evening's liturgy, after a long sermon detailing the death of Ali Asghar, the *jhula* is brought out in procession. While a dirge is chanted and the mourners beat their breasts in time, Hassan Abbas's nine-year-old son bears the tray about on his head in a slow circumambulation of the family courtyard. The boy's father and uncle flank him as he walks, extending their arms to steady the tray and help him with the burden. Men come forward as he passes and press their heads reverently against the tray; then the *jhula* is returned to the dais and covered with a veil. It is appropriate, onlookers explained to me, that a very young boy carry the cradle of the slain infant; this deepens the pathos of the liturgy.

The next guild I wish to introduce is the Anjuman-e Masoomeen (Association of the Immaculate Ones). The style and character of this guild are shaped largely by one person, the founder, secretary, and chief *nauha-khan* (reciter), Mir Sabir Ali Zawar. I will begin by sketching the early history of this *guruh* as related to me by Sabir himself in the course of two interviews at Masoomeen headquarters in July 1991.

Sabir is forty-one years old, well-to-do, and a landlord, apparently with considerable holdings in and around Hyderabad. By his own account he comes from a prominent family; his grandfather was an officer in the nizam's army. As a child Sabir belonged to a Persian-language *matami guruh* called Guruh-e Yathrib which had been founded by members of Sabir's family. His immediate family, relatives, and family friends comprised the membership. As a child, Sabir informed me, he was very active in this group and in the performance of the liturgical dirges that it sponsored. This self-assessment is confirmed by one of the most celebrated of Hyderabad's Muharram preachers, Allamah Akhtar Zaydi, who contributed an introductory essay to the chant-book of Muharram *nauhas* published by the Anjuman-e Masoomeen. In his essay Zaydi says the following of Sabir Ali:

> I have been acquainted with the founder and *nauha*-reciter of the Anjuman-e Masoomeen since he was ten or twelve years old, when he used to do *nauha*-reciting with other children of his age. Even at that time my estimate was that if Sabir were to offer his fine and heart-rending voice as a charitable donation for lamenting Husain, then very soon he would be counted among the most popular *nauha-khans*. And in fact this very thing has happened, so that today Sabir is counted among Hyderabad's recognized lamentation-reciters, and his style of *nauha*-chants, a style which was created by him, is also well liked.[10]

In the early 1960s Guruh-e Yathrib included some 250 adherents, but by 1969 the group no longer existed. Sabir attributed the demise to the dwindling knowledge of Persian among the younger members, who could not understand the language of the chants. Older Yathrib members drifted to other associations to perform *matam,* most notably Ja'fari (a logical choice, given its use of Persian-language chant). But in 1972 Sabir founded the Anjuman-e Masoomeen. From the start he decided to use Urdu *nauhas* only; the result was that he began to attract many young Shiites who knew nothing of Persian. At present the *guruh* now claims to have some five hundred registered members, who each must pay an annual membership fee of sixty rupees (although the officers told me they do not insist on full payment from impoverished members). From the beginning the new association was not defined in terms of family membership, but in fact (as with the other guilds I observed) family ties are reflected in the group's leadership posts: Sabir's older brother, Mir Mukhtar Ali, is president, his younger brother is one of the association's eight *nauha-khans,* and one of his childhood friends is co-secretary.

A visit to the guild's headquarters reveals a curious blend of traditional and modern motifs. The building's exterior is decorated with the group's insignia: a disk encircled by two *Dhul-fiqar* scimitars (fork-bladed swords of the type said to have been wielded by Ali, the first Imam). At the disk's center is a *panje,* a protective hand, fingers extended, with an eye displayed in its palm. Rays of light stream from the eye. Above the *panje* is a verse in Arabic, *wa-i' tasimu bi-habl Allah jami' an,* "and grip fast, all of you, the cable of God," a Quranic passage (3.103) generally accepted in Shiite *ta'wil* exegesis as a divine command for all Muslims to venerate the Prophet's family and the line of the Imams (a lineage described as "the cable of God" because of its exalted rank and the divine revelation conveyed directly from God to the Prophet. The Imams, recipients as they are of the Quranic *batin* and *zahir,* act as mediators in making this revelation available to Shiite believers, who "grip fast" in devotion to the *Ma'sumin* who lead them to God).[11] Encircling the *panje,* within the perimeter of the disk, are the fourteen names of the eponymous *Ma'sumin*: the Prophet, Fatima, and the Imams. Part Quranic text, part talismanic amulet, the guild's insignia combines symbols—eye, hand, sword—in a manner that is characteristic of popular Shiite piety.

After this display of traditional iconography over the doorway, the furnishings of the headquarters' interior come as something of a jolt. Barbells, wall mirrors, and wrestling mats crowd one end of the meeting hall; Sabir's office is decorated with a near-life-size wooden silhouette figure of a karate master posed for assault. This youth club/gymnasium ambience offers a first clue to the group's membership; for of all the *matami guruhan* in Hyderabad, Masoomeen seems by far the most popular and most successful among adolescents and young men. Most of the rank-and-file adherents range from twelve to seventeen years of age; the reciters and choir assistants are somewhat older, in their early to mid-twenties. The handful of middle-aged and elderly men whom I saw in attendance are primarily officers and family friends.

"We want to appeal to a new generation," Sabir stated during our conversations; the influence of his philosophy is plain to see in every aspect of his guild. The group's *nauhas* are direct, forceful, even martial in tone; there is nothing plaintive to these chants, so different from the mournful dirges of Parwaneh Shabbir or Ja'fari. As noted above, all of Masoomeen's *nauhas* are composed in Urdu; the phrasing is simple and accessible. And the breast-beating which accompanies Masoomeen's chants is performed with elan. Attending a liturgy in the company of these young men, the visitor glimpses Muharram from another perspective: the season of mourning is a conduit to channel and express adolescent energy.

Even the barbells serve the guild's purpose, for teenagers and younger boys wander in and out of the building and seem to feel free to exercise on the mats, chat, or congregate as they please. Another contrast with Parwaneh Shabbir: there, boys also come to the headquarters building and attend *majalis* and meetings, but (as I noted earlier) they are in their fathers' company and are understandably quiet and restrained, relating to adults rather than to each other. Here, the boys come in clusters of young friends, with few adults in attendance save the officers of Masoomeen. Before the start of a liturgy or rehearsal session there will be a certain amount of clowning among the youngest participants, who seem at first glance spirited but undisciplined. Yet when Sabir enters the hall with his assistants all hubbub dies. The founder and chief *nauha-khan,* through his fine chanting voice, his vision, his drive, dominates each liturgy and gathering; the boys' attention is rapt.

But the Anjuman-e Masoomeen takes a larger interest as well in the Shiite society of Hyderabad's Old City. In an essay prefacing the *nauhas* in the *guruh*'s chant-book, the officers of Masoomeen state:

> In the course of working towards the economic, social, and religious progress of the community, the guild and its members, through their actions and speech, have given proof that the organization is effective. The foundation of the religion is belief and action.[12]

The guild has demonstrated this interest in the community's welfare in various ways. During the Hyderabad riots of December 1990, Masoomeen was exceptional among the *matami guruhan* for the interest it showed in trying to provide financial assistance to the Old City victims of violence (the question of the 1990 Hyderabad riots will be discussed in a later section of this book). The organization plans a building program to serve the needs of the Dar al-Shifa'/Panjetan Colony neighborhood (the locality where Masoomeen's headquarters are located): projected construction plans include a mosque, *ashurkhana,* guest-house, and *madrasah* (school of religious instruction). At a ceremony on August 19, 1987, the foundation stone for the guild's community mosque, the *masjid-e Ma'sumin,* was laid by

Hujjat al-Islam S. Muhammad al-Musavi, acting as agent of the Ayatollah al-Uzma Abu al-Qasim al-Khui of Iraq. The agent's presence was significant because Ayatollah al-Khui is by far the most revered religious authority among Hyderabad's Shiites, many of whom consider him their *marja' al-taqlid.* On this occasion Hujjat al-Islam al-Musavi announced that the Ayatollah had granted permission for Hyderabad's Shiites to donate the *sahm-e Imam* directly to the Anjuman-e Masoomeen for the sake of supporting the association's building program.[13] This constituted a financial windfall for the guild. The *sahm-e Imam* (Imam's portion) is a religious tithe owed by individual believers to the occulted twelfth Imam; in his absence the tax is paid to one's *marja',* who disburses the money in accordance with the needs of the faith. The Anjuman-e Masoomeen was quick to take advantage of this decision. In a pamphlet listing the "By-laws of Anjuman-e Masoomeen . . . along with the Amendments made by the Administrative Body Meeting on 5th January 1988," the association trumpeted the Ayatollah's announcement and appealed to Hyderabad's businessmen to donate their *sahm-e Imam* to the *guruh's* building fund. And on August 15, 1989, Masoomeen furthered its prestige by hosting Ayatollah Khui's son, Hujjat al-Islam S. Taqi Musavi al-Khui, who visited the guild's headquarters and who (according to the association's printed flyer) "inspected . . . and appreciated the activities of Anjuman-e Masoomeen."

Given Masoomeen's reach and ambition, it is perhaps not surprising that this association is singled out for criticism in many discussions among Hyderabadi Muslims who find fault with the guilds for their use of *matam* and other controversial practices. These criticisms will be analyzed in a separate section below.

AN ASSOCIATION DEFINED BY ETHNIC LINEAGE: THE IRANIANS' GUILD

Some of the smaller *guruhan* are defined by locality or neighborhood, as has been noted above; other groups are shaped by ethnic identity or family ties. The Anjuman-e Ittihad-e Iraniyan-e Dekkan (Association of the Union of Iranians of the Deccan) is composed of ethnic Iranians resident in Hyderabad. They meet in a building known as Darbar-e Husayni in Purani Haveli. According to informants from this *anjuman,* most members have Iranian citizenship, although many of them were born and raised in Hyderabad. Members are conversant in both Urdu and Persian; their *majalis* and chants are conducted in Persian. I was told that non-Iranian Hyderabadi Shiites tend not to attend this group's *majalis* because of the Persian language barrier.

The Hyderabadi Iranian community contributes actively to Muharram liturgies in the city. On the ninth of Muharram, 1989, I witnessed a nighttime procession composed of some forty to fifty young men, primarily teenagers, from the Iranian guild. Departing from the Darbar-e Husayni as their starting point, they marched through the alleys of Dar al-Shifa' and Purani Haveli, carrying banners and chanting verses in honor of Husain. Beginning with the Inayat Jung palace, the young men visited a total of seven *ashurkhanas*; at each shrine they performed *matam*, striking their chests in time with the recitation of Persian verses. Two days before this procession, leaflets distributed in the Old City announced a "*matam* ceremony in honor of the Bridegroom of Karbala" for that night, the seventh of Muharram (the bridegroom honorific refers to Qasim ibn Hasan, son of the second Imam, who was wed to the daughter of Husain on the battlefield of Karbala). The leaflet announced the organizers of this *majlis* as the Intizami Komiti Nawjavanan-e Iraniyan Muqim Haydarabad (Organizational Committee of Iranian Youths Resident in Hyderabad). According to this leaflet, the *majlis* was to take place in the New City, near Nampally Station and opposite the Ayk Minar mosque, to be followed by a *matam* procession to the Sufi shrine of Yousufain.

Another example of contributions to Shiite devotionalism by the ethnic Iranian community of Hyderabad is a popular cassette recording of Muharram lamentation chants entitled *Gham-e javid* (Eternal Sorrow) sold at a number of bookstalls in the Old City. This tape was recorded by a Hyderabadi men's guild called the Anjuman-e Sineh Zanan-e Irani (the Association of Iranian Mourners).

There are indications that the government of the Islamic Republic of Iran takes an active interest in the Shiite community of Hyderabad. According to my Shiite informants in the Old City, in the summer of 1989 nine Shiites—*zakirs* (*majlis* preachers), scholars, and other prominent members of the Muslim community of Hyderabad—were invited to Teheran for the *chehelom* (a memorial service held on the fortieth day after a person's death) in honor of the recently deceased Ayatollah Khomeini, as guests of the Iranian Consulate of Hyderabad. In August of the same year, Mehdi Fatemian Mohammadi, shortly before relinquishing his post as Consul General of the Hyderabad branch of the Iranian Consulate, published a notice in one of the local newspapers thanking "the esteemed people of Hyderabad for their great hospitality shown towards me, especially the spiritual and religious personalities, professors of the Universities, poets and writers, the religious associations, Theological schools, and the Honourable authorities of the State of Andhra Pradesh."[14]

During the first ten days of Muharram in 1989 a four-page pamphlet in Urdu was circulated throughout the Old City by young men standing at the entrance to *ashurkhanas*. Printed at the bottom of the last page of each pamphlet was the notice "From the press section of the Consulate of the Islamic Republic of Iran, Hyderabad." The flyer opens with the announcement, "Peace be with you, O father of God's servant Husain. We shed tears for Imam Husain, and with this flood of tears we demolish the walls resisting Islam." The bulk of the text is an Urdu translation of a speech by the Ayatollah Khomeini which was delivered (according to the pamphlet's preface) during Muharram shortly after the initial success of the 1979 Iranian Revolution. The text includes a detailed discussion of the "benefits and significance of the *majalis* of lamentation" as well as criticism directed against the "adversaries of Muharram-mourning." Public Muharram processions are praised as "a manifestation of resistance to the Satanic forces of oppression and injustice." The conclusion reads as follows: "Directions from the leader of the Islamic Revolution. The Islamic Revolution of Iran constitutes one beam of light from the luminous sun of Lord Husain's uprising. Only through assemblies of lamentation is it possible to guard Husain's movement in an illustrious place and keep it alive in every age."

Apparently Iran is trying to bolster its prestige among Indian Shiites by linking the 1979 Revolution and Iran's Islamic government with Imam Husain and the Muharram liturgies celebrated throughout India in his honor. Nevertheless, pamphleteering and activities of this kind do not in my opinion signify that Iran is attempting to exert any overt political influence over Indian Shiites. It is apparently understood by all concerned that the Indian government would be swift in any case to deal with agitation in the field of politics among India's minority communities, and Teheran shows no signs to my knowledge of trying to direct the Shiites of Hyderabad against the Indian government. Rather, the Islamic Republic today seems to be courting Hyderabadi and other Indian Shiites in two ways: it seeks to consolidate a role for Iran as spiritual leader of the subcontinent's Shiites; and it wishes to revive Iran's traditional role as source of inspiration and point of orientation for Indian Muslim culture. Thus, for example, the Iran Culture House in Delhi, under the aegis of the Iranian Consulate, is publishing a series of catalogues describing Arabic and Persian manuscripts in Indian libraries; collections described to date in this series include the Nadwat al-ulama in Lucknow and the private manuscript holdings of the former Shiite maharaja of Mahmudabad.[15]

I had an opportunity to test my personal impressions concerning present-day Iranian cultural influences in India when I interviewed Agha Muhammad

Abidi, the Iranian vice-consul in Hyderabad, at the Consulate of the Islamic Republic in the elegant Banjara Hills locality. The interview took place during my second Muharram season in India, on July 19, 1991. That I succeeded in obtaining this interview was thanks only to the intercession of Hyderabadi Shiite friends who overcame the consulate's manifest suspicions with regard to inquisitive foreigners.

In our conversation Agha Abidi denied any knowledge of pamphleteering activities by the Iranian consulate among Hyderabad's Shiites. "In any case, eighty percent of India's Muslims are illiterate," he claimed. "No one here would bother to read this material if we printed it. This is not our job or business at the consulate, to distribute literature."

At this juncture I wondered aloud whether the Iranian government might not feel impelled to undertake a mission of religious education in Hyderabad, given the very evident Hindu influence on the form of Muharram observances in this city. "We have other things to do," he replied sharply, "rather than get involved in educational missions. In any case it would be wrong to interfere with the internal customs and traditions of our host country. This," he added pointedly, "would amount to imperialism." Abidi went on to say that in any case Hindus, too, love Husain, and that non-Islamic influences on Indian Shiism are the result of a policy among India's past rulers to prevent people from knowing their own religion fully. "But for a good religious education," he conceded, "Shiites here should send their children abroad."

When asked whether the Consulate has any ties with Hyderabad's community of Shiites of ethnic Iranian descent, the vice-consul admitted readily that "we do participate, we of the Consulate, in Muharram *majalis* at Darbar-e Husayni [where Hyderabad's Anjuman-e Ittihad-e Iraniyan-e Dekkan assembles]. The Consulate sponsors two or three Muharram *majalis* annually at this shrine in the Old City, and we pay the expenses involved. We hold *majalis* in both Farsi [Persian] and Urdu." Later, I spoke with local Shiites who mentioned having seen the Iranian vice-consul himself attend liturgies at Darbar-e Husayni during the 1991 Muharram season.

In general, Abidi asserted, the Consulate has very cordial relations with Hyderabad's ethnic Iranian community, but, he repeated, "we do not interfere in their own programs or their own traditional religious ways" (a point to which he reverted several times in our conversation). "I can explain our Consulate's policy with a quotation from Persian verse," Abidi smiled. "The poem says something to the effect that 'the Beloved must respond to the Lover in order for the Lover to succeed'. That is, we cannot have a relationship with the Shiites here if we try to force a relationship exclusively on our terms only."

The verse about Beloved and Lover in its own way, of course, is an acknowledgment of Iran's courtship of Hyderabadi Shiites. But the vice-consul's stated emphasis on noninterference shows the Consulate's awareness of potential charges of political meddling and influence-mongering. At any rate, the Indian Shiites I encountered seem to show approval— tinged with a certain ambivalence—for the Islamic Republic of Iran and its self-appointed role as spokesman for and most visible member of the world Shiite community. On the one hand, portraits of Imam Khomeini adorn the walls of many *madrasahs* and private homes in Hyderabad and Lucknow alike. And in 1989, during the forty-day period immediately after Khomeini's death, flags of mourning were visible throughout Shiite neighborhoods in both cities. Many Shiites I interviewed in Hyderabad and Lucknow expressed admiration for Khomeini because of his role in asserting the Shiite faith in the international community and for serving as a focal point of Shiite identity worldwide. On the other hand, in numerous homes and market-stalls, I also noticed calendar portraits of the Ayatollah Abu al-Qasim al-Khui of Najaf, and many Shiites with whom I spoke in 1989 said that they had always preferred to look to Khui rather than Khomeini as their *marja' al-taqlid*: Khomeini in their view had allowed the war with Iraq to drag on unnecessarily for years, thereby causing the death of thousands of Shiites, whereas Khui maintained neutrality and refused to endorse the continuation of this inter-Muslim conflict. When I returned to Hyderabad in 1991, Khui's influence seemed to have grown, and Shiites everywhere in the Old City were angrily aware that Khui had been confined under house arrest by Saddam Hussein.

AN ASSOCIATION DEFINED BY FAMILY LINEAGE: THE GURUH-E HUSAYNIYAH

Like the Iranian *anjuman* described in the previous section, the Guruh-e Husayniyah is also located in the Purani Haveli quarter of the Old City; it uses as its headquarters the Inayat Jung palace. This association claims some two hundred members; membership is restricted to descendants and relatives of the Nawab Inayat Jung, a nobleman and pious Shiite who served as advisor to Mir Osman Ali Khan, the last reigning nizam. Inayat Jung established his palace as a *waqf*; and the present *mutawalli* (supervisor-custodian), Seyyed Asghar Hussein Musawi, grandson of the Nawab, makes the *ashurkhana* situated within the palace available to the public for wedding celebrations, *majalis,* and other religious occasions. This palace is favored by numerous *guruhan*—in addition to the Guruh-e Husayniyah—who come here to perform *matam* during Muharram. On Ashura, during the Bibi ka alam procession that marks the high point of Muharram observances in Hyderabad, the Inayat Jung palace has the distinction of being one of the halting-points for the elephant bearing the Bibi ka alam (the standard of Lady Fatima). As *mutawalli* of the Inayat Jung *waqf* and supervisor of the Guruh-e Husayniyah, Seyyed Hussein offers garland-draped *dhatti*-cloths to the *alam*.

10

Lamentation Rituals: Shiite Justifications for *Matam* (Acts of Mourning and Self-mortification)

Before discussing in more detail the Shiite men's guilds of Hyderabad, it may be worthwhile to analyze briefly one of the principal activities associated with these organizations: the performance of *matam*, actions of mourning or condolence. Although the term can be used generically to refer to any kind of funeral lamentation, among the Shiites of Hyderabad, as elsewhere in the Shiite world, *matam* typically designates observances performed during Muharram in honor of Husain and the other martyrs of Karbala. More specifically, the term denotes the striking of oneself—either with the bare hand (as indicated by the Persian term *sineh-zani*, "chest-beating") or with some weapon or flail (as for example in the scourging known as *zanjir-zani*)—in an act of ritual mourning. In this study I use the term *matam* to refer specifically to these practices of chest-beating and/or self-mortification involving weapons.

It is important to make clear that *matam* is by no means restricted to the guilds alone; I attended a number of assemblies where congregants performed *matam* (at least in its simplest form of bare-handed *sineh-zani*) despite the absence of any formally organized men's association. But the *guruhan*—as will be seen from the discussion below—frequently provide a highly structured context for the performance of *matam*, a performance in which the community as a whole often participates.

Shiite Muslims are not alone in honoring Husain during Muharram; various Sunni and Hindu communities also participate to some extent. But *matam* is seen as a primarily Shiite form of observing Muharram. On two occasions in June and July 1989 I visited the shrine of the Sufi saint Hazrat Nizam al-Din Awliya in Delhi. While there I made the acquaintance of

Seyyed Aftab Ali Nizami and Seyyed Sabir Nizami, son and nephew respectively of the *sajjadeh-neshin* or master of the Chishti order in Delhi. In conversation with Seyyed Sabir I learned that the Chishtiya celebrate Ashura in honor of Imam Husain; the Chishti Sufis identify themselves as Sunnis, Seyyed Sabir told me, but they hold liturgies for Husain because Nizam al-Din was a "Husaini Seyyed," a descendant of Imam Husain.[1] Thus in venerating Husain during Muharram, he explained, the Chishti Sufis thereby honor Nizam al-Din himself, the most celebrated saint of the Chishti order, and in turn the Chishtiya thereby honor the present master of the order who is himself a descendant of Nizam al-Din. Annually on Ashura, according to my informant, the Chishtiya parade four large *tazias* through the quarter of Nizam al-Din (the neighborhood surrounding the shrine); then they take the *tazias* in procession to a field known as Karbala Aliganj, where garlands and votive cloths are stripped from the *tazias* and buried. But Seyyed Sabir was careful to point out that the Chishtiya do not perform *matam* during Muharram; *matam,* he insisted, is something only Shiites do.

I met with a similar response in an interview I conducted in August 1991 while visiting Darjeeling (West Bengal), at the Chhoti Masjid located near the Darjeeling Himalaya Railway station. I spoke with Hafez Razi Ahmed, the young imam of the mosque,who described himself and his mosque's congregation as entirely Sunni. The imam explained that his Sunni congregation does in fact participate in Darjeeling's observance of Muharram: this includes a procession with *tazias* on Ashura which culminates in the Chawq bus station area in the lower town. There, he informed me, Muslims engage in *lathi* stick-fighting as a reenactment of the battle of Karbala. Nevertheless, he insisted that no members of his congregation perform *matam* in the Muharram observances.

These interviews reinforce Ja'far Sharif's reference in his *Qanun-i-Islam* to Muharram breast-beating as "a Shi'a practice prohibited to Sunnis."[2] Likewise Syed Husain Ali Jaffri, in an essay entitled "Muharram Ceremonies in India," asserted that "Our Hanafi [i.e., Sunni] brethren and Sufis also celebrate with *ta'ziyeh,* hold *Majales-e Aza* to commemorate the memory of the *Shahedan-e Kerbela* (Martyrs of Kerbela), but do not do *sineh-zani* like Shi'a Muslims."[3]

Thus, given that many Indian Sunnis do observe Muharram in some fashion, then the ritual of *matam* becomes a distinguishing characteristic of Shiite Muharram liturgies. What reasons do Hyderabadi Shiites give for performing *matam* and other actions of lamentation for Husain? Some of the most educated of the Shiites whom I interviewed—S. Abbas Ali, founder of the Imam-e Zamana Mission, S. Ahmed Ali, president of Parwaneh Shabbir, and his brother Mir Hussein Ali, vice president of the guild and a retired librarian from Osmania University—took care to quote the Quran in support of the practice of *matam*. All cited Quran 42.23 as justification: "These are the things which God announces as good news to His servants who have believed and performed good works. Say: 'As recompense for this I ask nothing of you save devoted affection with regard to matters of kinship' (*la as'alukum alayhi ajran illa al-mawaddah fi al-qurba*)." This last Arabic phrase is susceptible to varied interpretations. Yusuf Ali's translation reads, "No reward do I ask of you for this except the love of those near of kin"; Mohammed Pickthall offers, "I ask of you no fee therefor, save lovingkindness among kinsfolk."[4] But in an interview at his business office in the Himayatnagar quarter of Hyderabad, Seyyed Abbas Ali made use of this Quranic text as follows: "*Matam* is supported in the Quran by a verse we call *ayat mawaddat al-qurba*. I can translate it into English roughly as follows, off the top of my head: 'I have asked nothing of my community in return for all I have done for them except love of my people'." Seyyed Abbas then went on to explain that the "love of my people" commanded by God in the Quran is simply love for *Ahl-e Bayt*, the family of the Prophet. "And *matam*," Seyyed Abbas continued, "is one way of showing love for *Ahl-e Bayt*." Upon questioning he conceded that the Quran does not explicitly mandate *matam* as a means of showing love for the Prophet's family. "It's true," he argued, "that a Sunni could object: 'There's no reference to *matam* in the Quran or books of law'; but we could reply that the Quran doesn't prescribe the form of *rak'ahs* either [*rak'ahs* are the repeated bowings and prostrations which constitute a part of Muslim prayer ritual]. The Quran tells us to love *Ahl-e Bayt*, and *matam* shows our love for them." By way of conclusion he added, "Since the Quran does not explicitly stipulate the performance of *matam*, we should regard *matam* as *mustahabb* rather than mandatory." *Mustahabb* is a term from Islamic law designating a given action as religiously commendable and meritorious but not obligatory.

In a conversation at Parwaneh Shabbir headquarters I asked guild members about Shiite justifications for *matam*. Hassan Abbas Rizvi replied, "Beating one's chest is a natural thing, a natural response when one hears about Karbala. We want to feel Husain's sorrow." By way of commentary on Seyyed Hassan's statement, other Parwaneh Shabbir officers cited a tradition relating to the Prophet's lifetime and the battle of Uhud undertaken against the Meccan Quraysh. During the fighting at Uhud, Muhammad was wounded in the mouth by a flung rock that smashed several of his teeth. In grief at the Prophet's wound, the guild members told me, one of his companions seized a stone and smashed it against his own teeth, out of a desire to experience the same pain as had Muhammad. Not surprisingly, the example of the past is often cited in justifications of *matam*. In an interview at the Hauzat al-Mahdi al-Ilmiyah, a Shiite religious school in the Purani Haveli quarter of the Old City, I received the following comment from Seyyed Naimatullah Moosavi, administrator of the school: "We do what the original Karbala mourners did, what Hazrat Zaynab did, who held the first *majlis* right in the palace of Yazid when she was held prisoner in Damascus after Karbala." In asking about *matam* I frequently encountered this emphasis on precedent and the example of authoritative figures from sacred history.

On July 7, 1991, I went to the Yaqutpura quarter of the Old City to visit with Ansar Hyder Abidi, an Assistant Commissioner of Police formerly active in Parwaneh Shabbir. Also present were Agha Abbasi, president of Guruh-e Ja'fari, and Ahmed Ali, president of Parwaneh Shabbir. All three of them joined in conversation to offer me their perspective on Muharram lamentations. The following is a summary of their comments:

> We do *matam* because we want to remind people of what happened to *Ahl-e Bayt*. It is a duty for us. When Fatima learned that Ali, Muhammad, she herself, and Hasan would all die before her son Husain in his battlefield death at Karbala, she cried out, "Who then will perform *matam* and weep for Husain when he dies?"
>
> In reply God sent to Fatima an angel who conveyed God's promise that He would create a community which would agree to assume the duty for all time of performing *matam* and weeping for Husain.

Thus the Shiite world community is conceptualized in terms of a historical event and the covenantal acceptance of a duty related to this event. This historical view can be seen as rooted in an Abrahamic religious perspective common to Judaism, Christianity, and Islam alike, where God is understood as actively intervening in human history and humans choose freely to respond to this divine intervention.

Another justification of *matam* emerges from a work published in Karachi called *The Importance of Weeping and Wailing*. The author, Syed Mohammed Ameed, cites traditions to the effect that the entire cosmos participated in bewailing Husain's death at Karbala: the sky shed tears of blood for forty days; wild beasts roamed the jungles in agitation; genies recited poems of lamentation; seventy thousand angels descended to Husain's grave to weep; the earth emitted blood in grief. In Ameed's interpretation, God caused these actions to be manifested in the world in order to make clear to us humans the overriding importance of remembering Husain and of commemorating his death in mourning. "The inescapable conclusion," Ameed argues, "is that weeping and wailing for Husain is a matter of extraordinary importance in the eyes of Allah. Otherwise he would not have made all His creatures to weep according to their own natural forms."[5]

Displays of grief at Muharram are also, in Ameed's view, a part of the process of strengthening and defining the Shiite community:

> The life, progress, and glory of any community depends upon a passion for unity among its members and their wise organization. The stronger the passion for unity and the wiser the organization the more progressive and glorious will be the community. What sows the seed of passion for unity and organization in the community and helps it to germinate and develop is this very practice of weeping and wailing which has earned for us the nickname 'the Community of Weepers'...
>
> All the symptoms of unity and co-operation in the community—the parties of breast-beaters, the bands of *Nauha* (i.e., versified expressions of sorrow for a departed soul)-reciters, annual condolence meetings and processions, organizations of volunteers for facing those who are opposed to our condolatory observance and counteracting their mischievous propaganda—are either the direct product or the indirect result of this same practice of weeping and wailing.[6]

For some of the Hyderabadi Shiites with whom I spoke, weeping alone is insufficient as a mark of sorrow for Husain. One of the young men I interviewed, a member of the Guruh-e Haydariyah and the manager of a garage and gasoline station, went so far as to say it is "childish" to shed tears only without also shedding one's own blood for Husain. When I asked him why he performed *matam* at Muharram, he replied, "We feel it our duty to shed our blood on Ashura. To prove we are with him, with Hazrat Imam Husain, we shed our blood, we use implements and cut ourselves." In a second conversation this young man stated, "We do *matam* not just to commemorate Hazrat Imam Husain but as a way of saying we are Shiites... by hurting myself, I show I am willing to protect my religion and do anything to protect the religion."

When I repeated this comment about "protecting the religion" to other members of Hyderabadi men's associations, they were quick to point out to me that the performance of *matam* and shedding of one's own blood should never lead to harming others. A teacher who is affiliated with the Guruh-e Ja'fari explained to me, "Husain's voluntary death shows us it's better to hurt ourselves than hurt others." Again and again in conversations with guild members I encountered this desire to express grief at Muharram while avoiding confrontation with other religious communities.

Some of the younger *guruh* members whom I interviewed seemed to view the more strenuous forms of *matam* as a kind of masculine endurance contest. The garage manager from Haydariyah quoted above expressed particular admiration for those men with the physical strength to scourge themselves at length and with great force. Over the course of several conversations a young member of Guruh-e Ja'fari offered me a comparison of the bare-handed *matam* styles of various *guruhan* (to be discussed in more detail in the following section). "If you watch the men from Guruh-e Ja'fari beating their chests," he claimed, "you'll see that we do *matam* in the *ajami* [Iranian] style. Our style is simple and manly. If you compare us with another group like Masoomeen, you'll see that our *matam* is much more demanding and exhausting than theirs."

I suspect that this pride in a demanding *matam* regimen is not confined to Hyderabad's Shiites. During a brief visit to Lahore in June 1991, I visited a number of Muslim monuments with a Sunni acquaintance. We passed by a Shiite shrine known as Karbala Game Shah, and our talk turned to the upcoming Muharram season. He offered the following comment on *matam*:

> One day some years ago when I was still quite young I went swimming with some Muslim friends of mine. I didn't know that some of them were Shiite, and so when we were in the water I was very surprised to see all the scars on the back and chest of one of my friends. He was very heavily scarred! I asked him about this, and he wasn't ashamed at all. He was very proud of these *matam* scars, and he said, "These are a mark of my bravery."

My informant seemed both impressed and disquieted as he recalled this incident. In seeking to interpret liturgical self-mortification, perhaps one can say that *matam* scars set apart the devout Shiite: he has shown himself brave enough to undertake a form of lamentation that most Muslims, for one reason or another, are unwilling to endure. Scourge-marks give a visible demonstration of the Shiite's unsurpassed love for *Ahl-e Bayt*.

In Hyderabad it is primarily the young men who engage in the severer forms of *matam* involving weapons and flails. This does not mean that older Shiites necessarily criticize the bloody varieties of self-mortification; in fact I spoke with several who defended the young men's actions, though they themselves performed nothing more strenuous than bare-handed *matam*. In one of our conversations Seyyed Abbas Ali (himself a man in his late fifties) stated, "For some men, being willing to cut themselves is a measure of their love for *Ahl-e Bayt*." By way of analogy he asked me to imagine a boy who has fallen in love with a girl. "How do you know how much the boy loves that girl? By what he does to show his love for her. Some young men, some older ones too, feel the same way about *Ahl-e Bayt*: they feel they must do the most difficult kinds of *matam* as a measure and display of their love. For myself, to show my love for *Ahl-e Bayt*, I personally will try to beat myself with one-handed breast-beating as hard as possible while the *nauha* is chanted. But nothing more severe than that. But perhaps another man will use implements on himself as his own way of expressing love for *Ahl-e Bayt*."

A similar opinion was voiced by Agha Muhammad Abidi, vice-consul at the Iranian Consulate in Hyderabad. Abidi said that he regarded all forms of *matam*, whether bare-handed or involving weapons, as sharing the essential attribute of being marks of respect for Imam Husain in his martyrdom. "Every individual has his own love for Husain. This love prompts some people to do things which strictly speaking are *haram* [forbidden by Islamic law], for example, shedding their own blood, which is polluting under normal circumstances. But it is their love for Husain which makes them do this." The vice-consul took care not to condemn any of these forms of *matam*; this diplomatic caution characterized all his comments to me concerning Muharram rituals in Hyderabad.

Another perspective on self-mortification was offered me by Seyyed Asghar Hussein Musawi, supervisor of the Guruh-e Husayniyah, who described *matam* as a way for today's Shiite community to express its sense of regret at not having been able to come to Husain's aid at Karbala. As Seyyed Hussein said to me in conversation:

> Why do Shiites do *matam*? Ali Zain al-Abidin, Hazrat Imam Husain's son, was sick and unable to fight at Karbala; for this reason he was not killed and was instead taken prisoner by the forces of Yazid. Zain al-Abidin's father, before dying, said to him, "When you get to Medina, tell my followers: The Imam says, 'I missed you—where were you?'" Doing *matam* today is a form of response to this last call of Hazrat Imam Husain, to show that if we had been there at Karbala we would have stood with him and shed our blood and died with him.

The feelings described above emphasize the community's sense of failure, regret, and desire for penitence; Seyyed Hussein's comments also imply a personal imaginative involvement in sacred history. What I mean thereby may be clarified by the comments made by a young Shiite during one of my interviews with the Imam-e Zamana Mission's Seyyed Abbas Ali; this young man (who identified himself only as Haydar), one of several present in the office and listening while I talked with Seyyed Abbas, could not resist offering his opinion when I broached the subject of self-mortification rituals: "What thought does a *matamdar* [mourner undertaking *matam*] have in mind when he does *matam*? Just this: If I had been there at Karbala, I would have fought for Imam Husain and died for him."

Again and again in discussions of *matam* I noted this desire to break down the barriers of time between the believer and the sacred event, between the twentieth century and the seventh. For the devout Shiite the rituals involving *matam* permit one to do precisely that, to "feel Husain's sorrow" (in the words quoted earlier of Parwaneh Shabbir's reciter), to be imaginatively present at Karbala.

But *matam* encourages one to look forward in time as well as to the past. Lahore's Shiite shrine of Karbala Game Shah bears the Arabic inscription: *kull ayn bakiyah yawm al-qiyamah illa ayn bakat ala al-Husayn fa-innaha dahikah mustabshirah bi-ghaym al-jannah,* "On the Day of Resurrection every eye will weep save that which has already wept for Husain; for the one who has wept for Husain will be gladdened and rejoice in the cloud of paradise." An eschatological glimpse of Judgment Day becomes possible for the *matamdar.*

The Shiites quoted earlier suggest that Muharram is characterized by a communal desire for penitence. The assembled mourners of Hyderabad, like mourners gathered elsewhere in the Shiite world, thus in some sense atone for the failure of the seventh-century Shiite community to come to Husain's aid in time. In this way, today's *matamdaran* are reminiscent of the *Tawwabun* ("Penitents") of seventh-century Kufa. Because of intimidation by the forces of the Umayyad governor, the Shiites of Kufa had failed to send help to Husain when he was besieged at Karbala; after his death the guilt-stricken Kufans gathered in a desire for collective atonement for their failure.

Ideally, Muharram rituals should inspire a personal as well as communal desire for penitence, as Haydar made clear in his comments: "*Matam,* the action of *matam,* opens your eyes; it awakens you to your sins of the past year, as you think about the *Ma'sumin* and compare them with yourself and the way you've been acting in your sinfulness."

Several other men whom I interviewed likewise commented on the personal motivations attending the performance of *matam.* They explained to me that Fatima is spiritually present at every *majlis* during Muharram; *matam* performed at the end of a *majlis* will lead her to intercede with God on behalf of the *matamdar*: she will be moved to intercession by the degree of devotion to her son Husain shown by the individual mourner. The men with whom I spoke acknowledged that the potential for abuses exists: they knew of Shiites who acted as if the zealous performance of *matam* at Muharram compensated for the failure to observe religious obligations during the rest of the year.[7]

Essays in publications distributed among the Shiite community of Hyderabad show an awareness of this problem. The *Ja'fari Times,* a Shiite newsletter published in Bombay that circulates widely in Hyderabad, published the following in an article entitled "The Importance of Mourning (*Azadari*)" for its Muharram 1409 (1988) issue:

> Imam Husain's objective was to reform the conditions of society and re-establish the forsaken laws of Islam. So we cannot claim to be a true *azadar* [mourner] if we neglect our obligatory duties such as *Namaz* [Quranically mandated prayer], fasting, kindness towards one's parents, etc. and indulge in forbidden acts such as listening to music, watching obscene films, etc.[8]

While in a Shiite-owned bookshop in Hyderabad, I came across a pamphlet entitled *The Leader of Martyrs.* The author records an Arabic legend to the effect that as Husain lay dying at Karbala he heard a divine voice proclaiming: "O Husain! Comfort yourself in that, for your sake, I shall forgive from among the number of sinners those who are your lovers, so that you may feel gratified." The author comments on this legend as follows:

> A question may herewith arise whether the promised forgiveness is a free license for the friends of the Imam to commit whatever sins they like. If so, then the threatened punishment for misdeeds in so many *Ayats* of the Holy Quran would become null and void.
>
> The fact is that a true lover is the one who does nothing that displeases his beloved. If all the great sacrifices made by the Imam were for the purpose of saving Islam and to uphold its rules of *Sharia,* then to flout them would be tantamount to displease [*sic*] our beloved Imam.[9]

In responding to criticisms of the practice of *matam*—especially those forms of *matam* involving bloodshed—defenders of the practice tend to emphasize the importance of *niyyat* (personal intention). As one Hyderabadi put it to me succinctly: *matam* should be done out of love for Husain, not to show off. "*Niyyat* transforms the act," commented Agha Mohammed Hussein, a prominent Hyderabadi businessman, an educated and sensitive Shiite, whom I interviewed at his home. "And this extends to *matam* when it involves shedding one's own blood" (it should be noted here that Shiite legislation involving *taharah* or ritual purity normally classes "spurting blood" with other emitted bodily fluids as *najis* or polluting).[10] Illustrating this principle of *niyyat* is an anecdote told to me by a local Shiite cleric concerning one of the sons of Ayatollah Khui who visited India and was taken on a tour of Hyderabad during Muharram. "A problem came up," my informant explained, laughing, "every time we'd visit a shrine where the *matamdaran* were cutting themselves and swinging their chains. Of course we kept getting sprayed with blood. And the Ayatollah's son insisted on being taken home to change each time his clothes were stained with blood. But for us Hyderabadis," he asserted, "our love for Imam Husain is such that this blood is pure, not *najis*."

Feeling at ease in our rapport, I took the risk of offending Agha Mohammed by asking him whether self-flagellation was really the most constructive outlet for young men's energy in Hyderabad's Shiite community. Might it be possible, I wondered aloud, to put all this communal *matam* energy into something more productive? Not at all put out, my informant replied enthusiastically, "We convert this energy into spiritual energy which becomes available to us only when we shed our blood. By losing physical energy we gain spiritual energy." In reply to the same question the Iranian vice-consul replied sharply, "These various forms of *matam* are all constructive because they express our love for Hazrat Husain, who resisted Yazid, leader of an aggressive superpower. Besides," he added in a revealing afterthought, "only through *matam* and *azadari* can one cause such huge crowds of people to gather voluntarily."

In general I was impressed by the reluctance of educated Shiites to condemn self-flagellation and other bloody forms of *matam,* even when these individuals themselves did not engage in such practices. Underlying such attitudes, as far as I could tell, was a desire to sustain communal solidarity concerning ritual practices universally identified as Shiite. This may be compared with the findings reported by Werner Ende in his study of *fatwas* issued by *ulama* in the Shiite communities of Lebanon and the Arab Middle East. According to Ende, some Shiite clerics have in fact condemned the various forms of extreme self-mortification as *bida'* (heretical innovations in religious practices); but other mullahs, together with the Shiite populace at large, have resisted any attempt to curb *matam* rituals. Resistance has been strengthened by the fact that Wahhabi Saudis and other Sunni Muslims have at times stridently criticized *matam*; retaining such practices thus becomes a way of asserting Shiite identity.[11]

11
—

Lamentation Rituals:
Liturgical Forms of *Matam*

As noted earlier, two basic forms of *matam* may be differentiated: *matam* using one's hands only, that is, *sineh-zani* or breast-beating; and *matam* "with implements" (to use the phrase commonly employed in English by Hyderabadi Shiites), that is, cutting oneself through the use of *zanjir, chaq chaqi,* and so on (to be discussed in more detail below). Both types of *matam* have two characteristics in common: they are generally performed in a group liturgical setting rather than in private by a single individual, and they are performed in time to a rhythm determined by the chanting of a *nauha* or lamentation poem.

The simplest form of bare-handed *sineh-zani* is *ayk dast-e matam* (one-handed *matam*), where the mourner strikes his breast over the heart with the open palm of his right hand. This is the style of *matam* most commonly used when one does not wish to exhaust oneself physically: thus I have noticed *ayk dast-e matam* performed by middle-aged and elderly men standing at the periphery of a crowd of mourners; by tired boys near the end of a long evening vigil; by poets and chorus who, as they chant for extended periods, tap their chests in a relatively perfunctory way, pouring their energy instead into the chants that furnish the cadence for fervent mourners; by mothers who keep a watchful eye on their children even as they themselves perform *matam.*

To the extent that I have been able to observe this, *ayk dast-e matam* also seems the form of *sineh-zani* most commonly used by women in general.[1] Hyderabadi women do in fact participate actively in *matam,* most typically in segregated quarters behind purdah. Moreover, in the summer of 1991 I heard that several women's associations have very recently come into existence; according to my informants, these groups hold Muharram *majalis* for women only, in which the liturgies are led by *zakirs* and reciters who are women. Men whom I questioned seemed reluctant to discuss the topic; the gender segregation prevalent in Hyderabadi Shiite religious gatherings hindered me from catching anything more than glimpses of women's liturgies. I recall blundering into what I had thought was an empty family shrine one Muharram afternoon, only to find some two dozen women grouped before the *alams* on the *ashurkhana* stage. Although I retreated quickly, I nevertheless saw that the participants were beating their breasts and chanting under the direction of a black-clad elderly woman. An entire untouched field of research awaits some scholar.

Shiite tradition does not permit women, so I was told, to use implements in their acts of *matam*. This prohibition, however, is not always respected. During my second Muharram season in Hyderabad, while visiting the shrine of Hazrat Abbas on the morning of Ashura 1991, I saw within the courtyard a few young women with bloodied foreheads who had wrapped white gauze bandages about their heads. When I pointed them out to my companions, I was told that these women had performed *shamshir-zani* (a form of *matam* described below), and that Hyderabadi women will occasionally vow to shed their own blood on Ashura in one of the severer forms of *matam* if their prayers to *Ahl-e Bayt* and the Karbala martyrs are answered. This conforms to Ja'far Sharif's observation with regard to Indian Islam in general that "women often make vows to be performed at the Muharram."[2]

Noteworthy also is a recent *fatwa* issued by a religious scholar, Hujjatul Islam Seyyed Mohammed al-Moosavi, in a readers' question-and-answer column in the *Ja'fari Times,* an Indian Shiite newsletter.[3] Someone had written the newsletter to ask whether it is permissible for women to watch men perform *matam* with implements, when the men have stripped to the waist so as to scourge themselves. The mullah's reply was that women should not watch acts of *matam* performed by men who are not family members. Despite such strictures, however, one cannot help but observe that at the great public *matam* ceremonies on Ashura, at the Hazrat Abbas ka dargah and all along the route of the Bibi ka alam procession, women and girls openly crowd rooftops, balconies, and stairwells to watch the flagellants.

The degree of physical intensity with which *sineh-zani* is performed can vary greatly. I attended four *majalis* in Banjara Hills where *ayk dast-e matam* was performed. The Shiites living there, a minority among the resident Hindus, Sunnis, and Christians, tend to be wealthier and more educated than the Shiite population of the Old City. In the *majalis* I observed in Banjara Hills, *matam* was performed in a very brief and restrained manner. The night before attending one of these *majalis*, however, on the eve of the first of

Muharram in 1989, I went to the Old City and visited the Bibi ka allava (the shrine where the Bibi ka alam, the standard of Lady Fatima, is stored). On this night one of the men's associations, the Guruh-e Matamdaran-e Shah-e Karbala (the Association of the Mourners of the King of Karbala), was present and performed *matam*. There were some twenty-five to thirty members there, most of them teenagers fifteen to seventeen years old, and they performed a simple bare-handed *sineh-zani* without implements. Yet so forcefully did they strike themselves that the vaulted porch overhead rang with the sound, as the pounding of hand against chest created a percussion accompaniment to the lamentation-chanting of the chorus. When I withdrew late in the evening, I could hear the cadenced echo of their beating for some distance along the alleys of the Old City. Thomas Lyell, British District Magistrate in Baghdad at the end of the First World War, reported a similar effect in his description of Muharram in Iraq:

> Each band forms a kind of choir, for, wherever it stops, the masses flock round and in their turn begin beating their breasts, led by the trained band . . . On a still night I have heard the dull thud of the breast-beating in Najaf, from a point in the desert over three miles distant.[4]

Members of various guilds drew my attention to the fact that particular forms of bare-handed *matam* are characteristic of each *guruh*. The types of *matam* favored by each group depend in part on the *nauhas* that form a part of its repertoire and are recited by its members. *Nauha* and *matam* together comprise a unit; participants select a style of *matam* which can easily be performed in time to the *nauha*-chant.

The Anjuman-e Ittihad-e Iraniyan-e Dekkan favors a type of *matam* known variously in Hyderabad as "*Irani*-style," *ajami* (Persian)-style or *do dast-e matam* (two-handed *matam*): the mourner extends both arms straight up over his head, then drops them forcefully, striking his chest with both hands at once. Iranian-style *matam* is also used by Guruh-e Ja'fari, an appropriate choice, given that this association, Hyderabad's oldest (founded in 1884, according to an Urdu document I was shown by a Ja'fari officer), prides itself on its repertoire of traditional Persian-language *nauha*-chants. This style is reputed (by members and nonmembers alike) to be one of the most physically demanding forms of bare-handed *matam*.

The style favored by the Anjuman-e Parwaneh Shabbir seems somewhat more complex. The first half of a chanted stanza will be accompanied by a slow-paced one-handed breast-beating; then the rhythm will quicken in the second half of the stanza, and participants initiate a two-handed *matam*, striking their chests with first their right hand, then their left, in turn. Then follows a brief refrain, furiously fast in pace, in which the men crouch forward intently while still standing and increase the rhythm of their two-handed *matam* to match the heightened intensity of the chant. The refrain abruptly ends, and the chanter reverts to the slow-paced stanza as the men regain their breath while keeping time with a gentle one-handed *matam*. In a conversation at Parwaneh Shabbir headquarters the guild's president explained that this manner of breast-beating is a modified form of what is known as "Punjabi-style" *matam,* a very slow and deliberate fashion of alternating-hand *matam* brought (according to my Parwaneh Shabbir informants) by Punjabi immigrants to Hyderabad.

A third example of *matam* is that used by the Guruh-e Sajjadiyah, an association, so my informants told me, restricted to Shiites who are descendants of the fourth Imam, Ali Zain al-Abidin. I saw this group perform *sineh-zani* within the *ashurkhana* of the Inayat Jung palace on the afternoon of Ashura in 1989. The men, some thirty of them, stood side by side in two lines. To the accompaniment of chanted *nauhas,* each man struck his chest with his right hand in time to the chant, while keeping his left hand placed on the hip of the man to his left (alternatively, some men gripped their neighbor's shirttail). The mourners stepped together in accord with the rhythm, a pace to the front, then an equal pace back, all of them bending forward slightly in unison as they beat their chests.

The *matam* style of Anjuman-e Masoomeen is as follows: the penitent lifts each arm in turn high over his head, then strikes a glancing blow to the chest, the arm then continuing down to swing behind the body. The torso sways from side to side as he strikes his chest, though the feet remain still. Rhythm in time to the *nauha*-chant is maintained in part by the swaying torso movement. Masoomeen's style, according to both members and nonmembers, is one of the less fatiguing forms of *matam,* characterized by rapid light slaps rather than Ja'fari's heavy *ajami* chest-blows. Guruh-e Haydariyah's *matam* style is very similar to that of Masoomeen; not surprising, given that Haydariyah derived from Masoomeen after a split in the membership within a year or two after the founding of Masoomeen. In terms of liturgical performance Haydariyah differs from its parent in its style of *nauha,* favoring staccato lyrics and fierce shouting on many refrains. The effect to me seemed strained, a striving after distinctiveness.

The above is no more than a sampling of forms, but it is worth emphasizing here that members of the *guruhan,* while acknowledging similarities of style among groups, themselves insist that distinctive patterns of *sineh-zani* comprise some of the most important characteristics distinguishing one guild from another. In fact the *matam-nauha* unit seems essential to each group's self-definition. Consider the responses I received when I asked officers of various guilds to explain to me why their association had been founded. Parwaneh Shabbir: "My brother and I wanted an organization with a separate style of *matam*, our own style. We were both attracted to Punjabi *matam*, so we modified that and made it the *matam* for Parwaneh Shabbir." Masoomeen: "We wanted to be in a *guruh* with a simple style of chanting and a simple style of *matam*, one that was less fatiguing, so that we could do *matam* for a long time at the end of each *majlis*. So we founded our own *guruh*." Haydariyah: "We founded our own group so our *nauha-khans* could express and develop their own *nauha* styles." Obviously much is left unsaid in such responses; to take but one example, with regard to Haydariyah, other respondents, members and nonmembers alike, conceded that quarrels and personality clashes in the Masoomeen leadership were a prime cause of the creation of Haydariyah. Nevertheless, *matam-nauha* styles offer each group a means of identifying and characterizing both itself and other *guruhan*.

Without fail in each conversation where I introduced the subject, virtually every man present took a keen sporting interest in *matam* styles, showing a good knowledge of the various forms favored by other associations across the Old City. Points of connoisseurship were endlessly debated: how does Guild X's *sineh-zani* compare with ours in terms of origin, history, technique, ease of performance, and so on?

By this point the reader may well be wondering what degree of participation in *matam* is expected of a non-Shiite observer at a Muharram *majlis*. Does one just stand about awkwardly feeling conspicuous? For my part I was at my most comfortable remaining with the older men at the periphery of the crowd; my age (nearing forty) made this grouping appropriate. I performed *matam* as they did, light one-handed breast-beating, a courtesy form, if you will, nothing strenuous. Nor was anything more expected: generally only very young men in their teens and early twenties go in for enthusiastic chest-pounding.

Bare-handed *sineh-zani* can be observed in Hyderabad beginning on the first of Muharram and continues well after Ashura throughout the season of mourning for the martyrs of Karbala. *Matam* with implements, however, the most exhausting form of self-mortification, is primarily confined to the eighth, ninth, and tenth of Muharram. Any of the following instruments may be used: *patti; chaq chaqi; zanjir;* daggers; or short swords. The *patti* is probably the most widely used form of cutting implement in Hyderabad: the term in this context refers simply to a naked razor blade. The mourner inserts razor blades between the fingers of his right hand; palm open, fingers stiffened, he then beats his breast, the cutting edge of the blades lacerating his chest at each stroke. A member of the Guruh-e Haydariyah explained to me, "The blood that gets on the blades helps keep them stuck in place between your fingers. You cut your chest, then if you like you remove the blades with your free hand and simply use your bare hand to do *matam* until the blood stops flowing. When you want to bleed more, then you use the blades again."

The *chaq chaqi* is a wooden disc that fits easily in the palm of one's hand; it is furnished with a handle on one side and is studded with nails on the other. Like the *patti* it is used for breast-beating but it has largely been superseded by the simpler razor. According to my informants, both implements have the advantage that they can safely be used in crowded processions without risk of harm to those nearby.

The *zanjir* is a scourge or flail. Four or five metal blades, each some six inches in length, are connected by chains to a wooden handle. The *zanjir* is used for lacerating one's back: the mourner takes a step or two away from his companions so as not to harm others, then, legs apart, left hand held high, he swings the flail smartly with his right hand in a rapid horizontal motion at chest level so that the blades strike his exposed back. Because of the potential harm to bystanders, *zanjir-zani* is not performed in tightly packed crowds such as the Bibi ka alam procession; I witnessed *zanjir-zani* in a separate ceremony in the streets outside the shrine of Hazrat Abbas on the morning of Ashura.

Knives and short swords are used to inflict wounds to one's scalp and forehead, a ritual identified by the Persian term *shamshir-zani*. Once blood begins to flow from these cuts the participant wraps a long white bandage around his head and wears it throughout Ashura; the bloodstained cloth serves as a token of devotion to Lord Husain (as noted above, in 1991 I saw several young women who had undertaken *shamshir-zani* and were wearing bloodstained head-cloths). When custodians bring forth the *alam* of Hazrat Abbas on the morning of Ashura for procession through the streets, young men press forward frantically to touch their daggers to the *alam* in an act of consecration to Abbas before initiating *shamshir-zani*.

One concluding note on this subject: on Tasu'a (the ninth of Muharram), vendors appear on the streets of the Old City, sharpening blades on whetstones and offering a display of knives and *zanjirs* for sale to those who wish to perform these types of *matam* on Ashura.

12

The *Majlis* Liturgy:
Sermon Topics and Shiite Self-definition

The activities of Hyderabad's *guruhan* are not confined to any one season. Throughout the year the men's associations supervise the holding of *jeshns* or festal celebrations on occasions such as the birthdays of the Prophet's family and the Twelve Imams, Id-e Ghadir, and Id-e Mubahela. But conversations with members of six associations confirmed my impression that the guilds are most active in the months of Muharram and Safar, during the time of the commemoration of Husain's death and the events surrounding Karbala.

One of the foremost functions of each guild is to provide a group setting within which devotion to Imam Husain may be expressed. Towards this end the men's associations sponsor many of the *majalis* held in the Old City during Muharram. When sponsoring an assembly, officers of the *guruh* take the responsibility for providing the orators and chanters who preside over the liturgy. The *majlis* typically begins with a *marsiyeh*, the reciting of funeral laments by a chorus of some half-dozen men. A sermon is then given by a *zakir* or preacher. The structure of the sermon is fixed according to tradition: invocation of God's blessings and praise of the Prophet's family; *faza' il*, description of the merits of the martyrs of Karbala, with reflections on how their virtues may guide our conduct today; *masa' ib*, evocation of the sufferings endured by the martyrs and the rapacious cruelty of their persecutors. The sermon may last from twenty minutes to somewhat over an hour; and the assembled congregation takes a very active role therein. As the *zakir* embarks on the *masa' ib* and his voice quivers with ever more emotion in recalling the sorrows of the martyrs, those listening express their grief: quietly at first, in low groans and sighs, then more and more loudly, till by the conclusion of the *masa' ib* virtually all are crying, slapping their thighs or heads, or concealing their faces with handkerchiefs as they sob. At this point the sermon will end. An emotional decrescendo is provided as all stand and ritual prayers are recited quietly in Arabic in honor of the twelve Imams; while standing, the participants bow, first in the direction of Najaf and Karbala, then to Meshhed, and finally to Samarra (these are shrines and burial sites associated with the Imams).

When I questioned members of Guruh-e Ja'fari about the importance of organizing and attending Muharram liturgies, they conceded that participation in *majalis* is not mandatory for Muslims in the same way as are the performance of *namaz* and attendance at Friday congregational service. *Majlis* attendance is voluntary rather than required, they explained, and this makes it all the more meritorious for the participant. One of the members, a well-educated and affable individual, offered me the following comment on what he sees as the value of Muharram *majalis*:

> The *majlis* is a religious act in which I'm not alone. I don't mean just because the preacher is there, and the *nauha-khan* and chorus and my other Shiite friends. For one of the fourteen *Ma'sumin*, Hazrat Fatima and possibly some of the Imams, will be present with me while I'm there, I mean invisibly present. The *Ma'sumin* will ensure that my act of devotion is perfect. In private prayer, in *namaz*, I can never be sure my prayer will be perfect. It's easy to be distracted; I may think about Wimbledon [local Hyderabad TV stations had broadcast the Steffi Graf-Gabrielle Sabatini 1991 tennis championship that past weekend], and God may throw my prayer back in my face as unacceptable. Also, *namaz* is in Arabic and pretty much incomprehensible, so it's easy to get distracted. Whereas the *majlis* is in Urdu and holds our attention. And the *majlis* is voluntary, so even if I fall asleep during the sermon for five minutes, it's still acceptable. *Matam* and weeping, when you do them with other people in a group, are easier to give your concentration to than is an Arabic *namaz*. *Majlis* is the one act of worship I can be sure is perfect and will earn me merit.

The preachers whom I interviewed emphasized that in their view the primary purpose of the *majlis* is to render the events of Karbala imaginatively present to the congregation, and that the preacher's responsibility in his sermon is to evoke the sufferings of the Karbala martyrs so powerfully as to make the congregation weep. In this way both *zakir* and congregation acquire *savab* or religious merit.

In August 1989 I talked with Seyyed Hyder Zaydi, a preacher and the son of the celebrated *zakir* Allamah Akhtar Zaydi. I had accompanied Seyyed Hyder one night to the shrine of Hazrat Abbas in the Old City, where he gave a sermon on the occasion of the eve of the first of Muharram. Immediately after the *majlis* I asked Hyder what techniques he favored for moving his audience to tears. "It's not so much the story I tell," he replied, "but the words I choose and the way I stress certain pathetic words and phrases. That's what makes people cry." My own impression, as I recollect *majalis* I attended in 1989 and 1991, is that Muharram *zakirs* favor the creation of word-pictures that seize on vivid details of the Karbala tragedy and thereby move a listener's heart. In one sermon the speaker imagined Zaynab in chains suffering imprisonment in Damascus; in another the preacher repeatedly cried *al-atash al-atash* ("Thirst! Thirst!") in a thin pitiful child's voice, to convey the sufferings of the guiltless infants of the Imam's family on the desert plains of Karbala; in a third homily, one detailing the aftermath of Karbala, the *zakir*'s voice rasped roughly as he recounted how Yazid's soldiers laid hands on the young girls of the Household, tearing the gold earrings from their ears so that blood spurted from the torn lobes. In each instance the audience's wailed response of grief testified to the homilist's success in evoking Karbala.

More remarkable still was an omission which I noticed over the course of two summers in Hyderabad. The Muharram preachers I observed consistently avoided any reference to contemporary political issues, whether local or international. In 1989 this tendency seemed to me to be part of the politically quietist orientation that I observed in Hyderabad's Shiite community (a point to which I return later); but when I returned in the summer of 1991 I expected to hear some echo at least of current international developments. The Persian Gulf War, the revolt of Iraq's Shiites against Saddam Hussein, the Republican Guard's bombardment of the shrines of Abbas and Husain at Karbala: for any homilist contemplating a sermon on Muharram and the sufferings of the seventh-century martyrs, the parallels abound. Yet in none of the performance genres I encountered—*marsiyeh*, sermon, or *nauha*—did I sense any reference to current political issues. A young physician with whom I discussed this point stated, "*Zakirs* avoid politics in their Muharram sermons so as not to risk their popularity. Politics and current local events are not what people come to hear about or want to learn about when they attend a *majlis*." A member of Guruh-e Ja'fari confirmed my impression of the apolitical nature of Hyderabad's Muharram sermons, stating, "Muharram is set aside in honor of Hazrat Imam Husain. The *nauhas* and sermons are for him, in his honor. It would be wrong to bring in references to Saddam and the Gulf War."

To a certain extent the topic discussed in a given homily is linked to events from the tragedy of Karbala traditionally commemorated on specific days of Muharram. The first through the third of Muharram are associated with

Husain's arrival at Karbala and his refusal to give allegiance to Yazid, while the fourth focuses on Hazrat Hurr, a commander in the Umayyad army who repented of his opposition to the holy Family and chose martyrdom with Husain. Aun and Muhammad, teenaged sons of Hazrat Zaynab (Husain's sister), are remembered on the fifth of Muharram: both were killed in the battle. The sixth is set aside by some congregations for Ali Asghar (the Imam's infant son, slain by an arrow in the fighting), while other Shiites dedicate the day to Ali Akbar (the eighteen-year-old son of Husain, killed in combat in his father's presence). The seventh of Muharram recalls the battlefield wedding of Qasim (son of Hasan, the second Imam) and Fatima Kubra (daughter of Husain). Abbas is honored on the eighth, while the ninth and tenth of Muharram provide an emotional climax as the death of Husain himself is contemplated.[1]

Such at least is the traditional framework for *majlis* sermon topics during the first ten days of Muharram. In practice, however, the *zakir* enjoys some latitude in his choice of topic. This is particularly true during the first few days of Muharram, when the speakers often range widely in their subject matter, going beyond the events of Karbala to ponder the significance of Muharram in general. Two sermons will illustrate this flexibility of theme. The first is a sermon given by Hyder Zaydi on August 3, 1989, the eve of the first of Muharram, at the shrine of Hazrat Abbas; in his talk Hyder narrated a story which can be summarized as follows:

> There was once a widow, old and blind, who lived alone save for one devoted daughter who cared for her. Every year at Muharram the daughter arranged the family *ashurkhana,* brought out the *alams* and oversaw preparations for the *majlis* to be held in the family shrine. But then one year, just before the onset of Muharram, the daughter died of a sudden illness. After her funeral the mother cried out, "Who will arrange my *majlis*? O God, this year Husain and his mother will not come to my home."
>
> Then came a knock on the door. Four women stood there, saying they were strangers and needed someplace to stay. The widow agreed to house them, but only if they would supervise the *majlis* to be held in her home. The four women accepted, and they arranged the lamentation assembly with such success that the walls themselves groaned aloud in grief at the sorrowful *marsiyehs* and sermon which were recited in that household. The old woman was very pleased, for all believers want weeping at their *majalis.*
>
> Afterwards, however, the widow could only offer *tabarruk* (pastry sweets traditionally prepared for guests at a *majlis*) by way of payment to the four women who had prepared the successful liturgy. The women accepted the food with thanks; and suddenly the strangers stood revealed as the Lady Fatima and

the women of Karbala: Zaynab, Umm Kulthum (sister of Zaynab) and Sakina (daughter of the Imam Husain). Holding aloft the *tabarruk* Fatima looked up and cried out, "See, my son, how your people venerate us!"

This pleasing tale (with its *xenodochia* motif reminiscent of Abraham's hospitality to the disguised angels in Genesis 18.1-8 and the Greek myth of Philemon and Baucis) was succinctly explicated to me after the sermon by the preacher himself: "I wanted to demonstrate the devotion that we should show today to the holy Family during Muharram."

My second sermon-example is one given by Sadiq Naqvi (who is not only a *zakir* but also a professor of history at Osmania University) on July 16, 1991, the third of Muharram, at a private *ashurkhana* in the Dar al-Shifa' quarter of Hyderabad's Old City. As in the sermon cited above, Professor Naqvi chose not to dwell on Karbala. Instead he examined the role in the divine plan played by the first Imam, Ali ibn Abi Talib. It is true, Naqvi argued, that the Quran constitutes the perfection of God's message, but without Hazrat Ali this message would never have been preserved for all mankind. In the battles he fought on behalf of Islam, by saving the Prophet's life repeatedly (Naqvi cited as one example Ali's staying behind in place of the Prophet at the dangerous moment of the *hijrah* from Mecca), Ali ensured that Muhammad would be safeguarded and the full message of the Quran revealed. Thus it is inappropriate to revere the Quran without also fully and properly revering the man who was instrumental in its revelation and preservation.

After the sermon a Shiite acquaintance, a man in his early forties who is the assistant principal at a *dini madrasah* (Shiite religious school), said to me by way of commentary, "Many Sunnis and Wahhabis fall into the mistake described by Professor Naqvi. They revere the Quran but fail to acknowledge the qualities of perfection in Hazrat Imam Ali and the other Imams. Sunnis refuse to recognize the infallibility and sinlessness of the Imams; they don't show respect to the Prophet's family and his descendants as fully as we do, we Shiites."

Common to these sermons is a theme I heard reiterated in one form or another in numerous other Muharram homilies: the need to give sufficient veneration to *Ahl-e Bayt*. Of course all Muslims of whatever persuasion would protest their love of the Prophet's family; as discussed earlier, many Sunnis do observe Muharram to some degree. But the extent of disagreement among Muslims over the veneration appropriate to *Ahl-e Bayt* may be gauged from a conversation I had in Hyderabad with a self-proclaimed Wahhabi who derided my interest in the Old City Shiite community and its Muharram practices. Without any attempt at masking his irritation, he asserted:

We Muslims feel sorrow at Husain's death, but there's no need for excessive
sorrow such as the Shiites show. God raised Husain to Himself; why should we
sorrow at this? *Matam* is *bid' ah* [religious innovation or heresy]; it's not in the
shari' ah. Husain should not be called a *shahid* [martyr]: the title is only earned
when Islam is being threatened and when someone is killed defending Islam.
But Islam was not being threatened at Karbala; there was Muslim rule, Muslims
were free to worship; at stake was only an issue of political rule. Husain did not
die defending the faith.

When I repeated this criticism to members of Anjuman-e Parwaneh
Shabbir, they retorted that such talk was typical of Wahhabis and even of
some more moderate Sunni Muslims who try to hurt Shiites by reducing the
status of the Imams. From the Shiite perspective, I think it is fair to say,
neglecting the memory of Karbala in any way devalues the sacrifice made
by Husain's family and the Prophet's household. At the level of popular
piety, Hyderabad's Shiites do not distinguish themselves from other Muslims
on the basis of doctrinal assertions represented by terms such as *ismah* or
imamah. The belief in *ismah,* the sinlessness and infallibility of the Prophet's
family, and the concept of *imamah,* the rightful status of Ali and the other
Imams as both political and spiritual leaders of the Islamic community: these
are essentially doctrinal articulations of a desire to honor *Ahl-e Bayt* as fully
as possible. Denying *Ahl-e Bayt* the rank of perfection becomes tantamount
then to a failure to love them fully. Shiite self-definition, at least as I
experienced it in Hyderabad, could perhaps be summarized as follows:
Shiites are those Muslims who excel beyond all others in their love for the
family of the Prophet.

13

The Role of Liturgy
in Reinforcing Communal Identity

In the previous chapter I remarked that the men's associations sponsor many of the Muharram *majalis* held in Hyderabad's Old City. A given *guruh* may also provide for the performance of *matam* immediately after the sermon and prayers are concluded. In such cases a *nauha-khan* or dirge-reciter from the guild will direct this portion of the liturgy. The *nauha-khan* recites lamentation poetry, accompanied usually by three or four assistants who chant responses or choruses for each poem. Members of the congregation who wish to participate fully in *matam*, primarily young men, will gather in a semicircle around the *nauha-khan*; older men and young children stand at the periphery of the crowd, while women cluster near the purdah to watch as best they can. The guild's chanter is thus the focal point of any *matam* liturgy sponsored by the men's association.

The above comments suggest how the *guruh* furnishes structure for acts of self-mortification. *Matam* first of all is done as part of a group, not individually. Its form (for example, *ayk dast-e matam* or *do dast-e matam*) is determined by the styles of *matam* performed by the given *guruh*; its pace is controlled by the rhythm of the dirge chanted by the *nauha-khan*. The *guruh*'s reciter also decides at what moment to accelerate the pace of the chant for the entire congregation: he will suddenly raise his arm while reciting, one of his assistants in the chorus will respond to this signal by crying "Ali!" and the tempo will abruptly quicken, the *matam* strokes falling more swiftly to keep time with the chanter's increasingly urgent call.

Worth noting too is that some of the larger *guruhan,* such as Parwaneh Shabbir and Masoomeen, also publish chapbook editions of the poems chanted in their *majalis* and *matam* liturgies. These poems are characterized by frequently recurring simple refrains; thematically they focus on the sufferings of the martyrs, the love felt for the Imams and the Prophet's family by the Shiite community, and the central importance for all humankind of the events of Karbala.

At each *majlis* sponsored by a *guruh,* members set up microphones for broadcasting chants throughout the *ashurkhana* (sometimes setting up amplifiers at the entrance so that the poems can be heard throughout the neighborhood). On Ashura rickshaws and large carts outfitted with microphones and sound systems accompany each guild in the Bibi ka alam procession, so that the reciter's chanting can be heard by the crowds along the procession route.

It should be emphasized here that *majalis* sponsored by the men's associations are not as a rule restricted to members only. Especially in public shrines and in liturgies performed outdoors, men will step in from the crowd on the street and join the *guruh* in the performance of *matam* for as long a period of time as they wish. But in my observations of such occurrences I noticed that nonmembers who participate in the guild's *matam* subject themselves to the structure determined by the guild: they copy the style and rhythm of *matam* being performed by the *guruh's* members in the circle surrounding the *nauha-khan.*

All participants in *matam,* whether guild members or the general public, benefit from other services furnished by the sponsoring men's association. On Ashura, when the *guruhan* oversee the performance of *matam* with implements, the associations provide older men who stand ready to restrain anyone who risks hurting himself too severely. Both in 1989 and 1991 I noticed that at the shrine of Hazrat Abbas no one was allowed to administer more than three or four slashes to his forehead or scalp in the ritual of *shamshir-zani*; in several instances older men would step in to wrestle a dagger away from an ecstatic teenager who failed to respond to pleas that he had shed enough of his blood in honor of *Ahl-e Bayt.* Volunteers from the organizations, armed with large metal canisters each labeled with the name of a guild, sprayed all the mourners performing *matam* from time to time with rose water. Furthermore, at many *majalis* the *guruh* will also offer refreshments, providing *tabarruk*—sweets, pastry, water, spiced milk—not just to members, but to whoever attends the assembly.

Obviously one need not be a member of a men's association to undertake *matam*; this is something that transcends the limits of any one guild. But the men's associations make three particular contributions to Hyderabad's Shiite community with regard to the performance of *matam*:

1. By sponsoring a *majlis* and providing a preacher, chanter, and chorus, the *guruh* creates a structured context within which the entire community—not just the guild—may perform *matam* to the degree considered appropriate for each person. Young men may choose to join the circle of *guruh* members surrounding the chanter; boys and older men will stand at the periphery and undertake *ayk dast-e matam*; women and girls watch from stairwells or from behind purdah and beat their breasts in time. One might also claim that the men's associations serve to socialize youths in the learning of *matam*: at many *majalis* I saw very young boys studying the adults' actions and imitating the older boys as best they could in performing *sineh-zani*.

2. To the extent that they are able, members of various *guruhan* informed me, the men's associations try to ensure that *matam* is performed continuously throughout the most solemn period of Muharram, from the seventh to the tenth of Muharram (marking the days of the Karbala martyrs' worst privations: they were deprived of water and food beginning on the seventh of Muharram during the fateful siege). In a given *majlis* the actual performance of *matam* by an individual guild, whether barehanded *sineh-zani* or *matam* with implements, normally lasts from twenty minutes to a maximum of one hour; more than this is beyond most men's endurance and is considered unsafe. Therefore the associations will take it in turn to perform *matam* at a particular shrine in honor of the martyrs. This practice is most in evidence at the Hazrat Abbas ka dargah on the ninth and tenth of Muharram, where one *guruh* after another claims the shrine's courtyard and leads all the congregants present in the performance of *matam*. The form and rhythm of *matam* at a given shrine on such an occasion will thus change from hour to hour as each *guruh*'s reciter and chorus take their turn in leading the liturgy of mourning.

3. As noted earlier, *matam* may be performed by anyone. But it is the guilds that, by assembling groups of young men armed with cutting implements, ensure that the severest permissible forms of *matam* will be undertaken on Tasu'a and Ashura. In this sense the *guruh* can be said to perform a liturgy of benefit to the entire Shiite community. For, as noted earlier, Lady Fatima, mother of Husain, is believed to be present at every Muharram assembly; according to my informants, acts of self-mortification lead to intercession not only on behalf of

the men wielding the *zanjirs* but also on behalf of all those present at the liturgy.[1]

Although some men may step forward from the onlooking crowd to join the guild in its performance of *matam* with implements on Ashura, the majority of those present and watching the *guruh* will not actually cut themselves, confining themselves instead to bare-handed *sineh-zani*. Thus the *guruhan* exceed the levels of self-mortification undertaken by most persons in the Shiite community. But there is a sense in which the activities of the guild can be said to be paradigmatic. The *guruh* symbolizes the community as a whole; it exemplifies the community's desire to identify fully with the sufferings of the martyrs of Karbala. There is an extravagance to *matam* when undertaken with daggers, razors, and flails—an extravagance that is admired for the generosity it shows in the sacrifice of one's blood, offered on behalf of the community as a mark of love for Lord Husain. It is the Shiite men's guilds that ensure that this liturgy of sacrifice and generosity is made publicly and as nearly continuously as possible during the foremost sacred days of Muharram.

14

Preparations for the Muharram Season: Rehearsal Sessions and the Training of the Chorus in a Shiite Men's Guild

During my second summer in Hyderabad, a chance rainstorm and a casual remark led me to glimpse another activity sponsored by the Shiite men's guilds: the rehearsals that prepare boys and teenagers for each Muharram season.

I had traveled with my friend Andreas by motor scooter one evening over the Afzal Ganj Bridge to the Old City to visit Ali Muhsin Khan, a factory manager in his forties who performs *matam* with Guruh-e Ja'fari. Muhsin is also president of the Elia Theological Association, a charitable group which dispenses interest-free business loans to needy Shiites. When we arrived a half-dozen petitioners were seated with Muhsin in the Elia office (a small detached cinderblock building in his family compound), but he waved us in at once and insisted that business could be postponed while he answered our questions. The rickshaw-drivers and other clients in the office listened keenly and offered comments to supplement Muhsin's answers. For my part I promised to curtail our visit and leave after half an hour, but within minutes a monsoon storm broke overhead and lashed the house for most of the evening. Muhsin would not hear of our hurrying away, and as Andreas and I had little desire to chance his scooter in the rain, we were happy to sit and chat.

At one point in our conversation our host remarked that since we were now in the last few days of the month of Dhul hijjah, rehearsal sessions would be well underway among the city's *matami guruhan*. My interest was aroused at once, and in reply to my questions he explained that the leaders of each *guruh* gathered young members to train them in the guild's *nauhas* and *matam*. But when I asked about the possibility of my attending a practice session, Muhsin indicated that the groups might be reluctant to welcome me:

AMK: Each year a *matami guruh* will try to introduce at least one or two new *nauhas*. These will be written by a poet who writes a *nauha* which he thinks will suit the *matam* style and the kind of rhythms favored by that group.

DP: Do the poets also write the melodies for the new *nauhas* they create?

AMK: Not usually. Usually what happens is that the poet writes the words for a new *nauha*. Then he gives it to the group's *nauha-khans*, the reciters, and he says, "I've written this; now you set a tune to it." And then the *nauha-khans* create the melody. After that the *guruh* practices the new *nauhas* in their practice sessions before Muharram. But they try to keep these sessions secret if they can. So they might not want you to come.

DP: In what way are the sessions secret? Why do they do this?

AMK: There's a certain amount of competition among the *matami guruhan*. Each group wants to surprise the congregation at the *majlis* with the new chant they've practiced for this year. So they try to keep the new *nauhas* secret till Muharram, so another group won't steal any ideas from them, the tune or the words and so forth. Let me give you an example. I have friends in Parwaneh Shabbir. One day I went to visit them, and they were in the middle of practicing their *nauhas* for Muharram. As soon as I walked in on them they stopped; they were friendly, but they stopped. You see, they know I go to *majalis* with Guruh-e Ja'fari and do my *matam* with Ja'fari. Anyway, after a few minutes I offered to leave and I excused myself. And they didn't stop me from going.

At times jealousies run so high among the guilds, Muhsin asserted, that some groups have been rumored to send out young toughs to intimidate or even beat up *nauha-khans* from rival groups. I could not confirm this rumor of violence; but it made sense to me that the groups would guard their new chants from outsiders till the moment of performance. Impressive public performances of *matam* and *nauhas* increase a guild's prestige; from this flow invitations to *majalis,* an accrual in membership, and further membership dues and contributions. A stranger might well be unwelcome at rehearsals.

Nevertheless I asked around among the Shiite community leaders whom I knew, and through their good offices was able to secure invitations to several practice sessions, one with Guruh-e Ja'fari and two with Anjuman-e Masoomeen. At each session those present were cordial and welcoming; as a foreigner and non-Muslim (so I imagined to myself) I probably seemed unlikely to disclose new melodies to rival *guruhan*. My visits with Masoomeen were particularly fruitful; their rehearsals are held in the group's *ashurkhana* in the Old City.

I began my first visit by interviewing the guild's secretary and founder, Mir Sabir Ali Zawar, in his office, which is adjacent to the *ashurkhana*:

DP: With a huge *guruh* like yours, I assume it's impossible to fit everyone in here for practice at the same time. Who comes to these practice sessions?

MSA: We try to get the members who will help lead the rest of the congregation during the Muharram *majlis*. Of course the *nauha-khans* come; we have eight of them. And then we pick out the young boys from our *guruh* who have the best voices and encourage them to come to all the rehearsals. We teach them the correct responses, the words to the refrain in each *nauha*, as well as the pace of the *matam* which accompanies each chant. The younger boys watch the *nauha-khans* and follow them; that's how they learn. Then, during the actual performance in public at the *majlis*, these young boys who have come to our practice sessions will stand in the crowd and lead the rhythm for the rest of the boys. This way there'll be two trained chorus-groups during the *majlis*, the *nauha-khans* who stand behind me facing the congregation, and the boys who stand in the crowd and who already know the *matam* rhythm and the refrain to each *nauha*.

DP: At what time in the year do you begin practicing your *nauhas* for Muharram?

MSA: We start practicing during the last three weeks of Dhul hijjah, and we continue through the third of Muharram. On the fourth of Muharram we go out as a group and do *matam* at the shrine of Hazrat Abbas. During our rehearsals we practice the new *nauhas* that have just been written for us, but also sometimes we'll go over some of the old chants as well. Because we still keep reciting the old *nauhas* as well. We combine old chants with new ones at each *majlis*.

After our conversation Sabir and his assistant Hyder Ali led me into the hall where practice was being held. Perhaps twenty young boys and teenagers, twelve to sixteen years in age, sat on the floor clustered around a half-dozen *nauha-khans*. The latter were young men in their early to mid-twenties. One monitored a portable tape player, which played a cassette recording of Masoomeen *nauhas*. He pressed the stop button frequently and replayed portions of the tape, interspersing comments on the melody. Meanwhile some of the boys whispered and poked at each other. Across the hall another member on a stepladder was adjusting a light fixture overhead; other young men steadied the ladder and chatted back and forth.

But when Sabir entered the group came to attention. The repairman clambered down and the ladder was put away; conversation died and the tape ceased. Sabir seated himself on a mat to one side of the hall, Hyder at his left; as the youths pressed forward, he motioned them to sit, and the circle re-formed with the founder at its center. For a moment, silence; then Sabir murmured a single word, "*Salwat*" (Benediction). At once the group cried a reply: "*Salla Allah ala Muhammad wa-al-e Muhammad*" (God's blessings on Muhammad and Muhammad's family). His invocation was the same as that used to convene a Muharram *majlis*; the call for benediction and its response lent even this rehearsal an air of liturgy.

Sabir unfolded a sheet of paper and placed it on the floor beside his assistant. "This is a new piece," he said to me in explanation. Hyder studied the sheet with its pencilled lyrics; they exchanged comments and Hyder nodded. Then the young man lifted his head and chanted slowly:

Ay alamdar
ay Husain ibn Ali
ay Ali
(O bearer of the battle-standard
O Husain son of Ali
O Ali)

Hyder repeated the words, this time joined by the leader; on the third repetition all the circle joined in. These lyrics, I realized, comprised the refrain. Then Sabir and Hyder left the refrain and together began singing the verse stanzas, the older man jabbing with his finger at the sheet to mark their place. But each verse was brief, and at the end of each stanza they repeated the refrain, in unison with the entire chorus of youths. The brevity of the stanzas and the frequent recurrence of the refrain served, I could tell, to keep the group's attention focused.

After a few verses Sabir suddenly quickened the rhythm, signalling the heightened tempo by slapping his thigh in time. In response the chorus raised their voices and began a forceful one-handed *matam*, the boys pounding their chests as they sang. But the two leaders and the older *nauha-khans* marked time with light slaps to the thigh, conserving their energy for the chant. The increased tempo was sustained for the rest of the song.

Abruptly Sabir ceased; he had evidently decided the group now had some feel for this particular piece. Once more he called for the *salwat*, and the boys cried out the prayer as before. The secretary paused, head down a moment, while the whole chorus watched him in eager silence. Then he looked up and announced the title of the next *nauha* to be rehearsed, *Karbala la ilah illa Allah*. This is an older hymn and is printed in Masoomeen's printed *nauha* pamphlet, *Du'a-e Fatimah*; at once the *nauha-khans* pulled down well-thumbed copies of the chant-book from a shelf and readied themselves.[1]

Slowly and deliberately Sabir and Hyder intoned the refrain:

Karbala la ilah illa Allah
(Karbala: no god is there save God)

The chorus responded by repeating the line. Twice more leader and group exchanged the refrain, call and response, call and response, still with the same solemn incantation.

Then (as with the previous song) came a sudden quickening of tempo: Sabir led the boys into the stanza and the whole chorus beat their chests with vigor. Gone now was the mournful mood of the chant's opening. The subject might be a tragic death on the field of war; but Masoomeen's delivery stressed the heroic rather than the pitiful aspects of this death:

Jan-e Zehra Ali ka nur-e negah
kawn hay juz Husayn din-e penah
Jis nay lakha hay khak-e maqtal par
Karbala la ilah illa Allah
(Offspring of the radiant one, light of the eye of Ali,
Who save Husain is protector of the faith?
He who has written on the dust of the place of killing:
Karbala: no god is there save God)

As with the refrain, Masoomeen's chanting of the first half of each stanza was antiphonal: the leaders sang a line and the chorus echoed a response. But the third line of each stanza brought a variation. The melody rose, and Sabir alone sang the words, a solo which made the massed choral response in the refrain all the more forceful, as two dozen male voices cried *Karbala la ilah illa Allah*.

In this rehearsal session the secretary had his chorus practice three more stanzas of the *nauha*:

The meaning of Karbala is: the holy war of unwavering faith
Loftier than the heavens is the earth of Karbala
On each dust-mote of which is written
Karbala: no god is there save God.

Karbala is the place of the Great Sacrifice
The place where truth and falsehood were apportioned

On the afternoon of Ashura this decree was made—
Karbala: no god is there save God.

The message of light in the night of injustice
The message of life in the moment of death
On the day of Ashura only this voice was heard—
Karbala: no god is there save God.

Sabir's voice trailed off, and he called once more for the *salwat*. Leaving the *nauha-khans* to continue rehearsing with the boys, he led me back to his office to talk some more.

To summarize my impressions: The chanting style I experienced that night was identical to what I encountered in the other Masoomeen rehearsal I witnessed and in the various *majalis* I attended with this *guruh*. Antiphony, frequent repetition of refrains, simplicity of verse structure, forceful *matam*-driven rhythms: all are suited to a guild whose membership is overwhelmingly that of boys and older adolescents.

15

Liturgy as Drama:
The Seventh of Muharram and the
Bridegroom of Karbala's Procession

Despite important differences of culture and historical era, to a limited extent the chant-activities of Hyderabad's *matami guruhan* invite comparison with the genre of tragedy in ancient Greek literature. Both the *matam-nauha* unit and tragedy involve the performance of choral lyric in a religious liturgical setting, *nauha* during the annual Muharram *majlis,* tragedy during the annual festivals honoring the ancient god Dionysus. Both are agonistic: the *choregoi* who financed the tragic productions assigned to them by the Greek *polis* competed enthusiastically for the prizes awarded for the best plays; and I have suggested that a certain competitiveness characterizes the Shiite guilds, for social prestige, membership enrollments, and coveted invitations to further *majalis* are all linked to the quality of the group's public performance during Muharram. In both cultures adolescent boys and young men had a particular role to play in the ceremonies. In India, under the training of the *nauha-khan,* the most talented of the guild's youths are trained to sing antiphonal responses and expend their energy in physically demanding breast-beating. In ancient Greece a *didaskalos* or poet-trainer was selected by the *choregos* to train the young men of the tragic chorus. John Winkler in a recent study has emphasized the role of the *ephebes* (late-adolescent males of military age) in Athenian dramatic festivals; it was they who were charged every year with carrying the statue of Dionysus in procession from the Academy to the temple and theatre of Dionysus on the south slope of the Acropolis.[1] And it was the ephebes, according to Winkler, who comprised the tragic chorus in Athenian drama, an appropriate role for young men, Winkler points out, given the strenuous physical demands of dramatic performance:

The younger boys' dances were evidently meant to develop their poise, strength, and stamina as future citizen-soldiers. The dancing of the *tragoidoi* [members of the tragic chorus] was a still harder exercise in the same qualities: just think of the sheer physical endurance required to peform all the singing and dancing of three tragedies and one satyr-play consecutively. Performing in a tragic chorus must have been an athletic feat as exacting and grueling as any of the Olympic competitions. Indeed, this is a strong reason for accepting the youth of such choruses as an across-the-board rule.[2]

Similarly, in all the Shiite *matami guruhan* I encountered, the most strenuous forms of *matam* are left to the adolescents and young men.

These parallels, between the Greek tragic chorus and the Shiite choral chanters of the *matami guruhan*, trigger the question: To what extent can Hyderabad's Muharram liturgies be considered dramatic, that is, performances involving the mimetic enactment or symbolic representation of the events of Karbala? True Muharram drama can be found, of course, in Iran, in the *ta'ziyeh* or "passion-play," where individuals don costumes and assume the roles of Husain, Abbas and so forth and play out to some extent the battlefield speeches and deaths of Karbala.[3] Hyderabad offers nothing as fully representational in its Muharram rituals. Nevertheless, I witnessed several Muharram liturgies staged by the *matami guruhan* which incorporated elements of what can be termed dramatic representation. The most remarkable is a procession on the seventh of Muharram in honor of *nawsha-ye Karbala*, the "bridegroom of Karbala." This title refers to Qasim ibn Hasan, the young son of the second Imam, who was wed to Husain's daughter, Fatima Kubra. Besieged at Karbala with their families, the couple were wed on the eve of Ashura; shortly thereafter, Qasim was killed in the final combat.

During my second visit to Hyderabad, on the seventh of Muharram (July 20, 1991), I attended a liturgy in honor of Hazrat Qasim sponsored by the Anjuman-e Parwaneh Shabbir. The ceremony was held in a private *ashurkhana* within the home of a Parwaneh Shabbir member, situated near the guild's headquarters in the Mir Alam Mandi locality of the Old City. In a brief sermon the preacher reminded his congregation of the hurried marriage and violent death of the second Imam's son. No sooner had the sermon ended than everyone rose and the gold alam of Hazrat Qasim emerged from a storeroom at the rear of the chapel. Like a bridegroom the battle-crest was heaped with garlands of red carnations and jasmine; then it was borne aloft through the crowd of men. Thereafter followed a line of boys carrying silver trays which contained heaped fruit, henna leaves, and rows of lighted candles. These are the accoutrements of what is known as the "*maynhdi* procession"; as the author Athar Abbas Rizvi explains in his survey of Muharram practices, "In India the *maynhdi* is carried from the bridegroom's to the bride's house before the actual wedding."[4] Thus the iconography of the seventh of Muharram involves a disjunction apparent to all observers who know the story of Qasim and Fatima Kubra. The flowers, henna and fruit are meant to render imaginatively present to us the joyous setting forth of a young man on his wedding day to encounter his bride; but the procession advances against a dark background of certain knowledge: our awareness of the violent death awaiting the bridegroom the next morning. The disjunction draws our attention to the frustrated hopes suffered by the Karbala martyrs and thus deepens the pathos of this liturgy.

To the accompaniment of chanted *nauhas* and breast-beating by the congregants, the procession traversed the roofed interior of the *ashurkhana*. Louder even than the *nauhas* came a cry from some of the mourners: "*Dulha! Dulha!*" ("Bridegroom, O bridegroom!"); the cry continued as men pressed forward to touch the *alam* for its blessing as it passed.

Reaching the shrine's open courtyard, the procession circumambulated the yard several times, the garlanded *alam* held high on its pole. Then the bearers crossed the square to the doorway of the *zenana* or women's quarters of the sponsor-family. The pole was briefly dipped and thrust through the purdah; and through the half-parted curtain I glimpsed bangled arms stretched forth to caress the worn metal. Then the battle-crest was withdrawn and once more raised aloft.

But now the bearers halted motionless. An old man stepped forward and snuffed the candles on their tray. At this the *alam* was slowly lowered from its upright position and placed reverently on a long wooden plank. This, then, was the martyr's bier. Two boys advanced with a long white cloth which was spotted all over with red stains. Gently mourners wrapped the *alam* and plank in this cloth. Then once more the *alam* was raised up; but now it rested horizontally on its bier. Numerous marchers stepped forward to join in carrying the prostrate *alam* on their shoulders as if it were a coffin. The procession retraced its steps from the courtyard to the roofed *ashurkhana*, then to the interior of the storeroom at the rear of the shrine. A moment later the mourners reemerged empty-handed and carefully locked the door shut. This *alam* would now remain hidden away till next year.[5]

Wedding procession, death, shrouding, entombment: the ritual actions of the seventh of Muharram comprise mimetic representations which can be characterized as a form of liturgical drama. In the light of such findings it seems advisable to widen the definition of Shiite drama beyond *ta'ziyeh* and to look beyond the geographic confines of Iran in future studies of Shiite drama.[6]

One further note from this liturgy merits discussion. As the bridegroom of Karbala's procession ended, Parwaneh Shabbir members recited a final dirge in honor of Qasim. Following are some of the verses from this *nauha*:

> Our hearts, too, are houses of lamentation for the king
> (*qalb bhi hamare hayn shah ke azakhane*)
> In lamentation for Qasim are gift-offerings of tears;
> O Ali, the cry has gone forth: Qasim has been slain! . . .

> This sound of *matam* (*yeh sada-ye matam*) is a message of wakefulness;
> for this reason flows the life-blood in our veins.
> Our life is lamentation for the king;
> he himself takes part in the *majlis*, innocent and wretched.
> O Ali, the cry has gone forth: Qasim has been slain! . . .

> O exalted one, in this sorrow there will arise a people who will beat their breasts
> (*ay rafi' is gham mayn qawm-e sineh zan hogi*)
> O Ali, the cry has gone forth: Qasim has been slain![7]

The language of this hymn for the bridegroom of Karbala prompts comparison with stanzas from two of the Anjuman-e Masoomeen's *nauhas*:

> This sound of *matam* which echoes forth
> is the announcement of victory over care and affliction.
> In the victory of truth is the oath made with tears:
> Karbala: no god is there save God.[8]

> O young men of lamentation (*ay naujavanan-e aza*),
> You embody the prayer of everyone's heart.
> Truly, till the gathering of humankind on the Day of Resurrection
> there will continue from breasts the sound of *matam* (*matam ki sada*).[9]

Note too the lyrics composed by Ali Javid Maqsud, a poet whose *nauhas* are used by various Hyderabadi guilds such as Parwaneh Shabbir and Masoomeen:

> This *matam* is Fatima's prayer;
> how could this *matam* ever be stopped?
> This *matam* is a cry of challenge;
> each tear is part of a passionate desire for victory.[10]

In such verses we find that (to borrow a comment from John Herington in his examination of choral lyric in ancient Sparta) "the chorus begins to sing to itself, and about itself."[11] These four *nauhas* dwell not just on the historical event of Karbala but on the liturgical commemoration of the event as enacted by the men's guilds. Many of the terms occurring in these poems—*matam* (mourning/breast-beating/self-mortification), *sineh-zani* (breast-beating), *majlis* (Muharram liturgy), *azakhane* (houses of lamentation, a synonym for the Hyderabadi term *ashurkhane*, Muharram-shrines)— are taken from the vocabulary of religious liturgy in current usage today. Such lyrics need to be evaluated in terms of their performance context. The poet has composed these verses to be sung by *guruhan* in a group liturgical setting, whether before fellow guild members only or in the presence of a larger Shiite public. In some phrases the chorus is made to specify itself (*ay naujavanan-e aza*: O young men of lamentation), but more common are references to ritual actions—cries, breast-beating, the shedding of tears—in which every person in the congregation will participate. Guild-adherents and other congregants alike are brought into the lyrics, in part through a technique of immediacy which breaks down the barriers of time: Qasim is described not as a victim from the remote past, but as if only recently slain; the bridegroom himself is said to be present now in the liturgy; the future is glimpsed as a continuum of mourning from now till Judgment Day.

Common to all four poems are references to breast-beating and the sound produced by the performance of *matam*. But this sound of breast-beating (*sada-ye matam, matam ki sada*) is not dismissed as mere noise or the expression of grief; the poets here describe it as a "message," an "announcement," a "cry of challenge." *Matam* communicates. It is not too fanciful, I think, to claim it as part of a meaningful language-system. Breast-beating, self-mortification, all the acts comprised under *matam*: these rituals announce the congregation's devotion to the bridegroom of Karbala and to all the Prophet's family while setting the congregation apart from all those, Muslims and non-Muslims, who do not perform *matam*. And thereby the language-act of *matam* helps define the Shiites as a coherent denominational unit. Poetic descriptions of *matam*, written for the men's guild and performed by its chorus in a public liturgical setting, can be said to encode self-references that contribute to building the communal identity of the Shiites of Hyderabad.

16

Cooperation and Competition Among the Men's Guilds

Throughout my two summers in Hyderabad I heard stories of disputes between various men's associations. Disagreements tend to arise especially it seems between a splinter group and its parent guild. Thus I heard from insiders and non-members alike of bad feeling between the Anjuman-e Masoomeen and Guruh-e Haydariyah (the latter was formed as the result of arguments among the leaders of Masoomeen). The flashpoint for quarrels, I was told, are the large public *ashurkhanas* in the Old City, such as the Hazrat Abbas ka dargah and Pari Mahal, where visitors throng and prestige is at stake for each of the groups that wish the distinction of leading the crowds in the performance of *matam*. At the great shrines the *guruhan* are expected to take turns in their devotions, succeeding each other with intervals of only minutes separating one group from the next. As one guild performs the next will be poised near the shrine's entrance, its members keyed up and expectant; tired and thirsty too, perhaps, from the round of liturgies experienced during the ten days culminating in Ashura.

Courtesy dictates that each group limit itself to some twenty to thirty minutes in the shrine and no more before yielding place to the group following; but at times, my informants claimed, a group might go overlong and eat into the next *guruh*'s allotted time. Unsurprisingly, tempers flare. A central committee known as the Markazi Anjuman-e Matami Guruhan tries to regulate the order of appearance of the guilds during major gatherings, such as the Bibi ka alam procession on the tenth of Muharram; but my impression is that in most circumstances discretion and deference associated wth tradition must serve as guides regulating behavior in public interactions. Thus, for example, Guruh-e Ja'fari is traditionally given precedence before all other guilds at liturgies because it is acknowledged as the oldest of Hyderabad's Shiite *guruhan*.

If I wished to see the interaction of the men's associations, my friends counseled me, I should begin with an evening's visit to the Hazrat Abbas ka dargah on the fourth of Muharram. If any place in Hyderabad can be described as the focal point of *matam* devotions, whether bare-handed or bloody, this is it. What happens here on the ninth and tenth of Muharram, when crowds converge from throughout the city and beyond, will be described later. But this shrine is of importance even earlier in the season. According to my informants in Parwaneh Shabbir, many *guruhan* conclude their rehearsal sessions annually on the third of Muharram; the next night, they begin the season's round of public liturgical appearances with a brief *matam* service at the shrine of Hazrat Abbas. An appropriate choice of locale, given that Abbas, "martyred in the prime of his youth," as one devotional pamphlet puts it, is considered a model for young men because of his impetuous generosity of spirit.[1]

During my second visit to Hyderabad I attended the liturgies held at this *ashurkhana* on the fourth of Muharram (July 17, 1991). The Hazrat Abbas ka dargah is located in the Old City near the Medina Building and the Afzal Ganj bridge. One enters from a narrow alley to find an open courtyard, in the center of which is a five-foot-high painted cement representation of the *mashk-e Sakinah*, the goatskin flask symbolic of Abbas in Shiite iconography (recall that Abbas was killed at Karbala in an attempt to bring water from the Euphrates to Sakina and the other thirsting children of Husain). Beyond the *mashk* is a raised platform with a *minbar* (pulpit) and a display stand containing *alams* which are coated with sandalwood paste. On the wall are framed pictures with vivid renderings of Karbala: Abbas on horseback, waterskin flung over his shoulder, sword in hand, charging through the enemy ranks; the Imam Husain cradling the dying Abbas in his arms. To the right of the *ashurkhana* stage is a roofed portico; to the left is an enclosed room with a purdah curtain, intended for women participants. Above the *zenana* is a second-floor gallery, its windows protected by latticed grillwork. All evening silhouettes of girls and women could be glimpsed behind this screen.

I arrived around seven o'clock that evening, an hour before services were to start, to find the shrine already a center of activity. Perhaps a hundred men and teenaged boys congregated in the courtyard or sat chatting on the portico steps. They kept back from the *ashurkhana* stage, yielding place to the young girls who darted in and out of the *zenana*. The girls, dressed in black for the season of mourning, called back and forth to each other excitedly as they attached red carnation garlands to the *alams* and lit incense sticks in urns. Vendors at the shrine's entrance, their stalls illumined by strings of overhead bulbs, offered votive wreaths and painted cloth banners. The number of visitors kept increasing.

The liturgy began at eight o'clock, when a cluster of reciters seated themselves in the *ashurkhana* to intone the opening *salaam* and chant *marsiyehs*. After some fifteen minutes the *marsiyeh-khans* abruptly ceased. At once a knot of older men in their thirties and forties pressed forward through the crowd to take possession of the central *ashurkhana* stage in front of the *alams*. Pounding their chests in a slow one-handed *matam*, they called out *ay alamdar ay Husain* ("O bearer of the battle-standard, O Husain") in hoarse low voices, over and over.

This was a kind of summons, it seemed; more men hurried forward to join those already on stage. "Guruh-e Ja'fari," murmured a companion, confirming my guess; as per custom, Ja'fari was being granted pride of place. By now the girls had retreated to their mothers in the *zenana*; the teenagers and other boys had withdrawn to the side portico, surrendering the stage with its *alams* to Ja'fari. "These boys are mostly members of Masoomeen," explained my companion. "Masoomeen comes after Ja'fari. They're waiting for Ja'fari to finish."

By now some forty men had gathered before the *alams*. The chant-rhythm quickened and the group displayed the Ja'fari signature-*matam*, its two-handed *ajami* stroke. Each man lifted both arms high overhead, then lowered his hands smartly in a fierce double strike to the chest. The blows were heavy and forceful; the vault overhead rang with the echo. Brief bursts of *ajami* pounding alternated with one-handed largo-tempo *matam*; the variation, it seemed, helped the *matamdaran* conserve their strength. Again and again they returned to the refrain:

Ya Abbas ya Sayyidi
Ya mazlum ya Sayyidi
(O Abbas, O my lord,
O wronged one, O my lord)

Through all this I stood watching in the courtyard with the elderly men and other members of the general public. But a half-dozen giggling boys in the side portico drew my attention. Flinging their arms wildly overhead, barely able to contain their suppressed laughter, they clearly were amusing themselves with a mocking mimicry of Ja'fari's *matam* style. But these pranksters were the exception. Almost all the Masoomeen onlookers kept time with the Guruh-e Ja'fari by tapping their chests in a light one-handed *matam.* Obviously they were saving energy for their own performance, and none of them attempted a serious imitation of Ja'fari's heavy two-handed stroke; still they understood the *adab,* the norms of comportment, appropriate to this public setting. One could guess that a suppressed eagerness gripped these boys, a desire to take the lead in front. Yet just as they had shown deference to Hyderabad's senior *guruh* by yielding center stage, so now they displayed respect for Ja'fari's liturgy by observing a token *matam* in time to the Ja'fari rhythm. This was all the more impressive given the lack of adult supervision at that moment: no Masoomeen officers or other older members from this group had yet appeared.

Within twenty minutes Guruh-e Ja'fari had concluded its performance; straightaway the men stepped down and withdrew from the shrine. At once Mir Sabir Ali, his *nauha-khans,* and other Masoomeen officers appeared and strode forward; throughout Ja'fari's liturgy, I learned later, they had been waiting out of sight outside the shrine's entrance.

From the portico the boys rushed up to the cleared platform in front of the *alams.* It was now their turn and their platform. But first Sabir motioned them to sit. The same *marsiyeh-khans* who had preceded Ja'fari intoned a dirge. Alert and silent, the boys listened, all trace of rowdiness gone; this attentive sitting, their very posture, it seemed to me, must be part of the discipline imposed by the Anjuman-e Masoomeen on its young members: the sequence of *majlis* rituals was to be respected by even the youngest *matamdaran.*

Thereafter, still seated, two teenagers from Masoomeen led the guild in a slow and haunting chant, while the other members tapped their breasts in time. Nonmembers in the courtyard responded in kind. The dirge completed, Sabir rose, and the boys sprang to their feet. Like Guruh-e Ja'fari, Masoomeen dispensed with any sermon in this particular liturgy, as the time allotted each *guruh* was so brief. A chanter cried out, "Husain, Husain!" A pause. Again: "Husain, Husain!" At once young men and boys throughout the shrine caught up the cry: "Husain, Husain; Husain, Husain." A throbbing one-handed *matam* echoed the name, while more youths, members and nonmembers both, surged onto the portico and *ashurkhana*'s stage. I guessed there to be over a hundred young men in the roofed portico of the shrine alone.

Flanked by his chorus, Sabir stood facing the crowded courtyard in front of the garlanded battle-crests. The shouting died; and Sabir's assistant Hyder began the chant:

Ay alamdar
Ay Husain ibn Ali
Ay Ali

As the group responded, I recognized, from the rehearsal of a few nights ago, both the *nauha* and the vigorous *matam* pattern that accompanied it. The youths flailed away at themselves with abandon—but for some five minutes only; the *nauha* ceased, and the secretary then led his guild in the brief staccato chant, *Shah salaamun alayk* (Peace be with you, O king), with which Masoomeen closes each of its public performances.[2] Their turn at an end, the young men left at once; few lingered in the shrine. Haydariyah was scheduled to be next; having heard of contention between the two groups, I imagined that Sabir wished to avoid potential problems.

In any event a good half hour elapsed before Haydariyah appeared; this hiatus, bystanders told me, was scheduled so as to minimize friction between the two groups.

These sequential liturgies were to continue at the shrine until late in the evening. I returned after midnight to find a dozen members of Parwaneh Shabbir clustered in the alley outside the entrance. Chatting and smoking, they waited as another *guruh* finished its turn.

In analyzing the guilds' interactions I can point to moments which may be interpreted as symptoms of competitive tension. In comparison with the rehearsals and intimate private liturgies I witnessed, there seemed to be an awkward self-consciousness in the groups' public performances. This came out especially in the noisy force with which some participants pounded themselves, as if they strove to impress non-members with the strength of the *matam* endured by their guild. And certainly the *guruh* members tended to avoid fraternizing with adherents of other guilds on this particular evening. Yet at least some guild-members performed *matam* in time with the group preceding them while awaiting their own turn. And each association and its leaders consistently showed patience in allowing their predecessor to complete a liturgy: no leader tried to compete by shouting a rival *nauha*-chant over that of the presiding *guruh*. One guild succeeded another without incident.

What is described above seems to be the most typical pattern of interaction when Shiite associations converge on the same shrine: a coordinated sequence of brief liturgies. A different situation prevailed, however, in the *majlis* I attended on the seventh of Muharram (August 10, 1989) at Pari Mahal (the "Fairy-Palace") in the Old City locality of Yaqutpura. This liturgy at Pari Mahal is one of the most heavily attended of the Muharram season

(I estimated there to be upwards of a thousand congregants at Pari Mahal during the 1989 service) and features a *mayhndi* procession in honor of Qasim and Fatima Kubra as well as sermons by popular orators. After the sermon three *guruhan*—Ja'fari, Parwaneh Shabbir, and Masoomeen—assembled in the large courtyard and performed *matam* simultaneously, each group claiming for itself a different portion of the yard. Onlookers participated by performing *matam* in time with the *guruh* nearest them.

The result was cacophony. Each circle of *nauha-khans* and chorus shouted to make itself heard above its neighbors. Some congregants insisted on pushing their way through the throng in an attempt to position themselves near their favorite *guruh*. A protective ring of guild-members formed around each chorus to guard the chanters from inadvertent jostling by supporters and participants. For my part I lost my footing more than once as I was urged through the crowd by Shiite friends eager for me to listen to each *guruh* in turn (we soon abandoned the effort).

An infelicitous arrangement, to say the least. Fortunately cooperation rather than competition characterizes the majority of jointly celebrated liturgies among the Shiite associations. Another instance of such interaction is the procession in honor of Hazrat Abbas held annually on the eighth of Muharram at the Husseini Kothi palace in the Old City. Husseini Kothi is the former estate of one of the Nizam's Shiite *nawabs*, who was known by the title of Shamsheer Jung; his descendants, six brothers and their families, inhabit the estate today and its extensive grounds and outbuildings. Hussein Ali Khan, one of the brothers, guided me through the palace in a visit at the beginning of the 1991 Muharram season and showed me the family *alams* which are paraded in the Abbas procession. This palace boasts a spacious *ashurkhana* with one of the finest collections of antique Shiite battle-standards in Hyderabad; one, a bronze dragon-headed *alam*, bore an incised date on its crest showing it to be some 225 years old.

The crowds attending the eighth of Muharram liturgy at Husseini Kothi in 1991 were more numerous than any I encountered save on Ashura. Hundreds made their way into the *ashurkhana* for the *marsiyeh* and sermon comprising the *majlis*; over a thousand waited outside for the procession to begin, filling the verandas and palace grounds. The sermon at an end, the *alams* were immediately taken outdoors via a long staircase leading from the *ashurkhana*. Youths in black mourning tunics formed up on either side of the staircase to beat their breasts as the *alams* descended. Here I saw the only violence committed that day. To clear a path on the staircase, attendants escorting the *alams* roughly pushed away any boys who rushed upward to touch the battle-crests for their *barakat* (blessing). Several young teenagers lost their balance in the scuffle and fell down the stone steps; the file continued its remorseless descent.

At the foot of the stairs the *alams* were transferred to two horses, referred to as "horses of Abbas" and intended to evoke the water-carrier's battlefield gallop to the Euphrates. Astride each mount sat a man and two small boys; the children perched uncertainly before the man, their fingers entwined in the horse's mane.

Waiting in the courtyard for the procession to begin were two *matami guruhan*. One, stationed immediately in front of the horses, was the Guruh-e Kazimi, a local association which draws its membership from the neighborhood surrounding Husseini Kothi. The second, which had taken up position some 150 feet away near the palace fountain and weathered elephant-gate, was the Anjuman-e Aun aur Muhammad. This group comprises almost exclusively young boys some eight to ten years of age (its name is derived from the two sons of Zaynab, who were among the youngest of the martyrs to be slain at Karbala).

Like lancers the riders sat poised a moment, crested poles held aloft; then they guided their horses slowly through the crowd. Unhurriedly the procession followed the dirt path circling the palace. The two *guruhan* led the way, Aun aur Muhammad in the van, Kazimi immediately preceding the horses. Both groups chanted *nauhas* and beat their breasts as they marched. Kazimi's *matam* was bare-handed, but the boys' *guruh* wielded razors, cutting their chests in stroke after stroke. Each group differed from the other in its *matam*-beat and chanted rhythms, so the potential existed for a situation such as I had seen at Pari Mahal, with each guild noisily competing for dominance and the onlookers' attention. But here the two groups avoided any such competition. Kazimi paced itself so as to stay some distance behind Aun aur Muhammad; as a result there was no shoving or elbowing in the line of procession, and relatively little dissonance.

One more instance of cooperation among Hyderabad's *matami guruhan* is worth citing in this context. This example is once more from the Hazrat Abbas ka dargah but involves the rituals attending Ashura, the tenth of Muharram. I have already mentioned that on Tasu'a and Ashura the men's associations take turns in performing *matam* with implements at the shrine of Abbas. I witnessed the Ashura rites at Hazrat Abbas in both 1989 and 1991; at no point did I see any serious conflicts among the groups. This is all the more remarkable given that at this point in the season, more than at any other time during Muharram, the possibility of conflict might be thought to exist, as the guilds mingle with each other then to a greater degree than on any other holyday of the season. This is because all the *guruhan* throng to the shops and stalls set up in the vicinity of the shrine on Tasu'a and Ashura: the sellers of knives and *zanjirs*; the blade-sharpeners with their whetstones; the vendors of garlands and votive-cloths; the gentlemen who ladle water from metal drums to passersby as largesse in imitation of Abbas's beau geste at Karbala. But the interactions I noticed at the stands and kiosks seemed peaceful and nonconfrontational.

This mingling of *matamdaran* from different guilds was especially noticeable at the Hyderi Medical Station, a first aid tent set up on Ashura at the entrance to the Abbas shrine by Ansar Hyder Abedi, a prominent Shiite community leader. The medics and volunteers stationed there treated penitents who had endangered themselves through excessive self-mortification: flagellation that left a man's back red from neck to waist; repeated sword-cuts to the forehead, leaving the scalp torn and bloody. Throughout the morning of Ashura the tent swarmed with hurrying figures, for many of the wounded flagellants were so severely hurt that they had to be carried in by fellow guild members, who beseeched the doctors loudly for help for their friends. The faces of the wounded registered various emotions: fear, exaltation, exhaustion; the friends accompanying them were far more agitated. Nevertheless, even in the hot crowded tent, in the urgent presence of uncontrolled bleeding and dagger wounds, the penitents from the various guilds retained some sense of *adab* and largely avoided arguments with each other as they each sought the medics' attention on behalf of a wounded friend.[3]

In any description of Ashura at Hazrat Abbas there is one other group of participants who must be mentioned: the *hijras*, Hyderabad's community of eunuchs.

The *hijras* make a living as drummers and dancers at birth celebrations and weddings; they live in small enclaves in the Old City localities of the High Court and Lud Bazaar. In the interviews recorded by the researchers Harriet Ronken Lynton and Mohini Rajan, Hyderabadi *hijras* refer to themselves as "the brotherhood."[4] Muslims and Hindus live together and pray together in the same household; religious identity is subordinate to their identity as eunuchs. The Shiites whom I asked claimed that the *hijras* give shelter to young boys who are homeless or abandoned; allowing the children to live with them for some years, the eunuchs permit them to decide whether they wish to remain with the brotherhood permanently. If the boy chooses to become a part of the community for good, I was told, then at some time before puberty he submits to castration. In one autobiographical statement recorded by Lynton and Rajan, a *hijra* described his boyhood: beaten by male elders for showing traces of effeminacy, tired of attempts to make him adhere to the gender expectations of society at large, the child fled his home. For a time, he stated, he tried living with the *zenanay* or transvestite whores, but the violence and abuse in that life sickened him. Unable to conform to the heterosexual model and unwilling to live as a male prostitute, he took refuge with the eunuchs. Castration seemed a small price to pay for acceptance.[5]

At about noon on Ashura 1991, shortly after the last of the *guruhan* had completed its *matam* at the Abbas *ashurkhana,* a group of some twenty-five *hijras* appeared at the shrine. The men's guilds had had their turn; now it was the turn of the eunuchs. Dressed in women's saris, makeup, and earrings, they nevertheless had lined mannish faces. Most of them seemed middle-aged or elderly. Occupying the now largely empty central courtyard before the *mashk,* the eunuchs stayed clustered closely together as they held their liturgy. A gentle one-handed *matam* characterized their rite: they beat their breasts slowly while chanting *nauhas* in thin falsetto voices.

Most interesting of all was the onlookers' response. Girls and women descended from the rooftops and gallery where they had watched the *guruhan* perform all morning; standing to one side of the courtyard, they beat their breasts in time to the eunuchs' chant. Nor was this all. Most of the flagellants and swordsmen had departed by now to join the Bibi ka alam procession; but some guild-members and other men lingered. The men did not abuse the *hijras* with sniggers or taunts; instead they stood quietly at the entrance to the shrine and, like the women, performed *matam* in time to the eunuchs' chant. The men had yielded the shrine to the *hijras.* For this brief period, at the very end of the Hazrat Abbas devotions, the eunuchs were allowed a liturgical role at the shrine's center.

In a sense it is as if Hyderabad's eunuchs are treated on Ashura as a distinct guild or *guruh* in their own right. They are given a turn in the round of *matam* devotions undertaken by the men's *guruhan* at the Old City's chief mortification shrine. True, they come in last place; but nevertheless they have a place. And the men and women who linger till the end at the shrine extend recognition to the eunuchs' liturgy by performing *matam* in time to the chant set by the eunuchs. The pattern of cooperation among the men's guilds, it can be asserted, is thus extended during Muharram to include those at the very periphery of Hyderabadi society.

17

Criticisms Directed Against the Men's Guilds

Given their popularity and public visibility, it is perhaps not surprising that the *matami guruhan* are a topic of controversy among many Hyderabadi Muslims. Criticisms from Sunnis tend to be general, directed against devotional practices embraced by the groups rather than against the *guruhan* themselves. Several persons whom I questioned asserted flatly that there is no Quranic warrant for the practice of *matam*, the devotion that defines the guilds. Wahhabi-minded Muslims went further, claiming that the guilds' veneration of Husain is so overdone as to elevate him to sainthood.

But the most pointed critiques arose from persons within the Shiite community itself. In the course of my work I met a half-dozen young Shiites, men in their twenties and early thirties, who frequently attend *majalis* sponsored by various *guruhan* but who told me that they have never taken the step of becoming formal members of a particular association. When questioned privately about this, several of them explained that many of the *guruhan* are notorious for wrangling with each other, most commonly over issues of authority and leadership. My informants felt that if they joined one particular organization they would be forced to take sides in such disputes. One respondent said that he attends many of the services organized by Parwaneh Shabbir; nevertheless, he declined membership so as to avoid what he called the obligation of participating in the *dawreh-ye majalis* or "round of liturgies": guild members will spend a long evening on several nights during Muharram wandering the city going to one *majlis* after another. "Once you're a member," he grimaced, "you're expected to do the whole *dawreh*. If you don't, people ask, 'Where were you?' I like to be able to go to as many *majalis* as I want without worrying what people will say."

When he voiced this complaint, I demurred and questioned whether there
was really so much social pressure on *guruh* adherents to attend liturgies;
but in a separate conversation another informant offered corroboration of
this complaint: "If I belonged to a *guruh,* then fellow members might get
angry whenever I went to someone else's *majlis* instead of theirs. By not
being a member of any *guruh* I keep my independence."

Older members of the Shiite community who found fault with the
guruhan tended to claim that guild-members are ignorant of Islam and of
shari'ah or the prescriptions of Islamic law. One such critic complained:

> The problem with these groups is that they have no idea of *wudu'* [ritual
> ablutions], no idea of *namaz* [Quranically mandated prayer] and all the regula-
> tions that go with it. Their idea of prayer is to fling off their shirts and start beating
> their chests as soon as they enter an *ashurkhana. Matam* is the only kind of prayer
> they know.

I tried to remind this critic that in any *guruh* members strip only in
undertaking *matam* with implements, an exercise reserved for the limited
period of the eighth through tenth of Muharram. He waved aside my
objection and persisted:

> The problem is that their level of education is low; they don't know Islam. What
> can you expect? A lot of these groups are made up mostly of boys; what do they
> know of Islam? Masoomeen's a good example. It's a bunch of boys, a gang of
> young rowdies.

I replied that Masoomeen members seemed disciplined rather than rowdy
in the *majalis* I had observed, but this did not deter him from his opinion at
all.

Another critic, a self-described traditionalist and a highly educated university graduate in his mid-thirties, objected to the very concept of ritualized
grief incorporated into the guild liturgies:

> What I don't like is the groups' idea of *matam* on schedule. *Matam* is supposed
> to be a spontaneous show of grief; how can you schedule it? These groups go
> around from one *ashurkhana* to another; they have one *matam-majlis* at seven,
> another at eight o'clock, another at nine. If *matam* means you feel real sorrow,
> how can you plan ahead of time to feel that way at seven o'clock and eight
> o'clock and so forth? How can you schedule your grief if it's real? Look, when
> you feel sorrow, when you hear of something terrible that's happened to someone
> in your family, someone you love, the way we love *Ahl-e Bayt,* you take out your

handkerchief and cover your face, you slap your leg and cry. That's what we do in the *majlis* when we hear the preacher tell about Karbala. And that's enough. Why all this fancy movement, everybody standing up and beating themselves in unison, doing the same thing at the same time? That's not how you show real grief. This group-scheduled breast-beating, it's showing off, it's not real *matam*. Group *matam* on schedule doesn't tell you a thing about a person's interior, what he's really feeling.

This critic offered another objection, one which tallied more nearly with my own observations:

By worrying so much about *matam*, these groups abandon knowledge and the chance to learn, they never get to hear the sermon and learn from it. Professor David, sometime if you're sitting in a *majlis*, turn around and look towards the entrance; you may find the young men of some group waiting outside for the sermon to end. That's when they come in and do *matam*, after the sermon's over. They've probably just arrived from doing *matam* at some other *majlis* while this majlis was going on. So they lose the opportunity for knowledge this way, rushing from *majlis* to *majlis* doing *matam* and missing one sermon after another.

His critique corresponded to my own observations of the *dawreh-ye majalis* practiced by Masoomeen and Parwaneh Shabbir. For any given evening in Muharram, a guild will often arrange its schedule so as to be invited to a string of successive liturgies at various *ashurkhanas* located in private homes and public shrines. Arrival at each *ashurkhana* is timed to coincide more or less with the end of the sermon (an abbreviated stay at each liturgy allows the *guruh* to squeeze more *majalis* into an evening). Rather than distract the congregation's attention with the sudden entrance of two dozen young men, the leader will station his entourage near the entrance and wait till the sermon is over. If congregational *matam* has been scheduled for a particular liturgy, it is always timed for the end of the sermon, when the listeners' sympathetic faculties have been freshly stimulated by the reevocation of the horrors of Karbala. At this moment the *guruh* steps in with its chorus to lead the gathering in *nauha* and *matam*. My informant was quite accurate in at least one part of his complaint: the structure of the *dawreh* dictates that the *guruh* often sacrifices full attention to the sermon for the sake of leading the communal performance of *matam*.

One final criticism should be mentioned. In July of 1991 I interviewed several Shiite community leaders, all men in their late sixties and seventies, after services in a private chapel in the Old City neighborhood of Dar al-Shifa'. One man complained that the chant-melodies and *nauhas* of

Anjuman-e Masoomeen are "too influenced by the new pop music; and they aren't even aware of it!" This led another elderly man to exclaim, "Guruh-e Ja'fari has pure *matam*, the old *matam*-style. But Masoomeen and Haydariyah, their *matam*-style is like dancing, too much moving about"— derisively he shook himself from side to side as he mimicked *matam* slaps—"too much swaying and moving about." His friends chuckled in agreement.

Equating any guild's *matam* style with dance is, of course, an insult and is meant to be understood as such. The old gentleman's taunt does have some foundation: more than any other guilds I observed, the *matam* of Masoomeen and Haydariyah might well be said to have affinities with dance: one's feet remain planted, but the style is governed by energetic bodily motions and patterned swayings of the torso in time to rhythmic chant.

Reflected in such gibes is a long-standing ambivalence within the Islamic tradition concerning the permissibility of music and dance in general. A treatise on music by Ibn Abi al-Dunya describes singing as an activity which "decreases shame, increases desire, and destroys *muru'ah* [manliness and the masculine virtues associated therewith], and indeed, takes the place of wine and what drunkenness does."[1] In the Shafii legal text *al-Tanbih* dancers and singers are classed with rag-pickers, scavengers, and those who urinate in public as persons whose testimony should not be allowed in a court of law.[2] The disapproval of music and dance found in such treatises stems from a concern on the part of the *ulama* to safeguard individuals from any possible loss of self-control triggered by an onslaught of rhythmic sound or rhythmic motion.

Throughout Islamic history dance has remained an object of suspicion even when performed in liturgical contexts as an act of worship. Controversy has focused in particular on the *sama'ha* or "spiritual concerts" associated with the Sufi tradition, wherein dervishes sway in whirling dancelike motions as they invoke the names of God. Many Sufi authorities have themselves cautioned their followers in this regard; the following is from the *Kashf al-mahjub* (The Unveiling of the Veiled), an eleventh-century treatise by Ali ibn Uthman al-Jullabi al-Hujwiri:

> You must know that dancing (*raqs*) has no foundation either in the religious law (of Islam) or in the path (of Sufism), because all reasonable men agree that it is a diversion when it is in earnest, and an impropriety (*laghwi*) when it is in jest. None of the *Shaykhs* has commended it . . . But since ecstatic movements and the practices of those who endeavour to induce ecstasy (*ahl-i tawajud*) resemble it, some frivolous imitators have indulged in it immoderately and have made it

a religion. I have met with a number of common people who adopted Sufism in the belief that it is this (dancing) and nothing more.[3]

That dance remains controversial even today is attested in the writings of Javad Nurbakhsh, present master of the Iranian Nimatullahi Sufi order. In a work published in 1983 entitled *Dar kharabat* (In the Tavern of Ruin), he devotes an essay to *sama'*, wherein he explains that dance is licit if it occurs as the result of mystic ecstasy, but that it should not be employed as a means of inducing or forcing this state:

> Bodily movement, dancing, and rending of one's clothes should overcome Sufis through no volition of their own while they are engaged in *sama'* . . . Dancing brings no one to the state of love; rather, it is the one who has already become a lover who, selfless and taken out of himself, engages in the dance.[4]

Given, then, the doubtful status of dance within the Islamic tradition, it is clear that the critic's dismissal of Masoomeen's *matam* as dancing was no compliment. But the criticisms directed by some Shiites against the guilds' performance of *matam*—that it lacks spontaneity, involves showing off in public, displays excessive motion or dancelike features—fail to take into account the guilds' collective achievement. Out of an instinctual display of grief (which is how Shiites repeatedly defined for me the act of breast-beating), and working within the constraints imposed by liturgical function (for in order to be welcomed publicly, the young men must serve the communal need for a ritualized display of grief over the Karbala martyrs), the *guruhan* can be said to have shaped something of beauty, a new genre of creative expression, in composing and articulating the *nauha-matam* unit. The presence of numerous men's associations in Hyderabad's Old City, this center of Shiite culture, has encouraged the creative development of *matam*. For under the pressure of the guilds' desire to differentiate themselves from each other, their *matam* styles have evolved into distinctive but interrelated forms, as surprising as the foliations and entwinements of Kufic lettering in a mosque. Like arabesque, *matam* can be regarded as an Islamic art form which has effloresced within religiously defined limits.

18

Muharram Liturgies and Hindu-Muslim Relations in Hyderabad

Although it is somewhat less celebrated than Lucknow as a center of Indian Shiite culture, Hyderabad in recent years has become arguably the best place in which to observe the celebration of Muharram in India. This is in part because of communal violence in other parts of the country. During the summer of 1989 no riots or other serious incidents marred Shiite observances in Hyderabad during the crucial first ten days of Muharram, whereas a number of other locations reported civil disturbances occurring especially on Ashura.[1] In Lucknow over 600 persons were reported arrested for defying a government ban on public Muharram processions.[2] Shiite community leaders had preached sermons in Lucknow calling for defiance of the ban; Kalbe Hussain, general secretary of the "youth wing" of the Shi'a Ali Congress, derided the prohibition on Muharram processions as a "partisan ban imposed on the Azadari processions in order to appease the Sunni lobby."[3] In describing the arrests in Lucknow, *The Times of India* reported that "responding to the call by the top Shia priest, Maulana Syed Kalbe Jawad, the protesters today [Ashura, August 13, 1989] raised anti-govern-ment slogans while courting arrest."[4]

In Benares, during the same period, some fifteen persons were wounded when police fired on members of a Muharram procession. The city govern-ment had tried to reroute the procession so it would not pass through certain neighborhoods where communal clashes were likely (as noted earlier in part I, this same problem had been faced by the Indian Civil Service in the days of the Raj); claiming the right to retain their traditional route, the marchers had tried to force their way through a police cordon. Following this incident, an "indefinite curfew" was imposed on various localities throughout Benares.[5] Similarly, violence resulting from Muharram clashes was reported from other parts of India: looting and rioting in two towns in Rajasthan; two persons killed and over a dozen injured near Krishnagar; and (according to one summary national report) "at least fifty-five people . . . injured in clashes across the country, as violence marred the observance of Moharrum."[6]

This is not to say that Hyderabad has itself by any means always been entirely free of communal discord. *The Imperial Gazetteer of India* in its volume on Hyderabad noted that in 1847 "a serious riot took place between the Shiahs and the Sunnis, in which about fifty persons lost their lives."[7] Another incident from nineteenth-century Hyderabad is recorded in Zahir Ahmed's biography of Sir Nizamat Jung (an official in the court of the Nizam of Hyderabad):

> An incident occurred which caused great terror in Hyderabad and completely upset all law and order for a few days. On the 10th Moharrum in the year 1885-86 there was a quarrel between some Arabs and policemen near the Purana Pul (Old Bridge) which gradually became a riot. It was said that some children belonging to the family of the great Arab Chief, Sultan Nawaz Jung, who were going on an elephant towards the river to see the alams were stopped by the police. The Arabs accompanying them at once made this a quarrel with the police, and as soon as the news reached Sultan Nawaz Jung, he is said to have given orders to his Arabs to attack the police wherever they could find them. The result was that in a few hours the Arabs were in possession of a number of police stations and the police were powerless against them. It was like an open revolt against constituted authority, and the disturbance was so serious and so widespread that special and strong measures had to be taken. The military was called in, but order was not restored until two or three days had passed.[8]

Incidents such as the above seem to have been sporadic and exceptional. Of more lasting consequence for the Old City were the Police Action of 1948 and the forcible incorporation of Hyderabad State into India. The effect on Hyderabadi Muslims was traumatic: a sudden end to Islamic political dominance, the disestablishment of the *jagirdar* landholding system, the cessation of the nizam's patronage system. Many wealthy Muslims abandoned Hyderabad and fled to Pakistan or overseas; the number of Hindu residents in the Old City increased sharply. Upon his release from prison in 1957, Qasim Razvi (former head of the paramilitary Razakar volunteer corps, which had resisted the Police Action and fought to retain Muslim supremacy in the Deccan) revived the Majlis Ittihad al-Muslimin (Council of the Union of Muslims) or MIM. This organization, founded in 1927 and once affiliated with the Razakars, has served ever since its revival as the focal point of Muslim communalism in Hyderabad. The MIM's confrontational attitude has been matched (and surpassed) by militant-minded Hindu organizations, such as the Bharatiya Janata Party (BJP) and the Arya Samaj. In such a climate it is not surprising that Hyderabad has suffered at times from extensive violence, notably in 1983 and again in 1984. These riots, although unrelated to Muharram, nevertheless harmed communal relations in the city.[9]

Both Muslim and Hindu militants have been opportunistic in shaping annual religious processions for the sake of communal politics. The BJP and Vishwa Hindu Parishad, another Hindu organization, have organized on a massive scale Hyderabad's Ganesh festivals, in which scores of elephant statues are paraded through the streets. Since 1978 the procession's path has been rerouted by the organizers so as to pass through Muslim neighborhoods in the Old City; frequent stops are scheduled in front of mosques, where male dancers writhe to drumbeats and blasts of music in what is announced as an assertion of Hindu identity. Muslims at prayer regard this as a calculated affront; tempers flare.[10]

Something similar has happened with the Bonalu procession in honor of the goddess Kali. Once a women's festival, it has now been largely taken over by men; like the Ganesh celebrations, its procession route was changed in the course of the 1980's so as to pass through Muslim localities in the Old City. In response to such displays the MIM has organized a new Muslim procession, called the Pankha, centered on the Sufi shrine of Yousufain. According to Ratna Naidu, a sociologist at the University of Hyderabad, this new Muslim celebration is timed so that it virtually coincides with the Ganesh festivities; at times the result has been the desecration of Hindu idols and consequent fistfights.[11]

Nor is that all. In December 1990 Hyderabad's Old City was torn by communal rioting that left some 150 persons dead and hundreds more wounded. A curfew was imposed and the Indian army given control throughout the Old City. Witnesses with whom I spoke in the summer of 1991 described this as the worst violence Hyderabad has suffered since the Police Action of 1948. Initial reports explained the killings as a spillover effect from the Ayodhya Mosque dispute (referring to the site of a sixteenth-century mosque in Uttar Pradesh where Hindu militants are insisting on their right to build a temple to the god Rama). Later, speculation grew among Hindus and Muslims alike that the bloodshed had been instigated by politicians eager to discredit Chief Minister M. Channa Reddy. Gangs of hired thugs, dressed in Hindu garb and shouting Hindu slogans, had made night forays into Muslim neighborhoods to waylay Muslim passersby; the same gang would change clothing and pass themselves off as Muslim militants when raiding Hindu localities. So the talk ran, corroborated by numerous trustworthy informants of diverse backgrounds whom I encountered throughout the city.[12]

Heightening the tension in early 1991 was the international situation: the Persian Gulf War, involving American military intervention in Muslim countries; a subsequent Iraqi Shiite uprising (encouraged and then abandoned by the American government) against Saddam Hussein; and the desecration of Shiite shrines in Najaf and Karbala at the hands of Saddam's Republican Guards. As I was to learn upon arrival, Hyderabadi Muslims, especially Shiites, had watched closely the unfolding of all these events.

Given these developments—the Ayodhya Mosque issue, Hyderabad's December riots, the Gulf War—I returned to Hyderabad in the summer of 1991 fearing what I might encounter during the Old City's Muharram liturgies: enflamed political rhetoric, disruption of the processions, even a banning of public observances. But the same pattern of events evolved as I had noted two years earlier. Elsewhere in India, Muharram triggered communal confrontation. According to the *Indian Express,* "Shia Muslims took out a procession to the BJP office in New Delhi on Sunday [July 14, 1991, the first of Muharram] demanding lifting of the ban on Muharram processions in Lucknow, where a BJP government is in power after the recent elections."[13] In several cities in Gujarat, *tazia* processions erupted in violence—shootings, stabbings and rock-throwing—leaving ten persons dead; an indefinite curfew was subsequently imposed. And in Bihar police fired on Muharram processionists said to be attempting an attack on a police station in Bhagalpur district.[14] Yet as in 1989, Hyderabad again enjoyed a relatively peaceful Muharram season in 1991: the municipal government did not impose any ban on public liturgies; as is the custom, people of all faiths mingled in the streets in the great Ashura processions, with no major incidents of violence resulting therefrom.

Why the success—hitherto at least—of Muharram observances in Hyderabad? For one thing, Muharram is a religious tradition of long standing in Hyderabad, untainted by politically motivated innovations of the type that have marred the Ganesh, Bonalu and Pankha celebrations. Muharram processions have not been re-routed so as to cause communal confrontations; in contrasting Muharram with the city's newer religious festivals, Naidu (who shows no particular bias in favor of Hyderabad's Muslim community) admits that "the Muharram procession seems to have retained its original character."[15] Furthermore, in Hyderabad's celebration of Muharram, Hindus have enjoyed a long-recognized role as active participants, whether as mendicants, entertainers, processionists, or even organizers of *majalis*. Hindus visit Old City *ashurkhanas* and venerate the *alams* displayed there (especially at the

Bibi ka allava, as will be explored further below); numerous Hindus line the roadside to watch the great Ashura processions.

Even today, I believe, despite recent attempts to set the communities at each others' throats, Hyderabad still has a residual tradition of communal harmony, one that predates the militants and revivalists, the BJP and MIM. Muharram in Hyderabad reflects this older tradition of peaceful communal interaction. Part of the wound inflicted on the city by the violence of December 1990 was the damage done to Hyderabadis' self-image as members of a community of interfaith tolerance. This came out in public responses to the Old City riots. Former Chief Minister N. T. Rama Rao said sadly that "this city was a monument to brotherhood, a glorious thing."[16] The *Indian Express* reported that

> many political parties, voluntary bodies, trade unions and some eminent citizens on Tuesday condemned the "brutal killing of innocent people" in the old city... They expressed their anguish over the attempts of the communal elements to tarnish the image of Hyderabad which always stood as an epitome of communal harmony.[17]

In another article, entitled "Riots Instigated for Political Gain," the *Express* printed an interview with the local head of the Communist Party of India:

> The CPI leader pointed out that despite such large-scale killings, there was amity between the people of the two communities. In many instances, Muslims have given shelter to Hindu families. This showed that the common man of both communities was not involved in the riots.[18]

In the face of occasional outbursts of violence and the confrontations that mar other public religious occasions in Hyderabad, Muharram has become all the more important as a symbol of the kind of city most Hyderabadis want to believe in. Shiites are proud of the fact that Muharram celebrations in Hyderabad continue to enjoy the reputation of being relatively peaceful. Muslims with whom I spoke in both Lucknow and Hyderabad agreed that Hyderabad's situation is in marked contrast to Lucknow, where Muharram observances from year to year are repeatedly marred by Sunni-Shiite tensions and government restrictions.

Informants in Hyderabad with whom I discussed the issue offered other reasons as well for the relative success of Muharram celebrations in the city, reasons related to the early history of Hyderabad. Some reminded me that it was a Shiite dynasty, the Qutb Shahi, which had founded Hyderabad, and

that the Qutb Shahis initiated an enduring tradition of government sponsor-
ship of Muharram liturgies, while also providing funds for the construction
of *ashurkhanas* and other buildings associated with the observance of
Muharram. Sadiq Naqvi, a professor of history at Osmania University in
Hyderabad, pointed out to me in the course of several conversations that the
Qutb Shahis consciously used Shiite public rituals to create a "common
cultural ethos" among the very diverse peoples of the Deccan—mercenary
soldiers of various origins, Kizilbash, Uzbek, Kabuli, Herati, Punjabi,
Rajput, and Bengali, together with the local Hindu populace. The resultant
form of Muharram celebrations shows the influence of numerous aspects of
both Muslim and Hindu devotionalism.[19]

Even during times of Sunni rule in the Deccan, Shiites made their
presence felt in government: thus during the era of the Asaf Jahis, from 1724
to 1948, the Sunni nizams frequently employed Shiite ministers, particularly
the celebrated Salar Jung family. Such patronage helped Hyderabadi Shiites
in identifying the government as their benefactor. The last reigning nizam,
Mir Osman Ali Khan, was known to be sympathetic to the Shiites and
frequently visited *ashurkhanas* and attended *majalis* in the Old City during
Muharram.[20] Many Shiites in Hyderabad repeated to me the rumor that the
nizam had secretly become a Shiite at some point and remained so for the
rest of his life (although Sunnis to whom I reported this scoffed at the idea).

There persists in Hyderabad, despite occasional outbreaks of violence, a
long-standing tradition for the relatively peaceful celebration of Muharram,
in which numerous faiths participate and the government acts as sponsor and
guarantor of security. According to a report published by the governmental
Census of India for 1971, the seventh nizam's reign, from 1911 to 1948, was
characterized overall by communal harmony, with the result that Muharram
was in general celebrated peacefully, especially from 1921 to the end of the
nizam's reign. Since the Police Action of 1948 and Hyderabad's incorporation into postindependence India, according to the government report,
Muharram observances in Hyderabad have continued without violence.[21]

At both the provincial and municipal levels the Indian government has
continued the nizam's policy of showing support for the Hyderabadi observance of Muharram. From among all the liturgies held at this time in the Old
City, the Bibi ka alam procession, most celebrated of all public rituals related
to Ashura, has been chosen by the city administration as the occasion on
which municipal officials acknowledge the importance of this Shiite holyday. Thereby the government continues the nizam's tradition of giving
special veneration to the Bibi ka alam. Thus on the day after Ashura in 1989,
Hyderabad's newspapers reported that the elephant bearing the Bibi ka alam

paused at the Mirchowk traffic police station, where the mayor and city police commissioner made votive offerings to the *alam* "as a mark of their respect," in the *Deccan Chronicle*'s words, "to those who offered their lives in the religious battle."[22] In 1991 the city police commissioner, a Hindu, wore black Shiite mourning garb for the *alam* ceremony at the Mirchowk station; his dress was duly noted in *The Hindu*'s news article concerning Ashura.[23]

Mir Osman Ali Khan's dynasty is still represented to this day in Hyderabad's observance of Muharram: Muffakham Jah, grandson of the last reigning nizam, was reported in both 1989 and 1991 as among those offering reverence and presenting *dhatti*-banners to the Bibi ka alam; newspaper accounts noted that "the H.E.H. Nizam's Trust, an agency handling the affairs of Bibi-ka-Alam to which Nizams of Hyderabad had donated jewels as offerings, made arrangements [for the Ashura procession of this *alam*] in consultation with Mr. Aliuddin Arif, Mutawalli."[24] And several Shiites informed me that the elephant which bears the Bibi ka alam on Ashura is maintained and fed at the Hyderabad Zoo throughout the year under the terms of a *waqf* or charitable trust established by the late nizam.

Public pronouncements in Hyderabad by municipal and state political figures on the occasion of Muharram tend to interpret the events of Karbala in a way consonant with the goals of communal harmony. They do so by emphasizing themes which transcend the concerns of any one religion. The following is the text of an article in Hyderabad's *Indian Express* reporting the 1989 public "Muharram message" by the Hindu politician N. T. Rama Rao, then chief minister of the state of Andhra Pradesh:

> Chief Minister N. T. Rama Rao in a message on Moharrum said that Moharrum the tenth day of the first lunar month of Hijra era is observed in commemoration of the supreme and heroic sacrifice rendered by the grandson of Prophet Mohammed Hazrat Imam Hussain. He said it is the day of mourning for the Muslim brethren and Moharrum reminds everyone of us that one could follow his conventions and faith without fear, provided we have a spirit of sacrifice.
>
> Mr. Rama Rao said that sacrifice, irrespective of caste and creed binds us all together as one man to work for the development of humanity. The sacrifice of Imam Hussain should inspire us even today in promoting oneness and brotherhood among all communities, he said.[25]

In 1991 I noticed that the same themes were sounded in the Ashura speech delivered in Hyderabad by the new chief minister:

Chief Minister N. Janardhan Reddy has appealed to the people to observe
Moharram in a big way as the day signifies the struggle for righteousness and
justice.

In his message, the Chief Minister said that Hazrat Imam Hussain sacrificed
his life for promoting justice and truth in society on this day and that it should
be remembered by all people.

The Chief Minister said Moharram would be observed in the city by
hundreds and thousands of people, irrespective of their religious beliefs and as
a true symbol of national integration and harmony.[26]

Numerous Indian publications have likewise registered praise for the
observance of Muharram as a means of uniting Muslim and Hindu popula-
tions and reconciling sectarian differences in an act of communal worship.[27]
The government's 1971 Census report on Muharram in Hyderabad stresses
this theme: "The performance of Moharrum festival today reflects the
composite character of the culture of the city and stands as a monument of
universal brotherhood."[28] A pamphlet published by the Imamia Mission in
Lucknow, entitled *Imam Husain and India,* seeks out points of contact
between Shiism and Hinduism, noting the presence of "Husaini Brahmins"
at the city of Pushkar in Rajasthan and comparing the events of Karbala with
scenes from classical Hindu literature:

Being the custodian of the sacred trust of Islam, Imam Husain preferred death
to a disgraceful life. His sacrifice was in keeping with the advice given by
Krishna to Arjuna on the occasion of Mahabharata: "But if thou will not carry
on this righteous warfare, then casting away thine own honour, thou will incur
sin."[29]

Public pronouncements on Muharram as a means of facilitating communal harmony seem—at least with regard to the city of Hyderabad—by no
means a mere rhetorical fiction. My informants in Hyderabad's Shiite
guruhan emphasized repeatedly in their talks with me how impressed they
are with the intense veneration shown during Muharram by Hindus in their
ziyarah or local pilgrimages to the *alams* displayed in the Shiite *ashurkhanas.* Seeking to give me tangible proof of such reverence, Aliuddin
Arif, custodian of the Bibi ka alam shrine, showed me a green satin purdah
on display in the *ashurkhana*; this covering, Aliuddin explained, was donated
by a local Hindu merchant who offers particular veneration to Lady Fatima.

I first heard of Hindu reverence for the Shiite shrines in 1989. When I
returned two years later I wondered whether the Shiites' opinion of Hindu
devotion to *Ahl-e Bayt* had soured in the aftermath of the December 1990

riots. Far from it: Shiite informants assured me that Hindus were still welcome and still very much in evidence at public processions and at major *ashurkhanas,* such as the Bibi ka allava. Mir Sabir Ali, secretary of the Anjuman-e Masoomeen, summed up what he described as the Hyderabadi Shiite attitude toward Hindu Muharram devotions: "Hazrat Imam Husain is for everyone. He doesn't care if you're Muslim, Christian, Hindu, as long as you love his family." Sabir offered me two pieces of evidence for the universality of Husain and of the devotion he inspires among Hindus. First, so greatly do some Hindus revere *Ahl-e Bayt* that they themselves sponsor Muharram *majalis* in their own homes. The second: certain Hindus who clasp Shiite *alams* in their arms while visiting *ashurkhanas* during Muharram will suddenly be granted powers of prophecy and are enabled to read anyone's fortune for as long as they go on grasping the *alam.*

The latter bit of evidence I could do no more than puzzle over; but the first I sampled personally. On the ninth of Muharram (July 22), 1991, I attended a *majlis* in the Old City locality of Dabirpura sponsored by Sudarshan Das, chairman of the Minorities Welfare Federation and a prominent Hindu community leader. Local Hindu politicians and government bureaucrats were in attendance; I recognized the Muslim custodian of the Bibi ka allava in the crowd. Clearly, it was a prestigious gathering. The *majlis* was conducted in the same fashion as a liturgy under Shiite patronage, introduced by *marsiyeh* recitation and followed by a sermon. Sudarshan had invited the Anjuman-e Masoomeen to include his liturgy in their *dawreh-ye majalis*; as soon as the sermon ended, Sabir Ali appeared, accompanied by some twenty-five young men. Masoomeen quickly led the congregation in a brief performance of *matam*; then, the *majlis* concluded, the guild members joined their host and the other Hindus present in a visit to the nearby Bibi ka allava. As we walked through the alleys of Dabirpura to the shrine I chatted with Sudarshan, who explained that for generations his family has had stewardship of one of the *alams* in the Bibi ka allava. When I asked him what this responsibility entails he replied with a smile that I should keep an eye out for him in the Ashura procession the next day. In the event he proved easy to spot: he was one of several dignitaries who rode camels in the procession. Sudarshan maintained both his dignity and his swaying balance as he guided his camel forward and held aloft his family's *alam.*

I glimpsed another instance of Hindu Muharram devotions when I visited the Hazrat Abbas ka dargah on the fourth of Muharram, 1991, to watch the Shiite *matami guruhan* take it in turn to honor Abbas with *matam* liturgies (an evening discussed in a previous chapter). During a lull between prayer-services a group of women and young teenaged boys entered the shrine's courtyard. "Hindus," commented a friend beside me; but this I could have guessed: resplendent in saris—orange, purple, metallic blue—the women brought a bright contrast to the somber Muharram black worn by Shiites. For a brief while they lingered gazing at the *alams,* which were grouped at the back of the *ashurkhana* stage. Incense sticks smoked in an urn placed before the crested standards. Quietly the women ascended the stairs and stepped up onto the low stage. Stooping over the urn, they rubbed incense ash onto their eyelids, and stared once more at the *alams.* Satisfied, they then withdrew from the shrine.

Worth mentioning also in this context are the numerous Hindu "fakirs" who appear in the alleys of the Old City on the morning of Ashura: their faces streaked with red paint, carrying drums and long whips, they make a display of scourging themselves, then crack their whips against the footpath and beg alms from the crowd assembled to watch. The fakirs also appear in advance of the official Bibi ka alam procession on the afternoon of Ashura and go begging among the crowds along the route. In my first encounter with the Hindu fakirs I was slow to offer them money; their show seemed the merest mimicry of the genuine flagellation carried out by Shiite *matamdaran.* But my Shiite friends had no such hesitation. "Because the Hindu fakirs beg in the name of Imam Husain," as one Shiite explained to me, "we give them money. They should be encouraged in their pious use of the Imam's name."

To sum up, my overall impression from my second visit is that, the Old City riots of December 1990 notwithstanding, Hindu attendance at Muharram processions and *ashurkhanas* continues at the same strength as before. I was told that Arya Samajists and other militants frown on Hindu participation in Muslim rites; if so, they have made few inroads to date. This tradition of Hindu-Shiite symbiosis helps explain the acceptance I experienced among the *matami guruhan*: Hyderabad's Shiites are accustomed to the presence of sympathetic outsiders at the periphery—and occasionally at the center as patrons—of their liturgies, outsiders who remain non-Muslim but who nonetheless show reverence for *Ahl-e Bayt.*

It may be of interest at this point to note the reaction of Hyderabad's *matami guruhan* to current political developments within India and abroad. All the events noted above—the recent Old City riots, the Ayodhya dispute, the Gulf War—might well be expected to stimulate some concerted response from the men's associations. I was keen to know in particular whether the Iraqi Shiite uprising against Saddam Hussein in February-March 1991 might be discussed in some way within the context of the guilds' Muharram liturgies. To me this would have seemed only natural. Upon questioning,

Hyderabadi guild members let me know that they were well aware of the damage inflicted on Najaf and Karbala by Saddam's Republican Guards in the course of the fighting. In fact, they told me, numerous Iraqi Shiite rebels had taken refuge within the very precincts of the tomb-shrines of Abbas and Husain at Karbala. For three days, encircled by Saddam's soldiers, the rebels withstood a siege; the army was apparently reluctant to force its way into the shrines. But then the Guards turned the full fury of artillery and automatic weapons fire on the defenders. Both mausolea suffered heavy damage: the gold-leafed dome of Husain's sanctuary pierced by cannon shells, the gates of Abbas's shrine shattered by the bombardment. Hundreds of the rebels were killed, the rest led away prisoners.[30] Like a *ta'ziyeh* drama the 1991 uprising reprised the long-ago defiance and death of the Imam himself, but this year's mime closed in bloodshed. And all of this enacted on the site of Karbala itself: surely, I thought, the guilds' preachers would discourse on the convergence of past and present in their sermons this summer and draw the obvious parallels between the sufferings of Husain's followers then and of Husain's followers now.

But such was not the case at all. During Hyderabad's 1991 Muharram season I attended numerous *majalis* sponsored by the *matami guruhan*; the sermons I heard consistently involved the standard fare of *faza'il* and *masa'ib*—enumeration of the virtues of *Ahl-e Bayt* and the evocation of their sufferings—with no trace that I could discern of any attempt at applying the lessons of the past to today's current events. Guild members and other Shiites with whom I spoke confirmed my impression of the sermons' nonpolitical content.

This tendency is linked to a larger pattern I noticed at work with regard to the *matami guruhan*. During Hyderabad's communal rioting in December 1990, to my knowledge only one *matam* group, the Anjuman-e Masoomeen, responded to the hardship inflicted on the Old City's population; Masoomeen tried to help with the distribution of money and food to riot victims living near the *anjuman*'s headquarters. In conversations with me, members of other groups admitted that their guilds had done nothing.

This is not to say that Hyderabad's Shiites lacked any means whatsoever of constructive collective response to the riots. There are, in fact, two private social welfare organizations within Hyderabad's Shiite community, the Elia Theological Association and the Imam-e Zamana Mission (IZM); both, however, are independent of the Old City's *matami guruhan* (although some individual guild members do belong to these two charitable associations). The IZM in particular took an active role in distributing food and clothing to riot victims throughout the Old City, to Hindus and Sunnis as well as to

Shiites, according to IZM officers. But most of the *matami guruhan*, geared as they are to liturgical functions, were apparently unprepared to respond to the Old City crisis.

The *matam* groups likewise kept a relatively low profile during the Gulf War. One demonstration against Saddam Hussein was held at Hyderabad's Government Secretariat building on June 25, 1991, and some guild adherents were in attendance.[31] A handful of men from various *guruhan*, I was told, also joined in taking a bus to Delhi in April of the same year so as to participate in an All-India Shia protest against Iraq; but that was all.

As far as I can tell, the largely apolitical attitude of the *matam* groups simply mirrors the largely apolitical attitude of Hyderabad's Old City Shiites as a whole. Why this collective attitude? The answer, I think, has to do with the Shiites' status as a minority within Hyderabad's Muslim community, who in turn are a small minority comprising no more than 10 to 15 percent of the city's total population. Shiites with whom I spoke said they wish to avoid drawing attention to themselves politically or antagonizing the city's Hindu majority. All this is happening at a time when (as noted earlier) Hindu militants in Hyderabad have become more aggressive in asserting Hindu communal identity, in part by promoting new religious festivals such as the Bonalu and Ganesh processions. The potential for confrontation is obvious. In the face of communal tension, and given their status as a small minority, the Shiites look to the municipal government for protection, an attitude which apparently has its roots in the benevolent interest once demonstrated by the nizam, Mir Osman Ali Khan, with regard to the Shiites of Hyderabad and their Muharram liturgies. For the government is perceived as playing a crucial beneficial role in the life of Hyderabad's Shiite community. Adherents of the men's associations asserted this view repeatedly in conversations with me as they discussed preparations for Ashura. As one *guruh* member remarked to me:

> The most important thing is for us to be allowed to hold our Muharram *majalis* and public processions. The Indian government is a friend. It protects our community when we hold our observances. Even when there is trouble, we're not prohibited from *azadari* [public liturgical mourning] the way Shiites are in Lucknow. We want to be left alone to hold our *majalis*, that's all.

Another guild-member expressed this attitude more succinctly: "The government doesn't interfere with us Shiites, and we don't interfere with the government."

This entente is given physical expression in the Bibi ka alam procession, when the Old City's Shiite *guruhan* assemble to march behind the elephant bearing the standard of Fatima, each group identified by its own banner, *tazias,* and *alams,* each group including in its ranks some 200 to 500 men performing *matam* in time to the chanting of the guild's *nauha-khan.* It is an impressive sight: thousands of mourners, guild-adherents and the general public alike, participate in this procession, in a parade that takes the better part of a day to make its way through the Old City. All of this devotional pageantry—the gathering of the *guruhan,* the performance of *matam,* the procession through the streets—derives its structure on Ashura from the shared reverence given the Bibi ka alam. And as noted above, it is this same *alam* to which votive offerings of garlands and *dhattis* are publicly made by both the nizam's family and the present municipal authorities: the *dhattis* thus become symbols of continuity linking past and present in the government's ongoing support for this communal liturgy. The government ensures moreover that more than symbolic support is given: mounted police in the vanguard clear a path for the procession, forcing the crowds to either side of the street as the marchers advance; an escort of soldiers and police clusters around the Bibi ka alam and accompanies it along the entire length of the procession.[32]

Based on the observations recorded in this chapter, I would venture to say that Hyderabad's *matami guruhan* seem to view the government as a protector guaranteeing the Shiites' right to hold their religious ceremonies in safety. As a minority community in a largely Hindu and Sunni population, the Shiites of Hyderabad seem glad of the very noticeable presence of police and municipal authorities at the principal Muharram observances. And the government for its part has chosen to capitalize on the opportunity presented by these religious occasions: by physically safeguarding Shiite celebrations in Hyderabad, by offering veneration publicly to objects of Shiite devotion, and by praising the Karbala martyrs as models for all humanity, state and municipal authorities lend support to Indian government pronouncements on the potential of actualizing communal harmony through the celebration of Muharram.

Part III

Conclusion

19

Hyderabad and the World Community of Shiite Islam

Friends asked, once I was back home after my second trip to India, what had impressed me most in my work with Hyderabad's Shiites. The hospitality, was my immediate reply; that, and the willingness of most of the men I encountered to talk to me and welcome me to their family chapels. Looking back now over two Muharram seasons, however, and having had more time for reflection, I would add something else: I was impressed by the immediacy of Karbala for Hyderabadi Shiites. Husain's death is no historical datum from the remote past; it generates a sense of injury, of something gone wrong with the world. This community guards a lively awareness of the violence inflicted on the Imam and the persecution visited on his followers down to the present day. Untiringly my hosts would recount for me each indignity suffered by Husain thirteen centuries ago, each blow that struck him and where it fell; and I sometimes had the feeling that we were talking about something from just yesterday, as if these were things that had befallen an immediate acquaintance or family member. And so in a sense they were. "We want the world to know, we want the world to see our side of things," as one informant said in describing the wrongful usurpation of the caliphate by the Umayyads; and in fact many of the men I interviewed were eager for me to write down notes and take photographs of the liturgies I witnessed.

The awareness of injury and wrong which characterizes Shiism is not necessarily expressed in violence (a point to which I will return shortly), but it does encourage Shiites to take the events of Karbala very seriously indeed. Karbala provokes tears even today because it continues to have relevance for the Shiite community. From generation to generation they have maintained the *silsileh-ye matamdaran*, the "chain of breast-beating mourners," across the centuries, and have passed on the responsibility of lamenting

Husain's death. By accepting this heritage Hyderabadi congregations also identify themselves to some extent with Husain's resistance to worldly powers and assume some share in the burden of persecution suffered by Husain's family and his descendants. Karbala thus becomes a model for explaining and giving theological meaning to sufferings encountered by the Shiite community today.

By accepting this heritage of mourning, Shiites feel they have the capacity to honor *Ahl-e Bayt* more fully than can Sunnis, because Shiites understand fully by direct participation what Husain suffered and why. Earlier I made the claim that Shiite self-definition might be summarized as follows: Shiites are those Muslims who excel beyond all others in their love for *Ahl-e Bayt*. As a proof of this love they assign sinlessness and infallibility to the Prophet's household and the Imams and in so doing they accentuate the contrast between the high reverence due the *Ma'sumin* and the abasement they were made to suffer. Shiites alone, then, fully appreciate the depths of affliction to which the Prophet's family was brought.

This awareness of injustice in the world order can be manifested in any one of a number of ways, which for convenience may be subsumed under the heading of either *qiyam* (insurrection, revolt) or *intizar* (expectation, waiting). Should one imitate Husain the rebel or await the Mahdi, who will one day heal the world's wrongs? Which image is truer to Husain's life, that of the fighter, setting forth sword in hand to battle tyrants, or that of the *dhibh azim,* the great sacrificial victim, surrendering himself like Ishmael in passive submission to the divine will? *Qiyam* characterized the early Alid partisans, the Zaydis of the eighth century, the *fedayeen* Assassins from the medieval militant phase of Ismaili history. Characteristic of Twelver Shiism for most of its history, however, has been *intizar,* a quietism in which rank-and-file believers avoided confrontation with the government while Shiite *ulama* either withdrew from public controversy or collaborated with the reigning hierarchy.

Mary Hegland has drawn attention to the multivalent significance of Karbala in an essay entitled "Two Images of Husain." She notes the mistaken belief held by many observers who tried to interpret the events of the 1979 Iranian Revolution, namely that the Shiite worldview and the content of Muharram liturgies automatically predispose Shiites to violent revolution and martyrdom. If anything, the opposite had been the case in prerevolutionary Iran, a country dominated by the Twelver form of Shiism and by a conception of Husain which encouraged political quietism. Husain was viewed as a powerful patron who, if approached with circumspection and propitiated by the believer, could be induced to intercede on the individual's behalf in the heavenly court of the Almighty. This model of hierarchical patronage reflected the highly stratified nature of traditional Iranian society, in which the only source of livelihood for many peasants was agriculture, and survival depended on the good will of powerful landlords. But the economic, religious, and educational innovations introduced by the Pahlevi shahs in the twentieth century changed Iran profoundly and weakened the traditional patronage system; as a result the dominant image of Husain as patron and intercessor lost some of its force. The rapid development of Iran's oil production and other industries led to new employment opportunities and the possibility of reshaping hierarchies of power; migration from country to city in search of jobs, however, left many workers feeling dislocated and eager to preserve some sense of their cultural identity. At the same time the policies of Mohammed Reza Shah Pahlevi (reigned 1941-1979) led many Iranians to reevaluate their attitudes towards the ruling government. The Shah's backing by the West, his attempt to consolidate power at the expense of the *ulama,* his disregard for traditional culture and willingness to make brutal use of the secret police to enforce his hurried modernization program: all these factors combined in such a way that the Shah and his supporters in the ruling hierarchy came gradually to be seen as oppressors rather than as patrons who might be counted on for help when propitiated. Accompanying this new view of the Iranian government and the Pahlevi dynasty came a perception of the Imam Husain as "example" (to borrow Hegland's term) rather than intercessor: he demonstrated how one could rebel actively against oppression by a tyrannous government.[1]

This shift in perception grew slowly in the course of the 1960's and 1970's, the product of efforts by Iranian intellectuals and certain members of the Shiite *ulama* who reinterpreted Karbala and Husain as a means of political resistance. Ali Shariati (d. 1977), a Paris-educated university professor who was imprisoned by the Pahlevi government, described the Imam Husain as a fighter who "bears witness to those who are martyred by the oppression in history, heir of all the leaders of freedom and equality and seekers of justice from Adam to himself, forever, the messenger of martyrdom, the manifestation of the blood revolution."[2]

Here Shariati transforms the familiar Islamic concept of the "chain of the prophets" and imagines instead what may be termed a "chain of revolutionaries," beginning with Adam and extending from age to age to Husain and beyond to all those in the present day who consent to be "messengers of martyrdom."

Shariati does not condemn traditional Muharram lamentation but instead reinterprets these practices, forsaking any notion of the individual merit to

be obtained by *matam* and emphasizing instead communal liturgies as a form
of social protest:

> Choose mourning for continuing the constant historical struggle of the Shiites
> against usurpation, treachery, cruelty . . . Remember Ashura to humiliate the
> ruling group who call themselves the inheritors of the traditions of the Prophet,
> for the remembrance of it will prove that they are the inheritors of the killers and
> murderers of the Prophet's family . . . Ashura recalls the teaching of this
> continuing fact that the present Islam is a criminal Islam in the dress of
> "tradition" and that the real Islam is the hidden Islam, hidden in the red cloak of
> martyrdom.[3]

Implicit here is a distinction recognizable at once to his Shiite audience:
the differentiation between *zahir* and *batin,* between the merely external
forms of Islam and the "hidden" concealed realities which the discerning
must seek out.

In a sense Shariati reverts to the earliest historical forms of Shiism, to a
political Shiism consonant with the Zaydi tradition (though his phrasing
shows influence from Marxist thought):

> Shiism was not just a revolutionary movement in history which opposed all the
> autocratic and class-conscious regimes of the Umayyad and Abbasid caliphate,
> . . . who had made the government version of the Sunni school their official
> religion . . . Like a revolutionary party, Shiism had a well-organized, informed,
> deep and well-defined ideology, with clear-cut and definite slogans and a
> disciplined and well-groomed organization. It led the deprived and oppressed
> masses in their movements for freedom and for the seeking of justice.[4]

Like Shariati numerous religious leaders in Iran participated in the
reevaluation of Karbala and its attendant commemorative liturgies. Morteza
Motahhary did not condemn the traditional rituals of Muharram lamentation;
instead he sought to make them relevant to contemporary social issues by
describing the inner disposition that should motivate congregants who
bewail Husain:

> A martyr creates the spirit of valour, and weeping for him means participation
> in his valour and in conformity with his longing for martyrdom . . .
> Another moral which the society should draw, is that whenever a situation
> demanding sacrifice arises, the people should have the feelings of a martyr and
> willingly follow his heroic example. Weeping for the martyr means association
> with his fervour, harmony with his spirit and conformity with his longing.[5]

The most famous exponent of such reinterpreted Shiism is the Ayatollah Ruhollah Khomeini:

> Islam is the religion of militant individuals who are committed to truth and justice. It is the religion of those who desire freedom and independence. It is the school of those who struggle against imperialism. But the servants of imperialism have presented Islam in a totally different light. They have created in men's minds a false notion of Islam. The defective version of Islam, which they have presented in the religious teaching institution, is intended to deprive Islam of its vital, revolutionary aspect.[6]

As noted earlier, the interpretation of Husain and Karbala as models for revolutionary confrontation had not prevailed in Iran before the Pahlevi era. Instead a quietist model of Shiite piety held sway; and because this did not suit the agenda of figures like Shariati and Khomeini, they reinterpreted Shiism to fit their political goals.

It is worth noting the way in which Khomeini chose to interpret the Shiite heritage in writings addressed to Sunni Arab audiences after the ouster of the Shah in 1979. As part of revolutionary Iran's ongoing bid for ideological hegemony in the Muslim world, the Ayatollah, in appeals directed to pilgrims at Mecca, sought to broaden the attractiveness of Iran's Islamic example by minimizing doctrinal differences and past historical disputes between Sunnis and Shiites. Arab nationalism and sectarian feuding were both to be avoided as divisive evils weakening the Islamic unity needed to counter the forces of secularism and Westernization.[7]

Such calls for solidarity have had some influence. I myself have occasionally encountered revivalist-minded Muslims who objected strongly to my inquiries about Sunni-Shiite differences and who disapproved even of any use of the words Sunni or Shiite. Such terms, they argued, represent an attempt to weaken Islam by dividing Muslims.

The latest manifestation of Iran's attempts at ideological rapprochement with non-Shiite Muslims can be seen in its extensive military aid to the Sudan, where the Sunni tradition prevails. The Sudanese military regime of Lieutenant General Omar Hassan al-Bashir is strongly influenced by Sheikh Hassan al-Tourabi, the Sudan's most prominent Muslim fundamentalist. Long an admirer of the Ayatollah Khomeini, Tourabi calls for the establishment of Islamic governments throughout the Middle East. Late in 1991, Teheran sent between one and two thousand Iranian Revolutionary Guards to the Sudan to act as military advisors. Training camps have now reportedly been established in the Sudan for the instruction of Muslim militants from throughout North Africa and the Persian Gulf region. According to Youssef

Ibrahim of *The New York Times,* "Tunisia, Egypt and Saudi Arabia have openly accused the Sudanese government of giving refuge, passports and logistical support to militant fundamentalist groups held responsible for terrorist attacks in those countries."[8]

But it is important to bear in mind that in contrast to these political developments, the form of Islam which continues to characterize Hyderabad's Shiite community today (at least as of this present writing in 1991) is the quietist Shiism typical of most of Twelver history rather than the revolutionary/confrontational model recently articulated in Iran.

Quietism need not imply apathy. As noted in part II of this study, Hyderabadi Shiites have created several charitable organizations that undertake educational and social welfare projects for the benefit of local Shiite communities. But as a small minority in a Hindu-majority city, Hyderabad's Shiites have tended to look to India's secular government for protection rather than confront it with demands for Islamic-oriented reforms. What the Hyderabadi community clings to is its right to hold Muharram liturgies; thereby Shiites fulfill the responsibility they have taken upon themselves, to hand from generation to generation the memory of the wrongs inflicted on Husain, to enter into his suffering for themselves through the rituals of *matam.* In the liturgies I attended, each Muharram *majlis* closed with an invocation to the twelfth Imam, whose return is awaited as the act which will finally right the injustice visited on the Prophet's family and heal the sorrows of his adherents. "*Intizar* is an act of worship in itself," as one Hyderabadi informant told me: to look for the coming of the Mahdi is to recall the historical events which cry out for healing at the end of time. The Shiites of Hyderabad's Old City neighborhoods, in their intense identification with their liturgical life, in their remembrance of historical expropriation and hopeful awaiting of eschatological restoration, share spiritual affinity in a sense with the Hasidim of Judaism. For the liturgy-centered life of Hyderabad's Shiites recalls the Hasidic *tikkun olam* (a concept developed in the kabbalistic speculations of Isaac Luria), the "repair of the world" to be effected by the observance of liturgical responsibilities.[9]

Study of the Hyderabadi community reminds one that there is nothing inherently militant or violent in the Shiite form of Islam. In America there seems to be an understandable popular tendency to judge Shiism by the political policies of the most highly visible national exponent of the faith, the Islamic Republic of Iran. It is true that the Khomeinist version of Shiism which shaped the Islamic Republic continues, even after the Ayatollah's death, to influence Shiites elsewhere in the world, most notably the

Hezbollah of Lebanon. But Hyderabad reminds us that there are different possible forms of Shiism, ranging from militancy to quietism.

A monolithic conception of Shiism as militant may have influenced American government policy towards the Iraqi Shiite rebellion against Saddam Hussein in February-March 1991, in the wake of the Persian Gulf War and the American-led Operation Desert Storm. Our government's reluctance to support the rebels (after initially encouraging them to revolt) seems to have stemmed from a fear that a fragmented Iraq might become an appanage of the Islamic Republic of Iran. Caution is not unreasonable: the majority of Iraq's population is Shiite; and Muhammad Baqir al-Hakim, one of the primary leaders of Iraqi Shiite opposition to Saddam and head of a Teheran-based government-in-exile, has called for the establishment of a Khomeinist Islamic administration in Iraq.[10]

Nevertheless, the February-March 1991 uprising may have been a missed opportunity for America. After Saddam had crushed the insurrection (in the process desecrating the Karbala shrines of Abbas and Husain), Hyderabadis complained to me bitterly of America's flip-flop—our encouraging and then abandoning the Shiite and Kurdish uprisings. American intervention on behalf of Iraq's Shiites after the Gulf War would have earned admiration and gratitude not only in southern Iraq but in Shiite communities in India and elsewhere in the world. A risk it would have been, certainly, with uncertain political consequences, but our aid might have represented a long step towards healing the mutual distrust prevailing after the Pahlevi era and the 1980 Iranian hostage crisis.

Anyone who attempts to understand Shiite Islam should not rest content with an examination of revolutionary militancy in Iran or Lebanon. Hyderabad's community reminds us that no single religious leader dictates political attitudes in Shiism, that the imagery of Karbala and Husain's death is multivalent and open to variable interpretation and application, that finally there are many ways of belonging to the Shiite tradition in Islam.

GLOSSARY

Ahl-e Bayt. Members of the Prophet's family and their immediate descendants, all of whom suffered violent persecution at the hands of the Umayyad and Abbasid caliphs.

Alam. A metal crest usually mounted on a pole and meant to suggest the battle-standards caried by the martyrs of Karbala. Usually incised with the names of Abu al-Fadl al-Abbas, Ali Akbar, or the *Ma'sumin, alams* are housed in *ashurkhanas* and exposed for veneration during Muharram.

Anjuman. "Association" or "group"; the word is used in Hyderabad in some contexts as an alternative designation for the *matami guruh.*

Ashura. The tenth day of the month of Muharram, the day on which Husain was killed at Karbala (A.D. 680). Ashura is the focal day of the annual Muharram observances.

Ashurkhana. The "Ashura-house," the shrine where *alams* are stored throughout the year and where *majalis* are held during Muharram. The *ashurkhana* may be as simple as a room in a private home containing the family's *alams* and partitioned by a black curtain from the rest of the house; or it may be as majestic as a walled compound with a courtyard, porticoes and a chapel housing relics associated with the Karbala martyrs.

Ayk dast-e matam. Literally, "one-handed *matam.*" The simplest form of ritual lamentation: breast-beating.

Azadari. Lamentation; specifically, lamentation during Muharram for the Karbala martyrs.

Batin. The interior, concealed or secret aspect of a thing. In Quranic interpretation *batin* refers to the esoteric or hidden meaning of a scriptural passage.

Da'i. In medieval Ismaili tradition, a missionary-preacher who sought to initiate selected Muslims into the esoteric dimensions of Quranic scripture.

Dhatti. A long votive-cloth which is fastened to an *alam* and draped along the length of the pole on which the *alam* is mounted. At Muharram *dhattis* are frequently offered to *alams* in an act of veneration which forms part of the *ziyarah.*

Dhul fiqar. Name of the fork-bladed sword carried by the Imam Ali ibn Abi Talib.

Fatwa. A written opinion on a specific legal/moral issue. *Fatwas* are issued by jurisconsults trained in Islamic law who are deemed competent to apply Quranic scripture to contemporary challenges.

Ghulat. "Doctrinal extremists," Muslims guilty of *ghuluww* and thus rejected as heretics by orthodox Shiites and Sunnis alike.

Ghuluww. Doctrinal extremism, beliefs rejected as heretical by orthodox Shiites and Sunnis alike. In Shiite religious history *ghuluww* has most typically involved attempts to deify the Imams or ascribe to them divine powers.

Hadith. A "report" or "account," specifically a description of things said or deeds undertaken by the Prophet Muhammad.

Hijrah. The Prophet Muhammad's withdrawal from Mecca (A.D. 622) northward to Medina, where he established a community of Muslims. The *hijrah* is taken as the point in time from which dates are reckoned in the Islamic calendar.

Ijma'. "Agreement" or "consensus," specifically the consensus of the Muslim community (as represented by its *ulama*) regarding a particular legal/moral issue of interest to the society at large.

Ijtihad. The use of independent reasoning, based on one's knowledge of Quranic scripture, the *hadith* literature, and the *shari'ah,* in order to arrive at a decision concerning a given moral/legal issue.

Imam. In its simplest meaning, one who leads a congregation in prayer; the word is used in this sense in both the Shiite and Sunni traditions. The term is additionally used in Shiism, however, to designate the descendants of the Prophet's family who were the rightful spiritual and worldly heirs of the

Prophet's authority and hence were the true leaders of the Muslim community.

Intizar. "Expectation" or "waiting," a term used to describe a quietist stance of avoiding political confrontation with the powers of this world as one awaits patiently the return of the Hidden Imam as the Mahdi.

Ismah. "Purity," a term used in Shiism to designate the state of perpetual sinlessness and infallibility inhering in the fourteen *Ma'sumin.*

Kafir. An unbeliever; one who refuses to acknowledge God's absolute sovereignty. In popular Islamic usage today the term is sometimes used simply to designate polytheists or pagans; some Muslims, however, apply the term as well to Jews and Christians, despite their shared spiritual ancestry as adherents of Abrahamic faiths.

Mahdi. "The one guided by God." In Twelver Shiite belief the messianic title to be assumed by the Hidden Imam when he returns at the end of time to preside over the Day of Final Judgment.

Majlis (pl. *majalis*). A "gathering" or "assembly". The term is used especially to indicate a Muharram liturgy held within an *ashurkhana.* In Hyderabad the *majlis* typically comprises *marsiyeh* recitation and a sermon and will sometimes conclude with congregational performance of *matam* to the chanted accompaniment of *nauhas.*

Marja' al-taqlid (pl. *maraji' al-taqlid*). A "reference point" or "model for imitation": a Shiite *alim* who is so outstanding for his learning and piety as to be worthy to serve as a moral exemplar for the generality of Shiite believers.

Marsiyeh. A lamentation-chant in honor of the Karbala martyrs, most typically recited near the beginning of a Muharram *majlis* just after the opening prayers of invocation and preceding the sermon.

Mashk. A leather waterskin, carried at Karbala by Husain's bodyguard Abbas when he tried to bring water from the Euphrates to the Imam's thirsting children. In Shiite iconography representations of the *mashk* evoke Abbas and his act of generosity.

Ma'sum. A term derived from the word *ismah* and used to designate a person protected from sin and error of any kind.

Ma'sumin. Plural of *ma'sum*; in Shiism *Ma'sumin* refers to the "fourteen Immaculate Ones," i.e. the Prophet Muhammad, his daughter Fatima, and the twelve Imams.

Matam. In general, an action expressing grief, loss, or condolence. In Shiite Islam the term describes ritual actions of lamentation for the Karbala martyrs. By far the most common form of *matam* is repeated breast-beating; but *matam* may include more extreme forms of self-mortification involving the use of razors, flails and knives. In Hyderabad *matam* is generally performed to the accompaniment of chanted *nauhas*.

Matamdar (pl. *matamdaran*). Specifically, one who undertakes *matam*. The term is used in general to designate active participants in communal rituals of mourning during Muharram.

Matami guruh (pl. *matami guruhan*). The *matami guruhan* are Shiite men's guilds organized especially for the purpose of performing *matam* in honor of the Karbala martyrs during the season of Muharram.

Mujtahid. A Shiite religious scholar who is considered sufficiently learned in Quranic sciences to undertake *ijtihad*.

Namaz. The Persian term for *salat,* the daily ritual prayer that all Muslims are obliged to perform.

Nauha. A lamentation-poem sung in honor of the Karbala martyrs, usually performed at the close of a Muharram liturgy. The *nauha* is chanted as an accompaniment to the performance of *matam* and thereby structures the rhythm and tempo of breast-beating and other forms of communal self-mortification.

Nauha-khan. The person who leads a congregation in the chanting of *nauhas*.

Panje. The representation of a hand, palm open, fingers and thumb pointing upward. In Shiite iconography the *panje* symbolizes the *Panjetan Pak* or "Pure Five," the Prophet, Fatima, Ali, Hasan, and Husain. *Alams* and other

Shiite insignia are often created in the form of a *panje,* a device believed to represent the divine protection offered to those who are devoted to *Ahl-e Bayt.* In Hyderabad *panje-alams* are often surmounted by a representation of Dhul fiqar, the fork-bladed sword of the Imam Ali ibn Abi Talib. B. D. Eerdmans, "Der Ursprung der Ceremonien des Hosein-Festes," *Zeitschrift für Assyriologie* 9 (1894), 280-307, traces the origin of the Muharram *panje* to ancient Mesopotamian fertility liturgies and to iconography associated with the vegetation-god Tammuz.

Panjetan Pak. The "pure five": the Prophet, his daughter Fatima, Ali, Hasan, and Husain.

Sabil. A booth where water, tea, and other refreshments are distributed as an act of charity to passersby on their way to and from Muharram *majalis.* Customarily situated near the most popular *ashurkhanas* and decorated with banners celebrating the slain Imams, the *sabil* is established by sponsors as a gesture of largesse in honor of the Karbala martyrs and in memory of the thirst they suffered on the battlefield.

Shahadah. The testimony of faith required of all Muslims, the assertion that "no god is there save God and Muhammad is the messenger of God." Sunnis and Shiites alike accept this formulation; but Shiites add the phrase, "and Ali is the beloved friend of God."

Shari'ah. Divine law, made manifest to humankind by God through the Quran and applied to Muslim society by the *ulama* who elaborate the legal/moral precepts encoded in Scripture.

Shirk. The sin of rejecting *tawhid* through a polytheistic ascription of divine partners to God.

Sineh-zani. "Chest-beating": Persian synonym for the term *matam.*

Sunnah. Customary behavior, either as pertaining to an individual or to a community. The *sunnah* of the Prophet Muhammad is recorded in the *hadith* and serves as a model of conduct for Muslims.

Tafsir. Commentary on passages from Quranic scripture.

Tariqah (pl. *turuq*). Literally "path" or "way". Used in popular Islamic devotion to designate a mystical order or Sufi brotherhood.

Tawhid. The doctrinal assertion of strict monotheism and divine unity: "no god is there save Allah."

Ta'wil. Esoteric interpretation of the Quran, whereby one penetrates Scripture's literal meaning to the *batin,* the text's hidden inner significance.

Tazia. A small-scale replica (made of metal or gilt wood) of the mausoleum-shrine of Husain or Hasan, the martyred Imams. *Tazias* are housed in *ashurkhanas* and carried in public processions on the tenth of Muharram. In Shiite iconography green-stained *tazias* symbolize Hasan (slain by poison); red *tazias* represent Husain (slain in combat).

Ta'ziyeh. The Iranian "passion-play" or dramatic representation of the battle of Karbala and other events from Shiite sacred history.

Ulama (sg. *alim*). Scholars learned in Quranic sciences who are thereby qualified to offer moral guidance to individuals and (at times) to Islamic society at large.

Zahir. The external, evident or readily manifest aspect of a thing. In Quranic interpretation *zahir* refers to the exterior or literal meaning of a scriptural passage.

Zakir. A preacher, specifically a preacher of sermons in Muharram *majalis.*

Ziyarah. Literally "visitation". The term is used in popular Islamic devotion to designate pilgrimage to local saints' shrines or (specifically in Shiism) visits to *ashurkhanas* during Muharram.

NOTES

Chapter One

1. In its simplest and most literal meaning the term "Imam" is used in both Sunni and Shiite Islam simply to designate an individual who leads a gathering of Muslims in congregational prayer. In Shiism the same word is also used to indicate the sinless and infallible descendants of the Prophet, spiritual leaders of the Shiite community. It is in this latter sense that the term "Imam" is used in the present study. Imam is used here with a capital "I" to designate one of the twelve infallible leaders of the Shiite community; "imam" with a small "i" designates the term in its wider sense, that of the prayer leader of a mosque congregation.
2. Abu al-Fath Muhammad al-Shahrastani, *Kitab al-milal wa-al-nihal* (Cairo: Maktabat Mustafa al-Babi, 1976), ed. Muhammad Sayyid Kilani, vol. 1, p. 146.
3. Relevant to this discussion of the Shiite *ulama*'s relationship with worldly governments is a discussion of "the ambiguity . . . at the heart of Iranian culture" in Roy Mottahedeh, *The Mantle of the Prophet* (New York: Pantheon Books, 1985), 161-165.
4. For a discussion of Iranian worldviews and Iranian perceptions of America and the West, see William O. Beeman, "Images of the Great Satan: Representations of the United States in the Iranian Revolution," in Nikki R. Keddie, ed., *Religion and Politics in Iran* (New Haven: Yale University Press, 1983), 191-217.

Chapter Two

1. W. Montgomery Watt, *Islamic Philosophy and Theology* (Edinburgh University Press, 1985), 25-27.
2. N. K. Sandars, trans., *The Epic of Gilgamesh* (Harmondsworth: Penguin Books, 1964), 89.
3. T. Emil Homerin, "Echoes of a Thirsty Owl: Death and Afterlife in Pre-Islamic Arabic Poetry," *Journal of Near Eastern Studies* 44 (1985), 167 and n. 10.
4. Ibid., 183.
5. Ibid., 182.
6. Tor Andrae, *Mohammed: The Man and His Faith* (New York: Harper & Row, 1960), 19.
7. Fazlur Rahman, *Islam,* 2nd ed. (Chicago: University of Chicago Press, 1979), 150, 153.
8. Moojan Momen, *An Introduction to Shi'i Islam* (New Haven: Yale University Press, 1985), 208-209.

9. Ibid., 116, 235.

10. Ibid., 116.

11. Abdullah Yusuf Ali, trans., *The Holy Qur'an* (Beirut: Dar al-Arabia, n.d.), 360 n. 1043.

12. For a discussion of *The City of Brass* see David Pinault, *Story-Telling Techniques in the Arabian Nights* (Leiden: E. J. Brill, 1992), 148-239.

13. Andrae, op. cit., 37-38; R. A. Nicholson, *A Literary History of the Arabs* (Cambridge University Press, 1977), 138; A. J. Wensinck, s.v. "Ka'ba," *Encyclopaedia of Islam*, 2nd ed. (Leiden: E. J. Brill, 1978), vol. 4, p. 320.

14. Jalal al-Din Abd al-Rahman al-Suyuti and Jalal al-Din Muhammad al-Mahalli, *Tafsir al-Jalalayn* (Beirut: Dar al-ma'rifah, n.d.), 174.

15. Mahmoud Ayoub, *Redemptive Suffering in Islam* (The Hague: Mouton Publishers, 1978), 73.

Chapter Three

1. H.A.R. Gibb, *Mohammedanism*, 2nd ed. (Oxford University Press, 1979), 50.

2. Moojan Momen, *An Introduction to Shi'i Islam* (New Haven: Yale University Press, 1985), 140, 289.

3. Recorded by al-Tanukhi, "The Table Talk of a Mesopotamian Judge," D. S. Margoliouth, trans., and included in the anthology entitled *Introduction to Classical Arabic Literature*, Ilse Lichtenstadter, ed., (New York: Twayne Publishers, 1974), 345-346.

4. For the passage in Mas'udi and the Harun al-Rashid tales see David Pinault, *Story-Telling Techniques in the Arabian Nights* (Leiden: E. J. Brill, 1992), 142-146.

5. Momen, op. cit., 148-153.

6. Abu Ishaq Ahmad al-Tha'labi, *Qisas al-anbiya'* (Beirut: al-Maktabah al-thaqafiyah, n.d.), 82-83; Jalal al-Din Abd al-Rahman al-Suyuti and Jalal al-Din Muhammad al-Mahalli, *Tafsir al-jalalayn* (Beirut: Dar al-ma'rifah, n.d.), 594.

7. Muhammad Husain al-Tabataba'i, *al-Mizan fi tafsir al-Qur'an* (Qum: Mu'assasah Matbu'ati Isma'iliyan, 1971-1974), vol. 13, p. 153; Mahmoud Ayoub, *Redemptive Suffering in Islam* (The Hague: Mouton Publishers, 1978), 235.

8. The Urdu text of this poem is printed in the chant-book of the Anjuman-e Masoomeen, *Du'a-e Fatimah: muntakhab-e nauhajat* (Hyderabad, n.d.), 9-10.

9. Ignaz Goldziher, "Neuplatonische und gnostische Elemente im Hadith," *Zeitschrift für Assyriologie* 22 (1909), 326-328.

10. Louis Massignon, *The Passion of al-Hallaj. Volume 1: The Life of al-Hallaj* (Princeton University Press, 1982), 295-330.

11. Abu al-Fath Muhammad al-Shahrastani, *Kitab al-milal wa-al-nihal* (Cairo: Maktabat Mustafa al-Babi, 1976), ed. Muhammad Sayyid Kilani, vol. 1, p. 173.

12. Abu Muhammad al-Hasan ibn Musa al-Nawbakhti, *Kitab firaq al-shi'ah*, ed. Hellmut Ritter (Istanbul: Matba'at al-dawlah, 1931), 55.

13. Shahrastani, op. cit., I, 176-177.

14. Annemarie Schimmel, *Mystical Dimensions of Islam* (Chapel Hill: University of North Carolina Press, 1975), 25, 177; Gershom Scholem, s.v. "Kabbalah," *Encyclopaedia Judaica* (Jerusalem: Macmillan, 1971), vol. 10, pp. 489-653.

15. Hans Jonas, *The Gnostic Religion*, 2nd ed. (Boston: Beacon Press, 1963), 181-194, 217-218.

16. Reinhold Loeffler, *Islam in Practice: Religious Beliefs in a Persian Village* (Albany: State University of New York Press, 1988), 40-41, 176-177.

17. Wilfred Madelung, s.v. "Isma'iliyya," *Encyclopaedia of Islam*, 2nd ed. (Leiden: E.J. Brill, 1978), vol. 4, 203-206; Bruce Borthwick, "The Ismailis and Islamization in Pakistan," *American Council for the Study of Islamic Societies Newsletter* 1 (Aug. 1990), 4-6; Sami Nasib Makarem, *The Doctrine of the Ismailis* (Beirut: Arab Institute for Research and Publishing, 1972), 35-47.

18. R. A. Nicholson, *A Literary History of the Arabs* (Cambridge University Press, 1977), 272-273; for the portrait of Jesus as an Ismaili *da'i* see David Pinault, "Images of Christ in Arabic Literature," *Die Welt des Islams* 27 (1987), 110 n. 5 and the sources cited therein.

19. Bernard Lewis, *The Assassins: A Radical Sect in Islam* (Oxford University Press, 1967), 72-73.

20. Makarem, op. cit., 73-75.

21. Muhammad Husain Tabataba'i, *Shi'ite Islam* (Albany: State University of New York Press, 1977), 83.

22. Fazlur Rahman, *Islam*, 2nd ed. (University of Chicago Press, 1979), 177-178.

23. Mustafa Ghalib, *al-Harakat al-batiniyah fi al-Islam* (Beirut: Dar al-Andalus, 1982), 273-274.

24. Muhammad Amin Ghalib al-Tawil, *Ta'rikh al-alawiyin* (Beirut: Dar al-Andalus, 1966), 535-537.

25. Fouad Ajami, *The Vanished Imam: Musa al-Sadr and the Shia of Lebanon* (Ithaca: Cornell University Press, 1986), 174.

Chapter Four

1. Farid al-Din Attar, *Mantiq al-tayr*, Ahmad Khoshnevis, ed. (Isfahan: Kitabkhaneh Sina'i, 1336 AH), 70-71.

2. Shams al-Din Hafez, *Diwan-e kamil-e Hafez-e Shiraz*, ed. Timur Burhan Limudhi (Teheran: Matbu'ati Kawiyan, 1363 AH), 39.

3. The text of Khomeini's poem is available in Michael Fischer and Mehdi Abedi, *Debating Muslims: Cultural Dialogues in Postmodernity and Tradition* (Madison: University of Wisconsin Press, 1990), 451-452.

4. Hermann Landolt, "Suhrawardi's 'Tales of Initiation'," *Journal of the American Oriental Society* 107 (1987), 482.

5. W. M. Thackston, Jr., trans., *The Mystical and Visionary Treatises of Shihabuddin Yahya Suhrawardi* (London: Octagon Press, 1982), 84-85.

6. Henry Corbin, *L'archange empourpré* (Paris: Librairie Fayard, 1976), 170.

7. Thackston, op. cit., 26-34.

8. Or as Corbin (p.242) elegantly describes Gabriel's role in *L'archange empourpré*: "C'est lui seul qui est l'herméneute, pour les hommes, du Silence divin des mondes supérieurs représentés par les autres Intelligences" ("He alone it is who guides men as interpreter of the divine Silence of the higher worlds represented by the other Intellects").
9. Thackston, op. cit., 35.

Chapter Five

1. Louis Massignon, "Die Ursprünge und die Bedeutung des Gnostizismus im Islam," *Eranos Jahrbuch* 1937 (Zurich: Rhein-Verlag, 1938), 56.
2. Abu Muhammad al-Hasan ibn Musa al-Nawbakhti, *Kitab firaq al-shi'ah*, ed. Hellmut Ritter (Istanbul: Matba'at al-dawlah, 1931), 16.
3. On the voluntary and sacrificial nature of Husain's death see also S. Husain M. Jafri, *Origins and Early Development of Shi'a Islam* (London: Longman, 1979), 203-205.

Chapter Six

1. Farid al-Din Attar, *The Conference of the Birds*, Afkham Darbandi and Dick Davis, translators (Harmondsworth: Penguin Books, 1984), 160-161.
2. John Norman Hollister, *Islam and Shia's Faith in India* (Delhi: Taj Publications, 1989), 103.
3. Ibid.
4. Saiyid Athar Abbas Rizvi, *A Socio-Intellectual History of the Isna 'Ashari Shi'is in India* (Canberra: Ma'rifat Publishing House, 1986), vol. 1, pp. 251-252.
5. Hollister, op. cit., 124.
6. According to my Hyderabadi informants this *tariqah* recognizes as its *qutb* (spiritual master) Shaykh Tabanday Husain Gunabadi of Iran.

Chapter Seven

1. Sir Arthur C. Lothian, *Kingdoms of Yesterday* (London: John Murray, 1951), 2.
2. Sir William H. Sleeman, *Rambles and Recollections of an Indian Official* (Karachi: Oxford University Press, 1973), 482-483. First published in 1844.
3. Philip Woodruff, *The Men Who Ruled India: The Guardians* (New York: St. Martin's Press, 1954), 179.
4. Ibid.
5. Ibid.
6. Rudyard Kipling, "The City of the Two Creeds," *Civil and Military Gazette* (Lahore), October 19, 1885. Reprinted in *The Readers' Guide to Rudyard*

Kipling's Work, ed. Roger L. Green and Alec Mason (Canterbury: Gibbs & Sons Ltd., 1961), vol. 1, 582-590.

7. Rudyard Kipling, "The City of the Two Creeds," *Civil and Military Gazette,* October 1, 1887. Reprinted in *Kipling's India: Uncollected Sketches 1884-88,* ed. Thomas Pinney (New York: Schocken Books, 1986), 265-269.

8. This story appeared in 1888 in a collection entitled *In Black and White.* The edition I consulted (New York: Doubleday, Page & Co., 1913) combines this volume with two other Kipling collections, *Soldiers Three* and *The Story of the Gadsbys. On the City Wall* appears on pp. 296-325.

9. Review of Kipling's *In Black and White,* in *The Athenaeum* (London), September 13, 1890, p. 348.

10. John Campbell Oman, *The Brahmans, Theists and Muslims of India* (London: T. Fisher Unwin, 1907). Oman's description of Muharram in Lahore occurs on pp. 279-310.

11. Ibid., p. 298.

12. Ibid., p. 300.

13. Ibid., pp. 300-301.

14. Ibid., p. 305.

15. A.E.W. Mason, *The Drum* (London: Hodder & Stoughton, 1937), 12.

16. Compare Mason, op. cit., p. ii, with Colonel Algernon Durand, *The Making of a Frontier: Five Years' Experiences and Adventures in Gilgit, Hunza Nagar, Chitral, and the Eastern Hindu-Kush* (London: Thomas Nelson & Sons, 1900), 281.

17. Durand, op. cit., 279-280, 285.

18. Mason, op. cit., 100-101.

19. Ibid., pp. 112, 114.

20. The 1938 movie version of *The Drum* (an Alex Korda London Film production) retained the setting of Muharram as the time appointed for the treacherous attack on the British (the chief Muslim plotter is played by a very villainous Raymond Massey). The film offers powerful and disturbing visual images: the camera pans from the severed head of a loyal Pathan servant (murdered through Muslim treachery) to a courtyard filled with Muslims performing ritual prayer while a muezzin cries out the *shahadah.*

Chapter Eight

1. For the Qutb Shahis and the early history of Hyderabad, see John N. Hollister, *Islam and Shia's Faith in India* (New Delhi: Taj Publications, 1989), 120-125; Akbar S. Ahmed, "Muslim Society in South India: the Case of Hyderabad," in *Hyderabad: After the Fall,* Omar Khalidi, ed. (Wichita: Hyderabad Historical Society, 1988), 173-187, offers a useful summary of early Hyderabadi history. For state patronage of Muharram ceremonies under the Asaf Jahi Nizams, see Hollister, op. cit., 169-171, and *Census of India 1971, Series 2, Andhra Pradesh: A Monograph on Muharram in Hyderabad City,* ed. T. Vedantam (Delhi: Government of India Press, 1977), 12-13.

2. The *Census of India*, 50-53, has a brief discussion of Shiite men's associations in Hyderabad; and the Rev. D. T. Lindell's article "Muharram in Hyderabad" in *al-Basheer: the Bulletin of the Christian Institute of Islamic Studies* 3, no.1 (Hyderabad, Jan.-Mar. 1974), 24, refers in passing to "associations of young men, each group identified by its own banner, who perform a special kind of *matam*." Ja'far Sharif, *Islam in India or the Qanun-i-Islam*, G. A. Herklots, trans. (London: Curzon Press reprint, 1972), 151-185 passim, cites Hyderabad occasionally in his description of Muharram in India. A useful description of the most prominent places of worship and relics associated with Muharram in Hyderabad is given by Sadiq Naqvi, *Qutb Shahi 'Ashurkhanas of Hyderabad City* (Hyderabad: Bab-ul-Ilm Society, 1987), 1-78.

3. The *Census of India*, 25, estimates the Shiite population of Hyderabad and nearby Secunderabad as being between twenty and forty thousand; it acknowledges the difficulty of making an exact determination because of the Shiite practice of *taqiyah* (dissimulation concerning one's religious identity, a practice permitted in Shiism when one fears persecution or harassment by non-Shiites for one's adherence to the faith). Shiites whom I interviewed in Hyderabad claim the number today is much higher, up to one hundred thousand.

4. The vocabulary I use here is characteristic of Hyderabad. In Lucknow the *ashurkhana* (literally, "the house of the tenth of Muharram") is known as an *imambara*; in Iran the term *tazia* or *ta'ziyeh* refers to the Shiite "passion play," a dramatized representation of the death of Husain and the events of Karbala. For clarity's sake I use the word *tazia* in this study to designate the processional tomb replicas and reserve *ta'ziyeh* for the Iranian passion play.

5. Naqvi, op. cit., 19-56.

6. Nadeem Hasnain and Abrar Husain, *Shias and Shia Islam in India* (Delhi: Harnam Publications, 1988), 146-148.

Chapter Nine

1. Richard Temple, *Journals Kept in Hyderabad, Kashmir, Sikkim, and Nepal* (Delhi: Cosmo Publications reprint, 1977). In two volumes; volume 1, 122. First published in 1887.

2. This is the period most actively observed by Shiites, but the time of mourning lasts till Arba'in on the twentieth of Safar (commemorating the fortieth day after the death of Imam Husain).

3. This phenomenon may be compared with Terence O'Donnell's description of Shiite men's associations in Iranian villages: "A *dasteh* is a religious brotherhood of the men of a neighborhood . . . Their principal activity is to walk in processions and flagellate themselves" during Muharram. *Garden of the Brave in War* (Chicago: University of Chicago Press, 1980), 94 et seq.

4. "Masoomeen" is the spelling favored by this guild in transliterating the title of their association. In this study I use *Masoomeen* to designate the guild and *Ma'sumin* to designate the "Immaculate Fourteen" (i.e., Muhammad, Fatima, and the twelve Imams).

5. A few Haydariyah members angrily denied this group's derivation from Masoomeen when I asked them about Haydariyah's history, but officers within Haydariyah whom I interviewed agreed with outsiders' assessments concerning the guild's origin as an offshoot of Masoomeen.

6. For the changes in Hyderabad's Muslim population after the 1948 Police Action see Ratna Naidu, *Old Cities, New Predicaments: A Study of Hyderabad* (Delhi: Sage Publications, 1990), 23-25.

7. For an example of moth/flame imagery from thirteenth-century Persian Sufi poetry, see Farid al-Din Attar, *Mantiq al-tayr*, lines 3987-4004; translated by Afkham Darbandi and Dick Davis in *The Conference of the Birds* (Harmondsworth: Penguin Books, 1984), 206.

8. Those interested in the subject may wish to consult Barbara Daly Metcalf, ed., *Moral Conduct and Authority: The Place of Adab in South Asian Islam* (Berkeley: University of California Press, 1984).

9. The admission criteria stipulated in Parwaneh Shabbir's application form—the promise of obedience and the emphasis on proper deportment towards fellow members—are to a limited extent reminiscent of the ideals of the urban *futuwwah* organizations once active at various periods in medieval Islamic history. See Claude Cahen and Fritz Taeschner, s.v. "Futuwwa," *Encyclopaedia of Islam*, 2nd ed. (Leiden: E. J. Brill, 1965), vol. 2, 961-969.

10. Akhtar Zaydi's essay was printed on the back cover of the Anjuman-e Masoomeen's chant-book, *Du'a-e Fatimah: muntakhab-e nauhajat* (Hyderabad, n.d.).

11. For an example of Shiite exegesis of this Quranic passage see A. F. Badshah Husain, *The Holy Quran: A Translation with Commentary According to Shia Traditions and Principles* (Lucknow: Madrasatul Waizeen, 1936), volume 2, p. 67. A copy of this text was very graciously presented to me as a gift in Lucknow by the Maharajkumar of Mahmudabad.

12. See the essay entitled *"Aghaz-e safar"* in *Du'a-e Fatimah*, p. ix.

13. Ibid., pp. ix-x.

14. *Deccan Chronicle* (Hyderabad), August 4, 1989, p. 16.

15. *Fihrist-e nuskheha-ye khatt-e arabi-ye kutubkhane-ye Nadwat al-ulama Lakhnau and A Catalogue of Arabic and Persian Manuscripts in Raja Mahmudabad Library, Lucknow*, both published in New Delhi by the Markaz-e tahqiqat-e zaban-e farsi dar Hind, the Iran Culture House, Islamic Republic of Iran, 1986.

Chapter Ten

1. Nizam al-Din's genealogy is given in Rukunuddin Nizami, *Hayaat-e-Nizami (Life of Hazrat K. Nizamuddin Aulia)*, (Delhi: Kutub Khana Mahboobi, 1979), 3-5.

2. Ja'far Sharif, *Islam in India or the Qanun-i-Islam*, G. A. Herklots, trans. (London: Curzon Press reprint, 1972), 159.

3. Syed Husain Ali Jaffri, "Muharram Ceremonies in India," in Peter Chelkowski, ed., *Ta'ziyeh: Ritual and Drama in Iran* (New York University Press, 1979), 225.
4. Abdullah Yusuf Ali, trans., *The Holy Quran* (Beirut: Dar al-Arabia, n.d.), 1312; Mohammed Marmaduke Pickthall, *The Meaning of the Glorious Koran* (New York: Mentor, n.d.), 346.
5. Syed Mohammed Ameed, *The Importance of Weeping and Wailing* (Karachi: Peermahomed Ebrahim Trust, 1973), 7-10.
6. Ibid., 75-76.
7. For a sampling of Iranian criticisms of *matam* as penance, see Reinhold Loeffler, *Islam in Practice: Religious Beliefs in a Persian Village* (Albany: State University of New York Press, 1988), 68, 75-76, 82. Thomas Lyell, a British civil servant in Iraq at the close of the First World War, records an intriguing conversation with a Shiite mourner on the question of the purpose of *matam*. See *The Ins and Outs of Mesopotamia* (London: A. M. Philpot Ltd., 1923), 74-75.
8. Mohammed Reza Karimi, "The Importance of Mourning (Azadari)," *Ja'fari Times* 2, no. 1 (Muharram 1409/Aug.-Sept. 1988), 13. This journal's name has since been changed to *Ja'fari Observer*.
9. Ahmed H. Sheriff, *The Leader of Martyrs* (Elmhurst, New York: Tahrike Tarsile Qur'an, 1986), 49-50.
10. For a discussion of *taharah* and blood see Ruhollah Mousavi Khomeini, *A Clarification of Questions (Resaleh Towzih al-Masael)* (Boulder: Westview, 1984), 12 and Muhammad Sarwar, trans., *Islamic Practical Laws Explained*, 3rd ed. (Bombay: Imaan Foundation, 1988), 30-31. The latter work is derived from the *fatwas* of the Ayatollah Abu al-Qasim al-Khui.
11. Werner Ende, "The Flagellations of Muharram and the Shi'ite Ulama," *Der Islam* 55 (1978), 34-35. I thank Wayne Husted of Pennsylvania State University for drawing my attention to this article. Another example of popular resistance to attempts by Shiite clerics to curb *matam* is cited by Emmanuel Sivan, "Sunni Radicalism in the Middle East and the Iranian Revolution," *International Journal of Middle East Studies* 21 (1989), 28: "Muhammad Fadlallah offered an olive branch to the Sunnis by trying to prohibit the self-mutilation so repugnant to Sunnis during the 1985 Ashura celebration in Beirut. But young Hezbollah zealots disregarded Fadlallah's prohibition with an outburst of frenzy." An informative description of Muhammad Hussein Fadlallah, spiritual mentor of the Lebanese Hezbollah (Party of God), is given in Fouad Ajami, *The Vanished Imam: Musa al-Sadr and the Shia of Lebanon* (Ithaca: Cornell University Press, 1986), 213-217.

Chapter Eleven

1. I base this remark in part on observations by Dr. Jody Rubin Pinault, who sat in purdah with Shiite women friends during a number of *majalis* in Hyderabad in August 1989.
2. Ja'far Sharif, *Islam in India or the Qanun-i-Islam*, G. A. Herklots, trans. (London: Curzon Press reprint, 1972), 181.

3. Seyyed Mohammed al-Moosavi, "Your Questions ... Our Answers," in *Ja'fari Times* 2, no. 1 (Muharram 1409/Aug.-Sept. 1988), 8.
4. Thomas Lyell, *The Ins and Outs of Mesopotamia* (London: A. M. Philpot Ltd., 1923), 65.

Chapter Twelve

1. See also T. Vedantam, ed., *Census of India 1971, Series 2, Andhra Pradesh: A Monograph on Muharram in Hyderabad City* (Delhi: Government of India Press, 1977), 74-75, for a list of sermon topics commonly presented in Hyderabad *majalis* during Muharram.

Chapter Thirteen

1. See Mahmoud Ayoub, *Redemptive Suffering in Islam* (The Hague: Mouton Publishers, 1978), 142-144 and 198-216, for a discussion of the intercessory benefits of bewailing the martyrs of Karbala.

Chapter Fourteen

1. Anjuman-e Masoomeen, *Du'a-e Fatimah: muntakhab-e nauhajat* (Hyderabad, n.d.), 9-12. The composer of this poem is listed in the book's table of contents as Mirza Farid Beg Farid.

Chapter Fifteen

1. John J. Winkler, "The Ephebes' Song: *Tragoidia* and *Polis*," in John J. Winkler and Froma I. Zeitlin, eds., *Nothing to Do with Dionysos?: Athenian Drama in its Social Context* (Princeton University Press, 1990), 36.
2. Ibid., p. 56.
3. For an introduction to the Iranian passion-play see Peter J. Chelkowski, ed., *Ta'ziyeh: Ritual and Drama in Iran* (New York University Press, 1979).
4. Saiyid Athar Abbas Rizvi, *A Socio-Intellectual History of the Isna 'Ashari Shi'is in India* (Canberra: Ma'rifat Publishing, 1986), vol. 2, 315 n. 74.
5. Participants seem very much aware of the symbolism inherent in these rituals. After the liturgy I walked with Hassan Abbas Rizvi, Parwaneh Shabbir's reciter, to his house for tea. Referring to what we had just witnessed, he said, "We assume the *alam* is a dead body; we wrap it in white cloth that's been stained with red spots and then take it from the war-field to the tomb."
6. Parwaneh Shabbir's Qasim procession is not unique in its mimetic characteristics. In 1989 I witnessed two similar *alam* processions, at the Bayt al-Qa'im on the seventh of Muharram and at the Inayat Jung Palace on Ashura (the latter ritual was celebrated by the Guruh-e Husayniyah). Like Parwaneh Shabbir's liturgy both these processions involved mimetic actions of exposition and

garland-decoration, shrouding, lamentation, and final "burial" in the chapel storeroom.

7. The text of this *nauha* appears in Parwaneh Shabbir's chant-book, *Karbala walay*, ed. Mir Ahmed Ali (Hyderabad: Maktab-e Turabia, 1989), 34-35.
8. Anjuman-e Masoomeen, *Du' a-e Fatimah: muntakhab-e nauhajat* (Hyderabad, n.d.), 11-12.
9. Ibid., 8.
10. Seyyed Ali Javid Maqsud, *Yeh matam kaysay ruk ja' ay* (Hyderabad: Maktab-e Turabia, n.d.), 9. Note too the discussion in this chapbook's introduction (pp. 1-2) of the use of Maqsud's poems by Hyderabadi *guruhan*.
11. John Herington, *Poetry into Drama: Early Tragedy and the Greek Poetic Tradition* (Berkeley: University of California Press, 1985), 21.

Chapter Sixteen

1. Yousuf N. Lalljee, *Hazrat Abbas* (Bombay: Esquire Press, 1982), 20.
2. The text of this *nauha* appears in Masoomeen's chant-book, *Du' a-e Fatimah: muntakhab-e nauhajat* (Hyderabad, n.d.), 109.
3. At the request of Ansar Hyder Abedi, sponsor and patron of the Hyderi Medical Station, I served as a volunteer paramedic (together with Andreas D'Souza of the Henry Martyn Institute and Klaus Schaefer of the Andhra Christian Theological College) on Ashura 1991 treating wounded flagellants in the first-aid tent at the entrance to the Abbas shrine. Our experiences there provided the basis for my remarks on the interaction of *matamdaran*.
4. Harriet Ronken Lynton and Mohini Rajan, *The Days of the Beloved* (Delhi: Orient Longman, 1987), 190-206.
5. Ibid., pp. 194-195.

Chapter Seventeen

1. Cited in Kristina Nelson, *The Art of Reciting the Qur' an* (Austin: University of Texas Press, 1985), 43.
2. Cited in Nelson, op. cit., 39.
3. Reynold A. Nicholson, trans., *The Kashf al-Mahjub of al-Hujwiri* (London: Luzac and Co., 1976), 416.
4. Javad Nurbakhsh, *Dar kharabat* (London: Khaniqahi Nimatullahi Publications, 1983), 86, 88.

Chapter Eighteen

1. See, for example, "Moharrum Procession Peaceful," *Indian Express* (Hyderabad), August 14, 1989, p. 1; and "Muharram Observed in Twin Cities," *Newstime* (Hyderabad), August 14, 1989, p. 3. This assertion is based also on

my personal observations of public processions and liturgies in Hyderabad at that time.

2. "Curfew Clamped in Varanasi Areas," *The Times of India* (Delhi), August 14, 1989, p. 1.
3. "Shias to Defy Ban Orders," *National Herald* (Lucknow), August 13, 1989, p. 3.
4. "Police Fire on Procession," *The Times of India* (Delhi), August 14, 1989, p. 7.
5. "Curfew Clamped in Varanasi Areas," *The Times of India* (Delhi), August 14, 1989, p. 1. For follow-up articles, see "Tension Continues in Varanasi," *The Times of India*, August 15, 1989, p. 5; "Curfew Relaxed in Varanasi," *The Hindustan Times* (Delhi), August 16, 1989, p. 7; "Curfew Relaxed in Varanasi," *Indian Express* (Delhi), August 16, 1989, p. 5; and "Varanasi Curfew Relaxed for 6 Hours," *The Times of India*, August 17, 1989, p. 9.
6. "2 Rajasthan Towns Tense," and "Two Killed in Muharram Clash," both in *The Times of India* (Delhi), August 15, 1989, pp. 5 and 17 respectively; "Curfew Clamped in Varanasi Areas," *The Times of India*, August 14, 1989, p. 1.
7. *Imperial Gazetteer of India. Provincial Series: Hyderabad State* (Calcutta: Superintendent of Government Printing, 1909; reprinted Delhi: Usha Publications, 1989), 17.
8. Zahir Ahmed, *Life's Yesterdays: Glimpses of Sir Nizamat Jung and His Times* (Bombay: Thacker & Co., Ltd., 1945), 198.
9. Asghar Ali Engineer, "Hyderabad Riots—An Analytical Report," in A. A. Engineer, ed., *Communal Riots in Post-Independence India* (Hyderabad: Sangam Books India, 1984), 288-295; Theodore P. Wright, Jr., "Revival of the Majlis Ittihad-ul-Muslimin of Hyderabad," in Omar Khalidi, ed., *Hyderabad: After the Fall* (Wichita: Hyderabad Historical Society, 1988), 132-141; Ratna Naidu, *Old Cities, New Predicaments: A Study of Hyderabad* (Delhi: Sage Publications, 1990), 23-27; "Three Dead in India in Scattered Clashes," *New York Times*, September 19, 1984, p. A11; "2 Die in Brawling in Turbulent Indian City," *New York Times*, September 24, 1984, p. A5.
10. Naidu, op. cit., pp. 125-133.
11. Ibid., pp. 132-133; Engineer, op. cit., p. 294.
12. "Hindu-Muslim Violence Persists in 2 Cities," *New York Times*, December 11, 1990, p. A6; Barbara Crossette, "In Hyderabad, a Pall Darkens 400th Birthday," *New York Times*, January 24, 1991, p. A9; Andreas D'Souza, "A City Gone Mad," *Outlook: Montfort Brothers of St. Gabriel, Province of Central India: Newsletter* (January-March 1991), 8-13.
13. *Indian Express* (Hyderabad), July 15, 1991, p. 1.
14. "10 Killed in Gujarat Violence," *The Hindu*, July 24, 1991, p. 9; "Police Open Fire on Moharram Marchers," *Indian Express*, July 24, 1991, p. 9; "9 Die in Moharram Clashes in Gujarat," *Deccan Chronicle*, July 24, 1991, p. 7.
15. Naidu, op. cit., p. 128.
16. Crossette, op. cit., p. A9.
17. "Communal Violence Condemned," *Indian Express*, Dec. 12, 1990.
18. "Riots Instigated for Political Gains," *Indian Express*, Dec. 13, 1990.

19. See also Sadiq Naqvi, *Qutb Shahi Ashurkhanas of Hyderabad City* (Hyderabad: Bab-ul-Ilm Society, 1987), 69-71.

20. T. Vedantam, ed., *Census of India 1971, Series 2, Andhra Pradesh: A Monograph on Muharram in Hyderabad City* (Delhi: Government of India Press, 1977), 12-13.

21. Ibid., p. 69.

22. "Moharrum Observed with Traditional Solemnity," *Deccan Chronicle*, August 14, 1989, p. 3.

23. "Muharram Observed with Fervour," *The Hindu*, July 24, 1991, p. 3.

24. Ibid.; "Moharrum Observed with Traditional Solemnity," *Deccan Chronicle*, August 14, 1989, p. 3.

25. "CM's Moharrum Message," *Indian Express*, August 13, 1989, p. 3.

26. "CM's Moharrum Message," *Deccan Chronicle*, July 23, 1991, p. 9.

27. See for example M. L. Nigam, "Indian Ashur Khanas: A Critical Appraisal," (where the author suggests that Bhakti devotionalism and ritual practices such as the *rathyatra* or public procession of idols helped incline Hindus to the acceptance of Shiite Muharram practices and the veneration of Husain); and Sadiq Naqvi, "The Socio-Cultural Impact of Karbala," both in *Red Sand*, Mehdi Nazmi, ed. (Delhi: Abu Talib Academy, 1984), 115-123 and 211-220. See also Nadeem Hasnain and Abrar Husain, *Shias and Shia Islam in India* (Delhi: Harnam Publications, 1988), 151-156.

28. *Census of India*, ix.

29. Z. H. Kazmi, *Imam Husain and India* (Lucknow: Imamia Mission, n.d.), 6-10.

30. Milton Viorst, "Report from Baghdad," *The New Yorker*, June 24, 1991, 72-73. On March 31, 1991, the Sunday *New York Times* carried a front-page photograph of the Karbala shrine of Husain, showing the damage inflicted by shellfire on the mausoleum.

31. "Iraq mayn mazalim kay khilaf Sakratariyat per ihtijaji muzahareh," *Ruznameh Siyasat* (Hyderabad), June 26, 1991, p. 2. I found no reference to this demonstration in any of Hyderabad's English-language dailies.

32. Prior to the 1989 Ashura processions newspapers in Hyderabad announced that twenty platoons of special police, plainclothesmen on rooftops, and "additional police pickets" would be posted on the tenth of Muharram all along the Bibi ka alam procession route in the Old City. See "Tight Security for Moharrum Procession," *Indian Express*, August 13, 1989, p. 3. Armed units were posted at the Bibi ka alam shrine to guard the standard during the liturgy of *ziyarah* on the eve of the first of Muharram; and (as I note in the text) mounted police escorted the elephant bearing the *alam* on Ashura. This protection is all the more appropriate, as my informants pointed out to me, in light of the decorations adorning the Bibi ka alam—emeralds, sapphires, and diamonds donated by the nizams of the past. See also "Moharrum Procession Peaceful," *Indian Express*, August 14, 1989, p. 1, for a newspaper reference to these jewels. In 1991 Hyderabad's newspapers likewise noted measures taken by the government to safeguard the Bibi ka alam procession. See for example "Muharram Observed with Fervour," *The Hindu*, July 24, 1991, p. 3: "Elaborate security

arrangements were made. Armed pickets were posted in sensitive localities and patrolling was organised all over Hyderabad." The *Deccan Chronicle* of July 24, 1991, p. 3, noted, "The city police made elaborate *bandobast* [arrangements] for Moharrum. The mounted police were pressed into service."

Chapter Nineteen

1. Mary Hegland, "Two Images of Husain: Accommodation and Revolution in an Iranian Village," in Nikki R. Keddie, ed., *Religion and Politics in Iran* (New Haven: Yale University Press, 1983), 218-235.
2. Ali Shariati, *Red Shi'ism* (Houston: Free Islamic Literatures, 1980), 8. Translated by Habib Shirazi.
3. Ibid., 9-10.
4. Ibid., 10.
5. Morteza Motahhary, *The Martyr* (Houston: Free Islamic Literatures, 1980), 17, 23.
6. Ruhollah Khomeini, *Islam and Revolution: Writings and Declarations of Imam Khomeini,* translated by Hamid Algar (Berkeley: Mizan Press, 1981), 28; cited by Gregory Rose, "*Velayat-e Faqih* and the Recovery of Islamic Identity in the Thought of Ayatollah Khomeini," in Keddie, op. cit., 166.
7. Emmanuel Sivan, "Sunni Radicalism in the Middle East and the Iranian Revolution," *International Journal of Middle East Studies* 21 (1989), 6.
8. Youssef M. Ibrahim, "Iran Shifting its Attention from Lebanon to Sudan," *The New York Times,* Dec. 13, 1991, p. A7.
9. Gershom Scholem, s.v. "Kabbalah," *Encyclopaedia Judaica* (Jerusalem: Macmillan, 1971), vol. 10, 588-601. For a highly readable introduction to the Lurianic Kabbalah and the concept of *tikkun olam* I recommend Lis Harris, *Holy Days: The World of a Hasidic Family* (New York: Collier Books, 1985), 40-43.
10. Elaine Sciolino, "Saudis Gather Ousted Iraqi Groups," *The New York Times,* Feb. 22, 1991, p. A8; George Joffe, "Still Divided," *Middle East International,* March 8, 1991, p. 5; Safa Haeri, "Close Eye on Iraq," *Middle East International,* March 8, 1991, pp. 18-19. For background information on Muhammad Baqir al-Hakim see Christine Moss Helms, *Iraq: Eastern Flank of the Arab World* (Washington, DC: The Brookings Institution, 1984), 28-29.

BIBLIOGRAPHY

Ahmed, Akbar S. "Muslim Society in South India: The Case of Hyderabad," in *Hyderabad: After the Fall,* edited by Omar Khalidi, 173-187. Wichita: Hyderabad Historical Society, 1988.

Ahmed, Zahir. *Life's Yesterdays: Glimpses of Sir Nizamat Jung and His Times.* Bombay: Thacker & Co., 1945.

Ajami, Fouad. *The Vanished Imam: Musa al-Sadr and the Shia of Lebanon.* Ithaca: Cornell University Press, 1986.

Ali, Abdullah Yusuf, trans. *The Holy Qur'an.* Beirut: Dar al-Arabia, n.d.

Ali, Mir Ahmed, ed. *Karbala walay.* Hyderabad: Maktab-e Turabia, 1989.

Ameed, Syed Mohammed. *The Importance of Weeping and Wailing.* Karachi: Peermahomed Ebrahim Trust, 1973.

Andrae, Tor. *Mohammed: The Man and His Faith.* New York: Harper & Row, 1960.

Anjuman-e Masoomeen. *Du'a-e Fatimah: muntakhab-e nauhajat.* Hyderabad, n.d.

Attar, Farid al-Din. *The Conference of the Birds.* Translated by Afkham Darbandi and Dick Davis. Harmondsworth: Penguin Books, 1984.

Attar, Farid al-Din. *Mantiq al-tayr.* Ahmad Khoshnevis Imad, ed. Isfahan: Kitabkhaneh Sina'i, 1336 AH.

Ayoub, Mahmoud. *Redemptive Suffering in Islam: a Study of the Devotional Aspects of Ashura in Twelver Shi'ism.* The Hague: Mouton Publishers, 1978.

Beeman, William O. "Images of the Great Satan: Representations of the United States in the Iranian Revolution." In *Religion and Politics in Iran: Shi'ism from Quietism to Revolution,* edited by Nikki R. Keddie, 191-217. New Haven: Yale University Press, 1983.

Borthwick, Bruce. "The Ismailis and Islamization in Pakistan." *American Council for the Study of Islamic Societies Newsletter* 1 (Aug. 1990), 4-6.

Cahen, Claude, and Fritz Taeschner. s.v. "Futuwwa." *Encyclopaedia of Islam,* 2nd ed., vol. 2. Leiden: E. J. Brill, 1965.

Chelkowski, Peter, ed. *Ta'ziyeh: Ritual and Drama in Iran.* New York University Press, 1979.

Crossette, Barbara. "In Hyderabad, a Pall Darkens 400th Birthday." *The New York Times,* January 24, 1991, p. A9.

D'Souza, Andreas. "A City Gone Mad." *Outlook: Montfort Brothers of St. Gabriel, Province of Central India: Newsletter* (Jan.-Mar. 1991), 8-13.

Durand, Colonel Algernon. *The Making of a Frontier: Five Years' Experiences and Adventures in Gilgit, Hunza Nagar, Chitral and the Eastern Hindu-Kush.* London: Thomas Nelson & Sons, 1900.

Eerdmans, B. D. "Der Ursprung der Ceremonien des Hosein-Festes." *Zeitschrift für Assyriologie* 9 (1894), 280-307.

Ende, Werner, "The Flagellations of Muharram and the Shi'ite Ulama," *Der Islam* 55 (1978), 19-36.

Engineer, Asghar Ali. "Hyderabad Riots—An Analytical Report." In *Communal Riots in Post-Independence India,* edited by A. A. Engineer, 288-295. Hyderabad: Sangam Books India, 1984.

Fischer, Michael and Abedi, Mehdi. *Debating Muslims: Cultural Dialogues in Postmodernity and Tradition.* Madison: University of Wisconsin Press, 1990.

Ghalib, Mustafa. *al-Harakat al-batiniyah fi al-Islam.* Beirut: Dar al-Andalus, 1982.

Gibb, H.A.R. *Mohammedanism.* 2nd ed. Oxford University Press, 1979.

Goldziher, Ignaz. "Neuplatonische und gnostische Elemente im Hadith." *Zeitschrift für Assyriologie* 22 (1909), 317-344.

Green, Roger L. and Mason, Alec. *The Readers' Guide to Rudyard Kipling's Work.* Canterbury: Gibbs & Sons Ltd., 1961.

Haeri, Safa. "Close Eye on Iraq." *Middle East International,* March 8, 1991, pp. 18-19.

Hafez, Shams al-Din. *Diwan-e kamil-e Hafez-e Shiraz.* Timur Burhan Limudhi, ed. Teheran: Matbu'ati Kawiyan, 1363 AH.

Hasnain, Nadeem and Husain, Abrar. *Shias and Shia Islam in India.* Delhi: Harnam Publications, 1988.

Hegland, Mary. "Two Images of Husain: Accommodation and Revolution in an Iranian Village." In *Religion and Politics in Iran: Shi'ism from Quietism to Revolution,* edited by Nikki R. Keddie, 218-235. New Haven: Yale University Press, 1983.

Helms, Christine Moss. *Iraq: Eastern Flank of the Arab World.* Washington, DC: The Brookings Institution, 1984.

Herington, John. *Poetry into Drama: Early Tragedy and the Greek Poetic Tradition.* Berkeley: University of California Press, 1985.

Hollister, John Norman. *Islam and Shia's Faith in India.* Delhi: Taj Publications, 1989.

Homerin, T. Emil. "Echoes of a Thirsty Owl: Death and Afterlife in Pre-Islamic Arabic Poetry." *Journal of Near Eastern Studies* 44 (1985), 165-184.

Husain, A. F. Badshah. *The Holy Quran: A Translation with Commentary According to Shia Traditions and Principles.* 2 vols. Lucknow: Madrasatul Waizeen, 1936.

Ibrahim, Youssef M. "Iran Shifting Its Attention from Lebanon to Sudan," *The New York Times,* December 13, 1991, p. A7.

Imperial Gazetteer of India. Provincial Series: Hyderabad State. Calcutta: Superintendent of Government Printing, 1909. Reprinted Delhi: Usha Publications, 1989.

Jaffri, Syed Husain Ali. "Muharram Ceremonies in India". In *Ta'ziyeh: Ritual and Drama in Iran,* edited by Peter Chelkowski, 222-227. New York University Press, 1979.

Jafri, S. Husain M. *Origins and Early Development of Shi'a Islam.* London: Longman, 1979.

Joffe, George. "Still Divided." *Middle East International,* March 8, 1991, p. 5.

Jonas, Hans. *The Gnostic Vision.* 2nd ed. Boston: Beacon Press, 1963.

Karimi, Mohammed Reza. "The Importance of Mourning (Azadari)." *Ja'fari Times* (Bombay) 2, no. 1 (Muharram 1409/Aug.-Sept. 1988), 4-13.

Kazmi, Z. H. *Imam Husain and India.* Lucknow: Imamia Mission, n.d.

Keddie, Nikki R., ed. *Religion and Politics in Iran: Shi'ism from Quietism to Revolution.* New Haven: Yale University Press, 1983.

Khalidi, Omar, ed. *Hyderabad: After the Fall.* Wichita: Hyderabad Historical Society, 1988.

Khomeini, Ruhollah Mousavi. *A Clarification of Questions (Resaleh Towzih al-Masael).* Translated by J. Borujerdi. Boulder: Westview Press, 1984.

Khomeini, Ruhollah Mousavi. *Islam and Revolution: Writings and Declarations of Imam Khomeini.* Translated by Hamid Algar. Berkeley: Mizan Press, 1981.

Kipling, Rudyard. *In Black and White.* New York: Doubleday, Page & Co., 1913.

Lalljee, Yousuf N. *Hazrat Abbas.* Bombay: Esquire Press, 1982.

Landolt, Hermann. "Suhrawardi's 'Tales of Initiation.'" *Journal of the American Oriental Society* 107 (1987), 475-486.

Lewis, Bernard. *The Assassins: A Radical Sect in Islam.* Oxford University Press, 1967.

Lichtenstadter, Ilse, ed. *Introduction to Classical Arabic Literature.* New York: Twayne Publishers, 1974.

Lindell, D. T. "Muharram in Hyderabad". *al-Basheer: the Bulletin of the Christian Institute of Islamic Studies* (Hyderabad) 3, no. 1 (Jan.-March 1974), 14-29.

Loeffler, Reinhold. *Islam in Practice: Religious Beliefs in a Persian Village.* Albany: State University of New York Press, 1988.

Lothian, Sir Arthur C. *Kingdoms of Yesterday.* London: John Murray, 1951.

Lyell, Thomas. *The Ins and Outs of Mesopotamia.* London: A. M. Philpot Ltd., 1923.

Lynton, Harriet Ronken and Mohini Rajan. *The Days of the Beloved.* Delhi: Orient Longman, 1987.

Madelung, Wilfred. s.v. "Isma'iliyya". *Encyclopaedia of Islam,* 2nd ed., vol. 4. Leiden: E. J. Brill, 1978.

Makarem, Sami Nasib. *The Doctrine of the Ismailis*. Beirut: Arab Institute for Research and Publishing, 1972.

Maqsud, Seyyed Ali Javid. *Yeh matam kaysay ruk ja' ay*. Hyderabad: Maktabe Turabia, n.d.

Mason, A.E.W. *The Drum*. London: Hodder & Stoughton, 1937.

Massignon, Louis. *The Passion of al-Hallaj*. Vol. 1: *The Life of al-Hallaj*. Princeton University Press, 1982.

Massignon, Louis. "Die Ursprünge und die Bedeutung des Gnostizismus im Islam". *Eranos Jahrbuch 1937* (Zurich: Rhein-Verlag, 1938), 55-77.

Momen, Moojan. *An Introduction to Shi'i Islam*. New Haven: Yale University Press, 1985.

al-Moosavi, Seyyed Mohammed. "Your Questions . . . Our Answers". *Ja'fari Times* (Bombay) 2, no. 1 (Muharram 1409/Aug.-Sept. 1988), 8.

Motahhary, Morteza. *The Martyr*. Houston: Free Islamic Literatures, 1980.

Mottahedeh, Roy. *The Mantle of the Prophet: Religion and Politics in Iran*. New York: Pantheon Books, 1985.

Naidu, Ratna. *Old Cities, New Predicaments: A Study of Hyderabad*. Delhi: Sage Publications, 1990.

Naqvi, Sadiq. *Qutb Shahi ashurkhanas of Hyderabad City*. Hyderabad: Bab-ul-Ilm Society, 1987.

Naqvi, Sadiq. "The Socio-Cultural Impact of Karbala". In *Red Sand*, edited by Mehdi Nazmi, 211-220. Delhi: Abu Talib Academy, 1984.

al-Nawbakhti, Abu Muhammad al-Hasan ibn Musa. *Kitab firaq al-shi'ah*. Hellmut Ritter, ed. Istanbul: Matba'at al-dawlah, 1931.

Nelson, Kristina. *The Art of Reciting the Qur'an*. Austin: University of Texas Press, 1985.

Nicholson, R. A., trans. *The Kashf al-Mahjub of al-Hujwiri*. London: Luzac and Co., 1976.

Nicholson, R. A. *A Literary History of the Arabs*. Cambridge University Press, 1977.

Nigam, M. L. "Indian Ashur Khanas: A Critical Appraisal". In *Red Sand,* edited by Mehdi Nazmi, 115-123. Delhi: Abu Talib Academy, 1984.

Nizami, Rukunuddin. *Hayaat-e-Nizami (Life of Hazrat K. Nizamuddin Aulia).* Delhi: Kutub Khana Mahboobi, 1979.

Nurbakhsh, Javad. *Dar kharabat.* London: Khaniqahi Nimatullahi Publications, 1983.

O'Donnell, Terence. *Garden of the Brave in War: Recollections of Iran.* Chicago: University of Chicago Press, 1980.

Oman, John Campbell. *The Brahmans, Theists and Muslims of India.* London: T. Fisher Unwin, 1907.

Pinault, David. "Images of Christ in Arabic Literature." *Die Welt des Islams* 27 (1987), 103-125.

Pinault, David. *Story-Telling Techniques in the Arabian Nights.* Leiden: E. J. Brill, 1992.

Pinney, Thomas, ed. *Kipling's India: Uncollected Sketches 1884-88.* New York: Schocken Books, 1986.

Rahman, Fazlur. *Islam.* 2nd ed. Chicago: University of Chicago Press, 1979.

Rizvi, Saiyid Athar Abbas. *A Socio-Intellectual History of the Isna 'Ashari Shi'is in India.* 2 vols. Canberra: Ma'rifat Publishing, 1986.

Sandars, N. K., trans. *The Epic of Gilgamesh.* Harmondsworth: Penguin Books, 1964.

Sarwar, Muhammad, trans. *Islamic Practical Laws Explained.* 3rd ed. Bombay: Imaan Foundation, 1988.

Schimmel, Annemarie. *Mystical Dimensions of Islam.* Chapel Hill: University of North Carolina Press, 1975.

Scholem, Gershom. s.v. "Kabbalah." *Encyclopaedia Judaica,* vol. 10. Jerusalem: Macmillan, 1971.

Sciolino, Elaine. "Saudis Gather Ousted Iraqi Groups." *The New York Times,* Feb. 22, 1991, p. A8.

al-Shahrastani, Abu al-Fath Muhammad. *Kitab al-milal wa-al-nihal.* 2 vols. Muhammad Sayyid Kilani, ed. Cairo: Maktabat Mustafa al-Babi, 1976.

Shariati, Ali. *Red Shi'ism.* Translated by Habib Shirazi. Houston: Free Islamic Literatures, 1980.

Sharif, Ja'far. *Islam in India or the Qanun-i-Islam.* Translated by G. A. Herklots. London: Curzon Press reprint, 1972.

Sheriff, Ahmed H. *The Leader of Martyrs.* Elmhurst, NY: Tahrike Tarsile Qur'an, 1986.

Sivan, Emmanuel. "Sunni Radicalism in the Middle East and the Iranian Revolution." *International Journal of Middle East Studies* 21 (1989), 1-30.

Sleeman, Sir William H. *Rambles and Recollections of an Indian Official.* Karachi: Oxford University Press, 1973. First published in 1844.

Sohravardi, Shihaboddin Yahya. *L'archange empourpré: quinze traités et récits mystiques.* Edited and translated by Henry Corbin. Paris: Librairie Fayard, 1976.

al-Suyuti, Jalal al-Din Abd al-Rahman, and al-Mahalli, Jalal al-Din Muhammad. *Tafsir al-jalalayn.* Beirut: Dar al-ma'rifah, n.d.

Tabataba'i, Muhammad Husayn. *al-Mizan fi tafsir al-Qur'an.* 20 vols. Qum: Mu'assasah Matbu'ati Isma'iliyan, 1971-1974.

Tabataba'i, Muhammad Husayn. *Shi'ite Islam.* Albany: State University of New York Press, 1977.

al-Tawil, Muhammad Amin Ghalib. *Ta'rikh al-alawiyin.* Beirut: Dar al-Andalus, 1966.

Temple, Richard. *Journals Kept in Hyderabad, Kashmir, Sikkim, and Nepal.* 2 vols. Delhi: Cosmo Publications reprint, 1977. First published in 1887.

Thackston, W. M., Jr., trans. and ed. *The Mystical and Visionary Treatises of Shihabuddin Yahya Suhrawardi.* London: Octagon Press, 1982.

al-Tha'labi, Abu Ishaq Ahmad. *Qisas al-anbiya'.* Beirut: al-Maktabah al-thaqafiyah, n.d.

Vedantam, T., ed. *Census of India 1971, Series 2, Andhra Pradesh: a Monograph on Muharram in Hyderabad City.* Delhi: Government of India Press, 1977.

Viorst, Milton. "Report from Baghdad." *The New Yorker,* June 24, 1991, 55-73.

Watt, W. Montgomery. *Islamic Philosophy and Theology: An Extended Survey.* 2nd ed. Edinburgh University Press, 1985.

Wensinck, A. J. s.v. "Ka'ba." *Encyclopaedia of Islam,* 2nd ed., vol. 4. Leiden: E. J. Brill, 1978.

Winkler, John J. "The Ephebes' Song: Tragoidia and Polis." In *Nothing to Do with Dionysos?: Athenian Drama in its Social Context,* edited by John J. Winkler and Froma I. Zeitlin, 20-62. Princeton University Press, 1990.

Woodruff, Philip. *The Men Who Ruled India: The Guardians.* New York: St. Martin's Press, 1954.

Wright, Theodore P., Jr. "Revival of the Majlis Ittihad-ul-Muslimin of Hyderabad." In *Hyderabad: After the Fall,* edited by Omar Khalidi. Wichita: Hyderabad Historical Society, 1988.

INDEX

Printed in the United States
95294LV00006B/1-3/A

"A valuable contribution to our understanding of the dynamics of Shiism today..."
—*Library Journal*

Shiite Islam is one of the world's major religions, with millions of adherents throughout the Middle East and South Asia. In the West, however, Shiite Islam has too often been misrepresented as a political movement. David Pinault's *The Shiites* describes what Shiism means to those who actually practice it and serves as both an excellent introduction to the subject and an original work of scholarship.

The author starts by outlining the defining events of early Shiite history—the struggle for the caliphate after the defeat of Muhammad, the battle of Karbala, and the persecution of the Imams—and explores how these events were interpreted by later generations of Muslim religious authorities to form a distinctive Shiite theology.

The second half of *The Shiites* looks at the particular example of the Shiite community in Hyderabad, India. Drawing on personal observations of the most important liturgies and extensive interviews with the participants, Dr. Pinault shows how the great rituals of Muharram—the public processions and self-mortification in honor of the Imam Husain, slain at the battle of Karbala—help define communal identity and illuminate Shiite cosmology and beliefs about the nature of voluntary suffering. Particular attention is given to the important role of the men's guilds that supervise the rituals.

All textual sources have been fully translated from Arabic, Persian, and Urdu into English. *The Shiites* is a uniquely accessible work of enormous value both to the general reader and to the specialist in Islamic studies.

DAVID PINAULT   University of
Pennsylvania   udies at the
University of
the Arabian

The cover phot
quarter, Ashur
Abbas!" Photo

RELIGION

9 780312 100247